Putting Knowledge to Work

Putting Knowledge to Work
Collaborating, influencing and learning for international development

Edited by Luc J.A. Mougeot

PRACTICAL ACTION
Publishing

International Development Research Centre
Ottawa • Cairo • Montevideo • Nairobi • New Delhi

Practical Action Publishing Ltd
The Schumacher Centre,
Bourton on Dunsmore, Rugby,
Warwickshire, CV23 9QZ, UK
www.practicalactionpublishing.org

A co-publication with
International Development Research Centre
PO Box 8500, Ottawa, ON, K1G 3H9, Canada
www.idrc.ca / info@idrc.ca
ISBN 978-1-55250-593-9 (IDRC e-book)

The research presented in this publication was carried out with the aid of a grant from the International Development Research Centre, Ottawa, Canada. The views expressed herein do not necessarily represent those of IDRC or its Board of Governors.

Product or corporate names may be trademarks or registered trademarks, and are used only for identification and explanation without intent to infringe.

A catalogue record for this book is available from the British Library.
A catalogue record for this book has been requested from the Library of Congress.

ISBN 9781853399589 Hardback
ISBN 9781853399596 Paperback
ISBN 9781780449593 eBook
ISBN 9781780449586 Library PDF

Citation: Mougeot, L.J.A. (ed.) (2017), *Putting Knowledge to Work: Collaborating, influencing and learning for international development,* Rugby, UK: Practical Action Publishing, <http://dx.doi.org/10.3362/9781780449586>

Cover design by Andrew Corbett
Typeset by Allzone Digital Services
Indexed by Elizabeth Ball
Printed by Replika Press Pvt Ltd, India

Contents

http://dx.doi.org/10.3362/9781780449586.000

List of illustrations

Figures

Photos

Tables

Acronyms and abbreviations

AIMS	African Institute for Mathematical Sciences
AQOCI	Association québécoise des organismes de coopération internationale
AUCC	Association of Universities and Colleges of Canada (now Universities Canada)
BCCIC	British Columbia Council for International Cooperation
CAWST	Centre for Affordable Water and Sanitation Technology
CPA	Country Programmable Aid
CCIC	Canadian Council for International Cooperation
CCSOs	Canadian civil society organizations
CESO	Canadian Executive Service Organization
CIDA	Canadian International Development Agency
CIFSRF	Canadian International Food Security Research Fund
CoP	Community of Practice
CP	Canadian Partnerships
CURA	Community–University Research Alliances
CSOs	civil society organizations
DAC	Development Assistance Committee
DFATD	Department of Foreign Affairs, Trade and Development
DFID	Department for International Development
DGIS	Dutch Directorate General for Development Cooperation
FDI	foreign direct investment
GAC	Global Affairs Canada
GACER	Global Alliance for Community-Engaged Research
GRIOT	Groupe de recherche pour l'innovation, l'organisation et le transfert d'Oxfam-Québec
HICs	high-income countries
HQ	headquarters
ICT	information and communication technology
ICURA	International Community–University Research Alliances
IDRC	International Development Research Centre
ILOs	international liaison officers
KFPE	Swiss Commission for Research Partnership with Developing Countries
KM	knowledge management
KMS	knowledge management system
LFA	Logical Framework Approach
LMICs	low- and middle- income countries

LO	learning organization
M&E	monitoring and evaluation
MDG	millennium development goal
MEL	monitoring, evaluation, and learning
MF	microfinance
MMRPs	multi-annual multi-disciplinary research programmes
NEI	Next Einstein Initiative
NGO	non-governmental organization
NOW	Netherlands Organization for Scientific Research
ODA	official development assistance
ODI	Overseas Development Institute
OECD	Organisation for Economic Co-operation and Development
OK	organizational knowledge
OL	organizational learning
R&D	International Centre for Human Rights and Democratic Development
RAWOO	Netherlands Development Assistance Research Council
RBM	results-based management
RMI	Latin American Network of Masters in Children's Rights and Social Policies
SCC	Save the Children Canada
SCI	Sustainable Cities International
SCSOs	Southern civil society organizations
SMEs	small and medium-sized enterprises
SSHRC	Social Sciences and Humanities Research Council
TNCs	transnational corporations
UNEC	Unidad de Negocios de Especias y Condimentos/Spice and Condiment Business Unit
WET	water expertise and training
WICI	Women in Cities International
WOTRO	Netherlands Foundation for the Advancement of Tropical Research

Foreword

While we may be moving from an economy of goods to an economy of knowledge, making the transition from the concept of knowledge economy to knowledge society and knowledge democracy remains a challenge we face. As defined in the UNESCO 2005 *World Report Towards Knowledge Societies,* 'Knowledge societies are about capabilities to identify, produce, process, transform, disseminate and use information to build and apply knowledge for human development.'

If knowledge is essential to advancing human development, putting it to work is quintessential. Globally, we know that the broad civil society sector plays a central role in building knowledge societies for advancing human development, through social movements, organizations, and coalitions thereof, as well as partnerships with other sectors. But there is now a renewed urgency for knowledge from the very praxis of the civil society sector, particularly non-academic organizations, to be acknowledged and recorded, to be distilled and leveraged, in order to help the sector remain significant in this role relative to other players. A 2.0 version of the civil society sector must be more knowledge-centred than ever.

Knowledge democracy is the discourse within which Rajesh Tandon and I work in our roles as co-chairs of the UNESCO Chair in Community-Based Research and Social Responsibility in Higher Education. Knowledge democracy moves forward even further from the knowledge society to say not only is the use of knowledge changing in our times of global challenge and uncertainty, but the very content of that knowledge is being challenged. This book lends support to the idea that civil society organisations (CSOs) by virtue of their location and purpose in society have knowledge about creating capacities and perspectives that most academic knowledge is slow or unwilling to recognize. As this book notes, advancing social, political, cultural, ecological, and even spiritual development calls for a deeper understanding of whose knowledge counts and how new forms of co-created knowledge can be generated.

More specifically, and given the deep transformations underway in the arena of international cooperation for development, Global North CSOs working in this arena are being challenged by funders and beneficiaries alike to be more agile and nimble in mustering knowledge and applying it to advance human rights, reduce inequality, and make our societies more inclusive, more just and more sustainable. Suddenly, there seems to be no future for civil society actors that will not invest more time and resources in knowledge to inform mission and mandate, structures and processes, actions and results. There will be no worthwhile innovation without it.

Somehow, CSOs engaged in international development now need to walk the cutting edge and keep their balance. The race is on to make more with less, tap more from knowledge wizards in their and other communities, transform business plans to enhance smartness, and venture into novel kinds of partnerships and alliances to improve both the overall value and reach of their actions.

This is precisely why *Putting Knowledge to Work* is a welcome contribution to understanding how CSOs engaged internationally are helping to build knowledge societies. The collection of chapters unveils the often under-rated role that knowledge plays in non-governmental organizations' work in international cooperation for development. How do they go about producing or accessing the knowledge which they need? How do they collaborate with others to grow their capacity and ability to do so? How do they strategize and apply knowledge to affect positive change locally and more broadly for development? How do they go about learning from their practice to keep evolving as development actors? The authors not only unpack tensions and challenges faced by small and medium-sized development NGOs in particular; they also case-review inspiring solutions devised by other such organizations to improve their own performance, often in the face of adversity.

I wish to congratulate the authors for bringing together this collection of work which, from the viewpoint of Global North CSOs, encompasses much of the spectrum of relationships which they thread day in and day out with donors, recipients, partners, local stakeholders, and communities. In doing so very distinctly, the collection examines the central role of knowledge in such relationships and their impact on it. The book not only fills a literature gap on the Canadian experience in particular; it also is a call for others to take on the relay for much needed similar efforts, this time from a Global South perspective.

Budd Hall, UNESCO Co-Chair in Community-Based Research and Social Responsibility in Higher Education

Founding Director of the Office of Community-Based Research, University of Victoria, Canada

Preface

Luc J.A. Mougeot, Megan Bradley,
Elena Chernikova, Stacie Travers, and Eric Smith

This publication revisits a series of original research pieces, bringing them together in a new format with an introductory essay to situate them in the current context. Our collected edition lends a rounded examination of strategies that civil society organizations (CSOs) active in international cooperation for development have been using to put knowledge to work: how they navigate donor–recipient relationships when setting the research agenda, how they collaborate among different types of organizations to create and access knowledge, how they apply knowledge to influencing policy and practice, and how they use knowledge to learn from their own ground-level experience and grow as organizations.

The original studies were carried out between 2007 and 2014, supported by research awards of Canada's International Development Research Centre (IDRC), partly to inform the Centre's own support of research collaboration among non-governmental organizations (NGOs) in Canada and in low- and middle-income countries (LMICs), as well as with higher learning institutions active in international development and cooperation. CSOs of all sizes are covered by the studies, active in sectors as diverse as agriculture and the environment, social and economic policies, health systems and science, and innovation. Earlier studies in the series informed subsequent ones, a dynamic that lends unity and is reflected in the order in which the chapters appear in this publication.

Three of the four studies counted on the collaboration of two national membership organizations representing universities and NGOs, Universities Canada and the Canadian Council for International Cooperation (CCIC). IDRC used the findings and recommendations from these studies to inform programming aimed at these two communities over the 2010–2015 period. This was done through extending support to emerging scholars, cross-sectoral projects, panels and publications, regional learning forums on issues such as excellence in action research and the design and use of virtual knowledge platforms, as well as supporting NGO communities of practice on topics such as project monitoring and evaluation, and gender-sensitive programming.

The latest step in a rapprochement that has intensified between the academic and practitioner communities in recent years is the announcement of a three-year partnership between the CCIC and the Canadian Association for the Study of International Development that is being launched in early 2017. This partnership aims to pilot novel approaches to cross-community synergies for knowledge creation, academic training and professional development, and advocacy and policy influence. Unprecedented in the history of these two communities, this is an experiment from which we stand to learn much over the coming years.

We believe the updated reports assembled here continue to have relevance and hold value, particularly as a collection, for three major reasons. Firstly, they provide an important historical perspective on current developments. Global North donors' influence on the agenda setting of Global South recipients is examined in Chapter 2 and remains a timely topic in light of a renewed emphasis by donor countries on aligning development with trade policies and prioritizing North–South research collaboration. In addition, at a time when NGOs are encouraged to collaborate more with universities, approaches not only need to acknowledge differences in organizational culture, structure, and outcomes, but also need to recognize the rich range of collaborations in existence, and the seeds that need to be deliberately nurtured to accelerate and expand such collaborations. Chapter 3 examines these collaborations between NGOs and universities, including the resources needed to ensure NGOs retain a measure of control over their own reflection and learning. Against donor pressure on recipients to produce measurable project-bound outcomes, studies are needed to educate policymakers on the transformative changes inherent to the mission of CSOs engaged in international cooperation for development. Chapter 4 addresses the elaborate strategies that international NGOs thread with Global South NGOs and others to apply knowledge and influence attitudes, practices, and policies. Their shifting roles in contexts where Global South partners become more structured and resourced are also examined. Finally, an insistence on civil society actors in international cooperation for development, particularly NGOs, becoming more innovative in 'delivering' development assistance highlights the essential role of learning in this process, and of the time, competence (or competencies), and resources required precisely for that purpose. Chapter 5 explores this role of learning and provides a previously absent focus on small and medium-sized NGOs, and the role of communities of practice collectives around particular issues.

Secondly, the studies remain highly pertinent as CSOs in high-income countries try to redefine their value in a new ecosystem. These studies fill a void created by the absence of systematic data on large numbers of CSOs and their models. In particular, literature searches carried out by the respective authors after the original studies were completed and during the preparation of this book point to a lack of knowledge sharing around the issues addressed. We believe this book, despite its emphasis on the Canadian scene, will be useful for academics and practitioners located in other countries in the Global North. They can be used for comparative purposes and encourage greater collaboration for the co-creation and use of knowledge by CSOs. Hopefully, the series will inspire similar studies on the experience of a growing number of Global South-based CSOs engaged in international cooperation for development.

Thirdly, combining these four studies under a same cover affords the reader a comprehensive view of how different relationships (funding, collaboration, influence, and impact) between development actors (donors, recipients, partners, stakeholders, and beneficiary communities) interact with one another to affect how knowledge is generated and applied. For instance, donor agencies' funding may affect recipients' ability to sustain long-term engagement with partners for durable influence, but also their ability to sustain learning strategies for their own organizational evolution. Just as North–South collaboration may not be the best way to support research in LMICs, insistence on more university–CSO collaboration should be context-specific, as all types of university–NGO collaboration are not equally relevant or beneficial, given differences in organizational cultures. More is not always better: knowledge will be of no use to influence if it is not timely, pertinent, and actionable. Similarly, NGOs' learning strategies will have little use if they need to rely mainly on academics to document and distil their organizational experience for change; NGOs must develop their own capacity to drive their own learning dynamics, individually or as collectives. Finally, learning from one's experience and that of others on how to navigate donor–recipient relationships, why and how best to collaborate across sectors for mutual benefit, and how best to influence positive change in particular contexts with available resources, are all essential for CSOs to grow as organizations and to remain relevant actors in the new ecosystem for international development (see Chapter 1).

We, the authors, are professionals who have worked or are working in different parts of this new ecosystem (as donors, in universities, and for NGOs). The viewpoints from which we address our respective topics in this book are diverse as they draw on a rich array of theoretical frameworks to knowledge creation and its use for development. Our respective emphases on some issues rather than on others are also driven by our own individual interests as professionals in the broad field of international cooperation for development.

We hope that this diversity, which enabled each one of us to appreciate one another's perspectives in developing this collection, will make its reading equally rewarding for the new generation of research activists and learned practitioners who are rising to make knowledge ever more central to development in both the Global North and the Global South.

About the editor

Luc J.A. Mougeot is a Senior Program Specialist with the Technology and Innovation Division of Canada's International Development Research Centre (IDRC) in Ottawa. From 2004 to 2014, he worked with IDRC's former Canadian Partnerships Program. Luc has been managing research grants to Canadian universities and their national associations, learned societies, and non-governmental organizations active in research and cooperation for international development. Luc led IDRC's Cities Feeding People Program (1996–2004) and was associate professor at the Federal University of Pará, in Belém, Brazil (1978–1989). He holds a doctorate in geography from Michigan State University, completed a post doctoral programme in Germany and the United Kindgom, and was seconded to the World Bank in Washington, DC, researching environmental and social impacts of large development projects. His latest publication (in *Integrated Urban Agriculture,* 2016, edited by Robert France) reviews lessons from collaborative research between scholars, non-governmental organizations and local governments for policy development.

CHAPTER 1

Introduction: Knowledge for civil society in the rapidly changing ecosystem for international development

Luc J.A. Mougeot

Abstract

Dramatic changes in the ecosystem for international development are pressing civil society organizations (CSOs) to invest more in knowledge to remain significant players within the system. While the need for creative thinking and experimentation is greater than ever, there is still very little research published on the challenges experienced and solutions found by CSOs. This book explores the knowledge relevance of working relationships, among and between development actors, with a focus on how CSOs in the Global North navigate these relationships to access and apply knowledge for them to remain effective in research and cooperation for development.

This introductory chapter reviews changes underway within this ecosystem, looking at how these affect Global North CSOs. It schematizes the chain of knowledge-relevant relationships between different categories of actors in this ecosystem, from donors to beneficiary communities. Specific chain links are covered in the following four chapters of this book: Chapter 2 examines the funding relationship between donors and recipients, and its impact on agenda-setting in North–South partnerships; Chapter 3 profiles the collaboration between different types of CSOs and its impact on the mutual building of capacity and information for practice; the use of knowledge in and by Global North and Global South partner CSOs to influence practices and policies of local stakeholders is studied in Chapter 4; finally, Chapter 5 outlines the role of knowledge in processes for CSOs' self and collective learning from the aforementioned relationships to improve themselves as organizations.

Keywords: international development, civil society organizations, knowledge, agenda-setting, collaboration, influence, learning

Introduction

Never before have civil society organizations (CSOs) engaged in international cooperation for development been so hard-pressed to put knowledge to work, compliments of dramatic changes over the last decade in the ecosystem in

http://dx.doi.org/10.3362/9781780449586.001

which they operate (King et al., 2016). These changes have been forcing the long-time actors to revise their relationships with one another, as well as engage with 'new kids on the block'. Everywhere, new approaches are being tested: to redress power imbalances between donors and recipients for more locally owned agendas; to magnify the impact of official development assistance (ODA) and its coherence with other policy objectives; to improve synergies between missions of the academic, other civil society, and private sector organizations involved; to inform and influence local dynamics for positive change at scale; to systematize and account for results that can be meaningful to all those involved; and finally, to learn from ground-level experience for organizations to remain relevant, effective, and efficient players within the new ecosystem. This flurry of experimentation is healthy, though challenging to many.

The field of interest at stake is complex and complicated, with pursuits often at odds with one another and opportunities for collaboration often overlooked. While the need for creative thinking and experimentation is greater than ever, there is still little research published on the challenges experienced and solutions found by CSOs, as they adjust to changes in the larger international development network.

This book is intended to help fill the void. It explores the shifting power dynamics between donors in the Global North and recipients in North–South development research partnerships; the difficult, yet mutually desired, research collaborations between Global North non-governmental organizations (NGOs) and Global North universities; and strategies devised by NGOs to create and use knowledge for influencing positive social change locally, as much as for improving themselves as organizations. It identifies and documents several inspiring practices to overcome specific challenges, drawing on the experiences of selected Canadian CSOs (CCSOs), including universities, NGOs, and coalitions thereof. These CSOs vary in size, field of expertise, mandate, and geographic focus; yet, they have all been developing different approaches to tackling challenges identified by their community in Canada. It is the hope of all the contributors to this book that such case studies will inspire others in tackling their own challenges and remaining significant players in international development.

The following sections introduce the concept of civil society that is central to this book, the changing global ecosystem for international development, and its implications for Global North CSOs. The focus is on relationships among and between CSOs, particularly development NGOs, and other actors in the Global North and Global South, and on the need for new knowledge to inform such relationships. Lastly, the various chapters assembled in this book are introduced. Emphasis is placed on their contribution to the state of knowledge, on past and recent developments which heighten their relevance to current conversations, as well as on literature reviews, primary data gathering, and original fieldwork on which analyses and conclusions are based.

Defining civil society

According to Dr Lester Salamon, director of the Center for Civil Society Studies at Johns Hopkins University, civil society is:

> a broad array of organizations that are essentially private, i.e. outside the institutional structures of government; that are not primarily commercial and do not exist primarily to distribute profits to their directors or 'owners'; that are self-governing; and that people are free to join or support voluntarily (Salamon et al., 2003: 3).

As key interlocutors, regulators, and funders of CSOs, governments' definitions circumscribe both the sector and the roles which governments expect organizations in this sector to play in their development assistance policy. For instance, the Canadian government's own definition borrows from that adopted by the Organisation for Economic Co-operation and Development (OECD):

> a wide range of non-governmental and non-profit-driven organizations through which people organize themselves to pursue shared interests or values in public life. In the international development context, these organizations and social movements can be found at the international, regional, national and local levels. Examples of civil society organizations include community-based organizations, environmental groups, women's rights groups, farmers' associations, faith-based organizations, philanthropic organizations, human rights groups, labour unions, co-operatives, independent research institutes, universities, diaspora groups, and the non-profit media. (GAC, 2015)

The changing ecosystem for international development

There is no denying that international cooperation and research for development have been undergoing dramatic and lasting changes over the past decade. Not only has the nature of development itself become more contested and its global geography decisively multi-polar, new actors have risen as major players and are now officially recognized as such. And yes, these many actors unsurprisingly often hold different, if not conflicting, understandings of what development is and how best it should be pursued.

In the Global North, longstanding OECD donors have been reducing ODA budgets and disbursing funds more selectively, while new donors have come to the fore. Following ODA reductions throughout the 1990s and after a recovery of ground lost throughout much of the last decade, the OECD's Development Assistance Committee (DAC) reported, in 2013, a continued return to decreases in net ODA, in both relative and absolute terms (OECD, 2016).

These reductions particularly affect flows to Africa and more generally to the least developed countries, with a continued shift toward bilateral activities and away from multilateralism. Programmes of the United Nations system have been affected, with several turning to their former 'regional anchoring partners' to take on full responsibility for the continuation of activities. While non-DAC donors more than compensated for this drop in DAC-related ODA, globally more of the larger country programmable aid (CPA) envelope (which includes the non-DAC donors' share) has been directed to middle-income countries in the Far East, as well as in South and Central Asia (where most of the world's poor now live). Meanwhile, the OECD was predicting a stagnation of CPA flows to countries with the largest Millennium Development Goal gaps and highest levels of poverty (OECD, 2016). It is still unclear to what extent this forecast might be redressed under the new Sustainable Development Goals agenda.

Developing and transition economies now constitute half of the top 20 countries attracting foreign direct investment (FDI) inflows. In 2013, FDI flows to developing economies reached a new high of US$778 billion, or 54 per cent of the total. Another $108 billion went to transition economies. FDI outflows from developing countries also reached a record level (UNCTAD, 2014). Despite some volatility, larger and growing volumes of FDI sourcing from both higher income and emerging economies against a declining ODA, are one reason why OECD governments are turning to private–public partnerships to maximize the economic and political outcomes of their development assistance, both at home and abroad. It is an argument which also underlies the pressure for Global North academia and other civil society ODA recipients to work more closely together, and with private corporate actors as well.

Further fuelling OECD donors' quest for inter-sector synergies, several recent statistical studies question the contribution of ODA deployment itself to even the most minimalist of all definitions of development: economic growth. In their 2013 analysis of the impact of FDI, remittances, and ODA on gross domestic product (GDP) growth in countries across various world regions between 1984 and 2008, Warwick Business School professor of international business Nigel Driffield and Aston Business School economist Chris Jones found that, in many regions, remittances were larger and more regular over time than ODA. More importantly, FDI had grown to be significantly larger than the other two sources of foreign capital over that period. Both FDI and migrant remittances had a positive impact on growth in developing countries, particularly so in better institutional environments. However, the relationship between ODA and economic growth overall was far from clear cut, as ODA was even observed to impact growth negatively in some places, while buttressing it where there was sufficient bureaucratic quality (better governance).

Driffield and Jones' suggestion that remittances are nearly as important as FDI for generating economic growth finds support in a 2013 study by Mamoun Benmamoun, public policy analyst with the John Cook School of Business at Saint Louis University, and Kevin Lehnert, professor of marketing with the Seidman College of Business, Grand Valley State University. Their analysis of 1990–2006 data focused on low-income countries and indicated that, although international remittances, FDI, and ODA were all positively and significantly associated with economic growth rates, international remittances contributed more to economic growth than ODA and FDI, even when countries were highly dependent on FDI. More recently, in a two-panel data model on the effect of ODA and microfinance (MF) on economic growth of 67 countries receiving ODA and with MF activity, Lacalle-Calderón et al. (2015) found that, over the decade from 2001–2011, while MF was positively and significantly associated with economic growth, namely through transmission mechanisms (private investment and private consumption), no such relationship could be found between ODA and economic growth, and this was true even when considering any of the potential transmission mechanisms (public investment, public consumption, and imports).

Unsurprisingly, business as usual in a context of declining ODA amounts and impact in many regions has become a non-starter, and policies nurturing greater synergies between the various categories of foreign capital flows at work now seem increasingly overdue (Benmamoun and Lehnert, 2013).

What does this mean for development cooperation? Various specialists have argued for a new framework for analysis and action, a re-definition of missions and roles, and a more coordinated and concerted approach to interventions. For instance, Brookings Institute fellow Laurence Chandy argues that for development cooperation to be more effective and justify itself to its various stakeholders, it must be markedly reframed through: (a) moving beyond the broad label of 'development' and devising a taxonomy of objectives (e.g. economic convergence, social welfare, and global public goods – not unlike what some post-development scholars propose); and (b) this in turn would call for a division of labour based on the comparative advantage of different flows, policies, and players. For instance, trade policy and equity flows would serve economic convergence, while remittances could support social welfare objectives. Funds for climate change mitigation would be applied to generating public goods (Chandy, 2011: 12), such as more resilient natural ecosystems, more robust infrastructure, and public strategies for reducing the vulnerability of certain groups to risk.

Given this, and in order to deliver development assistance that is more consistent with OECD-agreed effectiveness principles and better serves whole-of-government policy coherence and public spending accountability, OECD governments have been introducing new policies for integrating CSOs into their development assistance strategy. Since the 2008 financial crisis, some OECD countries have moved faster than others on this front, some even before 2008 (the Netherlands), and this transition to a new approach has not gone without uncertainty and losses to the CSO sector, affecting particularly those more heavily dependent on funding from their own government. Competitive calls open to all sectors especially put at a disadvantage the smaller development NGOs that need to raise their core operating funds out of project grants, unlike major NGOs and public institutions such as universities.

Brown et al. (2016) have reviewed Canadian ODA's foundations, geographic and theme foci, and its relationship to other government priorities and to new providers of aid. A major ODA provider (Heidrich et al., 2013), Canada reduced its international development assistance envelope after 2012, which affected grants and contributions available to CSOs through its Partnerships with Canadians programme (DFATD, 2014). Still, following lengthy and close consultations with the civil society sector, the government's Department of Foreign Affairs, Trade and Development (DFATD), renamed Global Affairs Canada in late 2015, issued a new partnership policy (DFATD, 2015). This recognizes CSOs' roles as programme implementers, awareness raisers, procurers of funds and volunteers, human rights supporters, participants in research, dialogue and advocacy, pilots of innovative approaches, and co-investors in partnerships.

How relevant are these new donor strategies to this book? Knowledge will be critical for CSOs to participate in new development assistance policies, and this adds purpose to this collection quite conspicuously in the Canadian context. Among the many objectives pursued under its new policy, the Canadian government expects CCSOs to lead innovation in the field of international development through incubating, testing, and scaling up new approaches for effective and efficient results aligned with its aid priorities. Partnerships will be particularly demanding of business processes that make more efficient use of resources, as well as of arrangements which encourage CSOs to collaborate with other development actors at home and abroad. In this book a couple of business-inspired NGOs are examined. Chapter 4 (Travers, 2016) looks at a development network created by a collective of agricultural cooperatives, while Chapter 5 (Smith, 2016) reviews the business model of another NGO created by industry professionals.

Implications for civil society organizations

Changes in the Global North domain of the ecosystem for international development have several other implications for the Global North (and South) CSOs involved. Actors which had been playing second fiddle for a long time, such as private and corporate foundations and private capital investors, are now becoming major players in defining and funding both research and cooperation for development in low- and middle-income countries (LMICs), as noted by Bradley (2016) in Chapter 2 of this book. They are also strong competitors for universities and other CSOs applying for ODA funds, as governments look for partnerships which will take ODA to generate results on foreign policy fronts like economic growth and international trade (Grady, 2014).

As a result, CSOs are having to reach out to other types of actors and compromise with their different, often divergent, interests and expectations. Major conferences and studies over the last five years have reviewed the role of civil society in development and its challenges in the face of changes in the arena. Noteworthy is the 'Civil Society @ Crossroads' study completed in 2012 by a consortium of CSOs based in South Africa, Tanzania, India, the United Kingdom, the Netherlands, and Uruguay, which produced case studies of NGOs based in 18 Global South countries, on the roles, capacities, contributions, and limitations of civil society in the changing local and global contexts (Tandon, 2012).

Scholars have argued that different actors now lend to the concept of civil society itself so many different, and often conflicting, meanings that the very usefulness of the concept can be questioned. For political scientist Neera Chandhoke (2007), director of the Developing Countries Research Centre at the University of Delhi – who has written extensively on civil society – this has turned from a contested to a consensual concept, its meaning somewhat 'flattened out' by multilateral and donor agencies, scholars, and activists.

Civil society and donor governments

As a result of ecosystemic changes to date, governments have been demanding that civil society recipients provide more accountability and impact on a larger scale, so as to sustain domestic political support for ODA programming aimed at civil society's development activities. From within and without (including competition from CSOs abroad), Global North CSOs are being pressed to professionalize their personnel, introduce new business models (for instance, combining development aid with commercial consultancy, as I witnessed in countries such as Ecuador, Nicaragua, Senegal, and Zimbabwe during the 1990s downturn of ODA) and knowledge management systems for constant learning, and seek new partnerships to grow the impact of interventions – and to do it all with fewer resources.

In Canada, over the last decade, several graduate programmes have been launched by higher education institutions in order to cater to this growing CSO demand, including Laval University's Bachelor of Business Administration in International Development and Humanitarian Assistance (with field internships provided by Managers Without Borders) and Humber College's International Development Ontario Graduate Certificate programme. Recent graduates from Humber's programme have taken positions such as: liaison to the US Mission at World Food Programme, based in Rome; relief coordinator for Samaritan's Purse, based in Calgary; communications officer for World Vision Canada, based in Mississauga; programme manager for a major UK charity, based in Moshi, Tanzania; and founder of their own NGO, based in Toronto and Nairobi, Kenya. Chapter 3 in this book (Chernikova, 2016) discusses the case of a university certificate programme designed with input from several development NGOs.

The contracting ODA resource base in Global North countries has been reshaping civil society roles and relations with government and business in their countries. Shifts in donor policies have affected NGOs based in the North and more so those in the South, argue Dr Rajesh Tandon, founder and president of the Society for Participatory Research in Asia, and L. David Brown, senior research fellow at Harvard University's Hauser Center for Nonprofit Organizations. In the South, many NGOs have engaged in microfinance and social enterprise activities, following market-based principles. Others are approaching the growing sector of individual and corporate philanthropy. As Tandon and Brown caution, engaging in service delivery can hinder advocacy, while social entrepreneurship requires NGOs to pay attention to markets first and foremost. In the North, partnerships increasingly equate with contracting ruled by market mechanisms, as ODA funding for civil society is under increased scrutiny. Pressure for greater efficiency and effectiveness, largely through management approaches imported from the corporate sector, can be useful in large-scale service delivery, but may distract many NGOs from their mission for local empowerment, capacity building, and systemic change (Tandon and Brown, 2013).

More information is needed on how some Global South CSOs may have been able to combine for-profit and not-for-profit activities, the former subsidizing the latter, which could inform similar hybrid models in the Global North.

Global South counterparts

It should come as no surprise that changes in management and reporting practices pressed upon North-based CSOs by OECD donors have had a domino effect on their South-based counterparts. Mike Powell (2006), international consultant and adjunct professor at the University of Alberta, quotes a study funded by the UK's Department for International Development (DFID) on the impact of new NGO management practices (Wallace et al., 2006): by 2006, many Northern NGOs were already imposing on their Southern 'partners' standard methodologies for planning and reporting work.

Case in point, Megan Bradley (Chapter 2) found that while the vast majority of researchers whom she interviewed hoped their work would make a real contribution to improving wellbeing and combating inequality, many stressed the difficulty of crafting agendas that could meet donors' demands for concrete and ideally immediate results in terms of poverty alleviation. In one of few such studies, economist Miguel Pickard (2007), with the Centro de Investigaciones Económicas y Políticas de Acción Comunitaria in Mexico, reflected on the nature of North–South partnerships involving five NGOs in Southern Mexico. He explains how shifts in Northern governments' policies in the early 2000s were passed on to Northern NGOs, which in turn were compelled to change the meaning and purpose of their partnerships with Global South counterparts. NGOs in Southern Mexico have experienced a shift in purpose (away from reducing poverty toward alleviating it, or simply attending to the poor), with greater priority being given to select themes of interest to Northern governments, plus an insistence on monitoring quantitative indicators of short-term success. Although the need for greater accountability was not questioned by these NGOs, the appropriateness of the methods used was.

Pickard's case study echoes Powell's broader-based assessment, questioning the value of knowledge produced under these new partnership frameworks:

'the tools that have been produced are based on linear processes of the service industry, rather than the complex interactions of a knowledge industry' (Powell 2006: 526). Powell, who became a director of the influential Information and Knowledge Management Emergent research programme (2007–2012) funded by the Dutch Ministry of Foreign Affairs, examined the Northern offices of development organizations which oversee policy development and exercise overall control of many programmes and budgets. Their growing preference for meeting targets through sets of contractual relations and upward reporting lends credence to a view of development as a set of deliverables, at the end of which development has taken place.

Knowledge as justified true belief (gained through separation of observer from what is being observed) underpins most Western scientific thought, yet is far from unchallenged, as no explicit knowledge is meaningful unless connected with the tacit knowledge held by the user. The very concept of log-frame analysis is based on Anglo–Nordic perceptions of reality, arguably untranslatable into most languages and understandings of reality around the globe.

> The development sector is increasingly dominated by the English language. As such, it is disempowering itself by ensuring its ignorance of vitally important mainstream intellectual traditions; as such, they do not value the relationships among different types of knowledge. (Powell, 2006: 526)

Likewise, Thomas Parks (2008), a regional director for Conflict and Governance at The Asia Foundation, reviewed the experience of NGOs in Asian countries where funding fluctuated due to constantly shifting priorities of international donors. He found evidence that such shifts often undermined the credibility and effectiveness of the very NGOs which donors were trying to strengthen. In countries where the domestic funding environment was more supportive, as was the case in Thailand in the mid-1990s, NGOs with reputation and leadership were able to continue, but not so in the Philippines or Cambodia. Beyond well-known factors that explain shifts in bilateral donors' priorities, the increasing fragmentation of development assistance itself further exacerbates the volatility of aid flows.

The Civil Society @ Crossroads Initiative, a major project that concluded in 2013, stresses the need to support research, for CSOs to redefine their identity and mission and explore new forms of resource mobilization, as well as to promote experimentation and innovation. Policymakers need to support partnerships within and across North–South boundaries for civil society knowledge sharing and solidarity, and to invest in long-term capacities for reflection, analysis, and learning in civil society (Tandon and Brown, 2013: 794). In recent years, several Canadian NGO coalitions have invested in collective multi-year exercises to review individual practices, identify alternative scenarios, and develop tools to improve themselves in partnership-building, gender mainstreaming, and outcome evaluation (see Chapter 5).

For instance, the Canadian Coalition for Global Health Research (CCGHR), jointly with BRAC (previously known as the Bangladesh Rehabilitation Assistance Committee), the Universidad Andina Simón Bolivar (Ecuador), and the Armauer Hansen Research Institute (Ethiopia), designed and successfully tested, with regional communities of practice, a Partnership Assessment Tool which enables parties to review and adjust their partnership throughout its duration (CCGHR, 2014). A group of 10 member organizations of the Canadian Council for International Cooperation (CCIC), led by Canada World Youth, reviewed various planning, monitoring, and evaluation methods used by participating organizations, and developed knowledge management systems that cater to both their learning and accountability objectives, including innovations in monitoring and evaluation (Buckles, 2013). Also, the Association québécoise des organismes de coopération internationale's community of practice on equality between women and men has been generating tools and methods to assist organizations in mainstreaming and auditing gender-equality programming (AQOCI, 2013). Hopefully, this trend will deepen in the coming years, given official policy expectations that this sector should continue to innovate.

Civil society and private sector

Another implication of OECD donors' new approach to ODA has been to require Global North CSOs to engage more with the private sector, particularly with its corporate actors investing overseas. In the interest of integrating development assistance with other foreign and domestic policy pursuits, particularly where economic growth is a priority, donor governments are pressing for greater collaboration between domestic civil society and private-sector actors.

As a result, CSOs in donor countries have been reviewing their past experience with the private sector writ large, in order to guide scenarios of more deliberate engagement in the future. In Canada, for instance, the CCIC has published at least 13 documents since 1996 on civil society–private sector relations in the context of development cooperation. The CCIC also carried out a survey in Canada, inspired and adapted from a similar process initiated by the European CSO confederation for relief and development (CONCORD), following the Fourth High-level Forum on Aid Effectiveness in late 2011. The CCIC survey received responses from 62 CSOs or 10 per cent of the target membership, with large and very large CSOs (with annual budgets over C$5 million) making up half of the final sample. Some CSOs, particularly the larger ones, have been engaging for some time through a mix of approaches with a wide range of private-sector actors, mostly with corporations in Canada and with small and medium-sized enterprises (SMEs) in Global South countries. They have been doing so as connectors, educators, conveners, contractors, and grantees. Despite differences in organizational cultures and power dynamics (priorities, operational modalities, and expectations), respondents recognized that this sort of engagement can be beneficial and they have already developed several processes, policies, and tools – considered useful, although insufficient – to govern such engagements, including for deciding on whether or not these are advisable (Klassen and Reilly-King, 2014).

While CSO–private sector partnerships undoubtedly can be extremely useful (Kindornay et al., 2014), they can also raise some ethical concerns. A review of OECD and UN policies and strategy papers by Carney (2014) has elicited key ethical principles held and actions taken by OECD and UN agencies in such partnerships, including existing practices which should be emulated to improve these partnerships. Beyond this generic guidance, actors in different sectors have started to develop together codes of conduct for cross-sector partnerships in specific fields, such as food and nutrition (Alexander et al., 2015).

Increasing our understanding of different organizational cultures, new tools for engagement, and research and capacity building will become critical for such partnerships to spur mutual benefits in the new ecosystem.

Non-governmental organizations and academic institutions

OECD donors' new approach to ODA is also pressing for greater collaboration between NGOs and academic institutions. Recent Canadian experience in research collaboration is examined by Elena Chernikova (Chapter 3), and growing CSO demand for formal and tailored training of personnel has been noted. But the student volunteering stream to Global South host partners of North-based sending organizations also merits further scrutiny. Its composition and nature is changing rapidly, as North-based diasporas participate more in such flows and Global North sending organizations complement these with volunteers drawn from Global South countries themselves. For one, CUSO (Canadian University Services Overseas) has been resorting increasingly to volunteers from Latin America to fill project vacancies in countries of that region.

NGOs act as direct recruiters for their own staff and as student/intern placement facilitators for educational institutions. In Canada, as elsewhere, both universities and NGOs grapple with how best to select, prepare, and mentor these placements. Recent research shows that for a number of reasons, academic placements from Canada to Global South universities tend to be of shorter duration, often at odds with the preferences and needs of Global South host organizations, motivated as they can be more by individuals' or sending organizations' interests than out of genuine solidarity or reciprocity with hosting entities and communities in the Global South. While sending organizations may be eager to measure contributions of mobility programmes to their own missions, more attention should be paid to monitoring and evaluating cost and returns to both the sending and hosting organizations and communities, both in the North and in the South (Tiessen and Huish, 2014).

In particular, NGOs and universities can do more to ensure student volunteers' placements maximize the impact of a student's research project for the NGO's programme (Hobbins et al., 2015). NGO–university partnerships can help NGOs integrate long-term research into their country programming and plan the build-up of individual pieces of research over time to drive real progress in the NGO's interventions on the ground. Travers (Chapter 4) discusses the case of SOCODEVI, an NGO based in Quebec, which has been using this strategy very effectively to develop agro-industrial cooperatives in Bolivia. Framing more deliberately the through-flow of individual placements within mutually agreed long-term partnerships is an approach to knowledge management which should merit greater attention on the part of both universities and NGOs in the future.

Universities themselves need to promote internship formulas which marry faculty and student engagement, particularly for mobility to LMICs. In a survey of 167 community–university engagement initiatives (local and international) in 37 countries worldwide, Granados and Puig (2014) found that interactions between service-learning and engaged scholarship activities were limited. This gap is particularly detrimental to attracting students to credit-worthy placements in LMICs, where risks, rightly or wrongly, are perceived to be higher by Global North students. In Canada, very few universities have institution-wide career incentives for faculty that engage in international work, like leading student placements (AUCC, 2014: 30). Such incentives for faculty could reduce students' perception of risk and encourage greater participation in culturally different academic systems (Rashid, 2014).

As noted at a 2015 national workshop on North–South student mobility organized by Universities Canada, a still incipient trend which may attract more attention in the future is that such exchanges sometimes lead to the creation of social enterprises in Global South countries; these in turn may continue to act as hosts for placements, both domestic and international. It is unclear how this entrepreneurial vein is tapping into the unravelling global community of social impact investors. This is rapidly changing the arena in which development CSOs worldwide will be operating over the next decades, as it diversifies options at hand to capture in-kind or in-cash resources for development projects.

Online portals and exchanges connect donors and investors directly to recipient organizations and ventures with unprecedented immediacy. These have been mushrooming in numbers and scale over the past decade, handling financial resources (Kiva, 2016), commodities, and services (Volunteer Match, 2016). Of interest, Kiva allows 'far-away' small-scale social entrepreneurs to access loans from socially oriented investors in high-income countries. Over seven years, Kiva has facilitated over US$360 million in loans from over 800,000 individuals to nearly 900,000 entrepreneurs (82 per cent women). The repayment rate is reportedly almost 99 per cent. By 2010, the former TechSouth Global had distributed US$6.6 billion worth of tech products to 133,000 organizations. For its part, EntrepreneurCountry Global (2016) acts as a catalyst for digital start-ups to engage with corporate counterparts and co-create opportunities which leverage each other's strengths. This type of portal has room to grow, as it has not yet reached a scale that rivals mainline contribution mechanisms (Salamon, 2014).

Official donors and foundations are increasingly interested in migrating some of their funding from a traditional granting model to a new lending model, with varying participation of other social investment actors. In Canada, AQOCI has been proposing the creation of a new provincial public fund for solidarity investment (loans and loan guarantees) in SMEs of the Global South. This facility would tap into the extensive domestic experience with social enterprise financing in the province of Quebec (Favreau, 2015). A small-scale version of this fund is now being piloted.

Such developments are bound to recast the added value which Global North CSOs bring or can bring to their Global South sisters' strategies to muster external support. But what do we know from these so far? Still not much.

Changes in the Global South field of the ecosystem

And since we are talking about Global North CSOs' value-adding, several changes have been taking place in the Global South which are affecting their niche, roles, and impact. The previous section has hinted at some, but more are in store.

For one, non-OECD governments have been supporting more CSOs at home and have launched their own bilateral agencies or programmes for international development cooperation. They are contributing more to global ODA flows and are actually making a significant difference. Also, emerging economies are investing more abroad. Transnational corporations (TNCs) from middle-income countries are acquiring foreign interests, including owning firms based in high-income countries (HICs) – Canada included – and in other LMICs. A quantum leap: in 2013 developing and transition economies together invested $553 billion abroad, or 39 per cent of global FDI outflows, compared with only 12 per cent at the start of this century (UNCTAD, 2014). At home, such corporations often create foundations which can support a wide range of CSOs for research and development pertinent to their areas of interest. In Brazil, for instance, GIFE (Grupo de Institutos, Fundaçoes e Empresas) was created by a group of entrepreneurs and executives back in 1989, then was formalized in 1995 by 25 organizations, and now has 130 associate businesses and social investors (Do Carmo et al., 2016).

Civil society coalitions which monitor the development impacts of foreign corporations in LMICs traditionally have been led by Global North NGOs, since most TNCs have been based in northern countries. But in the future, CSOs based in emerging economies, where more TNCs are seated or active, may become more important advocacy players in such coalitions. As a result, international coalitions may find themselves in need of capacity and research expertise transfer from some parts of their networks to others.

Also, development assistance itself is becoming increasingly fragmented, encouraged by rising economies. Several authors, including Ngaire Woods, Dean of the Blavatnik School of Government and professor of Global Economic Governance at Oxford University, argue that emerging economies are subtly changing the rules of foreign aid, with lasting impact on the role of multilateral institutions and of conditionality. Their approach becomes attractive in light of traditional donors' failure to increase aid, reduce conditionality, better coordinate and align aid, and reform its architecture. A silent revolution may be taking place, whereby emerging donors are 'quietly offering alternatives to aid-receiving countries, they are weakening the bargaining position of western donors. The resulting tensions underscore the urgency of reforming the multilateral aid system' (Woods, 2008).

A blurring of North–South boundaries in more than one way is clearly underway and will only become more pronounced in the future. But it already poses new challenges to North-based CSOs and their Global South counterparts. Few international CSOs have worked in their countries of origin, but some are now applying lessons from their international work to domestic issues (participatory budgeting and urban planning, community-led monitoring). On the other hand, CSOs in emerging countries are often unaware of the international activities of their country's government and businesses and need to acquire a greater understanding of global issues to complement their domestic experience (Tandon and Brown, 2013).

Is it fair to predict that Global South scholars will have greater influence on Global South CSOs' approaches to their development work? In the Global South, many universities and other CSOs, including think tanks, are now more capable of informing and influencing domestic policy, even assuming regional leadership. As regards CSOs, the 2013 *Global Journal* ranked the top 100 NGOs worldwide, out of a pool of 450 assessed according to criteria such as impact, innovation, and sustainability. A third of the 100 NGOs featured are based in 'developing' countries, led by India (6), Brazil (5), and Kenya (4). 'Only the United Kingdom (11) and Switzerland (9) outperformed these emerging actors, while major donors like France (2) and Germany (1) had only a marginal presence on the list.' (The Global Journal, 2013). In its 2015 ranking, new LMIC-based NGOs joined the top 100, including Garden of Hope from Taiwan, the African Ushahidi, Techo from Chile, and Kimse Yok Mu from Turkey (The Global Journal, 2013). Do Carmo et al. (2015) review the case of three major Brazilian NGOs whose production of social and practical knowledge, often jointly with research institutions, is credited for having heightened their influence in Brazilian civil society. Without a doubt, large NGOs in Global South countries will increasingly be leading coalitions to address development challenges rooted in policies of their own and other governments.

Research institutes and study centres concerned with development issues, both domestic and international, are springing up, especially in Latin America and Asia. Think tanks have also multiplied in the Global South (University of Pennsylvania, 2016), working on issues as diverse as development, economics and governance, social policy, food and agriculture, the environment, and natural (mineral) resources. They can be found not only in emerging economies such as India, Pakistan, Nigeria, Ghana, and Peru, but also in Nepal, Sri Lanka, Bangladesh, Rwanda, and Ethiopia, as well as in Honduras, Bolivia, and Paraguay. For instance, over 600 think tanks from 23 LMICs applied originally to the International Development Research Centre's Think Tank Initiative, of which over 40 are now supported with multi-year core grants funded by a donor consortium (Think Tank Initiative, 2016).

Both the sophistication of Global South organizations and the growing numbers of scholars and practitioners from the Global South now working in Global North organizations are leading Global North organizations to revisit a fieldwork fixation on 'developing countries', to acknowledge development problems which their own societies face, and to uncover the similarity, if not the connectedness, of many challenges across the high-income and low/ middle-income divide.

Over the last five years or so, more and more papers presented at congresses of Canadian learned societies, such as the Canadian Association for the Study of International Development and the Canadian Association for Latin American and Caribbean Studies, have been comparing Canadian and Global South realities on shared development issues, or analysing the development impact of activities by Canadian organizations in Global South settings (natural resources, agriculture, trade, labour and human rights, volunteering, fiscal policy, etc.). Development problems traditionally characterizing the Global South are of growing concern in the Global North: unemployment and growing income inequalities (OECD, 2011; on Canadian cities, see Hulchanski, 2010), the growing economy of organized crime (Schneider, 2010), youth electoral disengagement (Blais and Loewen, 2011), fiscal evasion and avoidance (Deneault, 2014, on a Canadian perspective), and the weakening role of the state in social service provision (Dunlop, 2006).

A new generation of Global South development thinkers and practitioners is questioning the dominance of externally driven models of development worldwide. It is not only the concept of development itself that continues to be assailed (Powell, 2006; Ziai, 2013) but, more to the point, there are renewed arguments from Global South academics and practitioners to move from exogenous to endogenous development in donor–recipient partnerships (Holcombe, 2014; Malunga and Holcombe, 2014). Professor Aram Ziai from Kassell University's International Center for Development and Decent Work argues that foundational assumptions of development theory and policy born out of 19th-century evolutionism have endured despite revisions since then. These assumptions are: existential (development as an organizing concept), normative (change is good, stagnation is bad), practical (development can be achieved all over the world), and methodological (development comparisons can be made using a universal scale).

Others have been added to these: specification of goal (the industrialized countries as models), of process (economic growth, industrialization, modernization), and its legitimation (interventions based on expert knowledge). The normative assumption in particular reflects the Eurocentric and evolutionist baggage of the concept and, more astoundingly, the 'transformation of geo-cultural differences into historical stages' (Nandy, 1992: 146, cited by Ziai, 2013: 128). Historical processes undergone by European societies are seen not as contingent but as universal, despite many aspects of 'developed' societies being unattractive to many, if not a majority, of non-European societies.

The concept obscures inequalities and conflicts at various levels, assuming that social problems can be solved with technocratic solutions, largely unconcerned with politics, relations of power, and conflicts of interest. Depoliticizing implications of the concept are still very influential. Despite attempts to introduce participation, ownership, and empowerment into development policy since the 1980s, Parks (2008) observes that participation remains confined, due to institutional constraints of the development industry. Ziai cautions that language use should be more careful and precise. Instead of a vague notion of development, scholars should refer, for instance, to processes of de-industrialization, redistribution on an international scale, amelioration of justice, solidarity, and human rights, or the reduction of global social inequality. Linked to this plea in the field of practice must be another for more precise upstream practice, in the way the field of development studies itself unpacks and communicates the concept, so as to make it a currency more useful to other fields (Currie-Alder, 2016).

Global South scholars bring to the conversation a widening spectrum of cultural values, development experiences, and intellectual perspectives. In Africa, East Asia, and Brazil, new patterns of local leadership are emerging, and cultural and traditional strengths are gaining new recognition and validity to support modern development (Malunga and Holcombe, 2014). In 2014, *Development in Practice* published a special issue on exogenous and endogenous development, mostly authored by scholars and practitioners from Africa (Holcombe, 2014). In the face of what many view as a less predictable and more invasive world order, endogenous development stresses locally defined, led, and controlled efforts to expand human choice, human dignity, and self-respect; it is rooted within the particular context and culture it serves. Adaptation and learning from outside may be desirable, but change must be led from within.

In this context, philosopher–economist Amartya Sen's appraisal of the concept remains as valid as ever:

> The concept of development is by no means unproblematic. The different problems underlying the concept have become clearer over the years on the basis of conceptual discussions as well as from insights emerging from empirical work. Insofar as these problems have become clearer, something of substance has in fact been achieved, and the demise of the brashness which characterized the initiation of development economics need not be seen entirely as a loss. A clearer recognition of the difficulties

and problems is certainly a step in the direction of enhancing our ability to tackle them. (Sen, 1988: 23)

Few would disagree that the very concept of development has always been contested. What makes the debate different today is the size and global reach of the intellectual capital engaged in the contention, as well as the scale and resemblance of development challenges faced and recognized by both the Global North and the Global South. Just as the globalization of communications exposes us more than ever before to more facts, and to more details, angles, and meanings of particular facts – no one can claim the full story anymore – reasons grow for much less hubris than 10 or 20 years ago, and for greater openness to what development means to different societies, and what to do and not to do in order to support it.

Central to the distinction between endogenous and exogenous is a different relationship between the giver and the receiver. Exogenous approaches are not to be discarded altogether, but there is certainly a need to ask whether this model works well and, if so, under which conditions. This is why Megan Bradley (Chapter 2) in her fieldwork queried Global South researchers on their approaches to North–South partnership opportunities. In the words of Sue Holcombe (2014), professor of practice at Brandeis University's Heller School for Social Policy and Management, the debate over exogenous and endogenous development would spring from growing dissatisfaction with assumptions buried in the prevailing concept of development, with upwards short-term accountability to the detriment of locally empowering and longer term impacts, as well as evidence that growth can be achieved and inequalities reduced without substantial foreign aid.

And surely enough, OECD's DAC has been working with recipient countries to articulate principles of donor–recipient engagement consistent with a more endogenous development approach. This stresses participation, local capacity, and knowledge and ownership, as well as a deeper level of using historical and cultural experience of a people to inform their development goals and shape its path (Holcombe, 2014: 751). Pioneering this OECD initiative, innovations by Dutch and British donor agencies in the area of research collaborations, as reviewed by Bradley (Chapter 2), point to constraints faced by North–South dynamics for endogenously led agendas.

Indeed, the road to more endogenous approaches to development should not be romanticized, as it is fraught with challenges, including Western aid and development philosophies. This came out loud and clear from The Listening Project, for instance, which collected opinions of more than 6,000 foreign aid recipients regarding their interactions with the international aid system (Anderson et al., 2012).

But some barriers also do exist in the Global South, namely governance and globalization, not the least being the influence exerted by major corporations over countries' governance and many political leaders' inclination to oblige (George, 2014). In order to bridge these barriers on a continent like Africa, Holcombe assigns a central role to investing in education and deploying a growing body of African professionals to provide endogenous leadership in government, the private sector, and in civil society. This includes supporting university programmes that encourage critical thinking and problem solving, locally appropriate innovation, and support to returning graduates, associations, and connections (Holcombe, 2014). Five years earlier, based on their review of the first cohort of a pan-African leadership development programme delivered to 300 participants from 19 sub-Saharan countries, Richard Bolden, director of the Bristol Leadership Centre, and his University of West England colleague Philip Kirk were calling for such programmes to step outside dominant paradigms and adopt an Africa-centric perspective, where participants can enhance their sense of self in community, challenge repressive power relations, and innovate culturally relevant forms of leadership (Bolden and Kirk, 2009).

Such recommendations have found an ear among several donor agencies, including Canada's International Development Research Centre (IDRC). For instance, the African Institute for Mathematical Sciences (AIMS), created in Cape Town in 2003, launched The Next Einstein Initiative (NEI) in 2010, which by February 2015 had graduated 748 African students from 42 countries, nearly a third of whom are women. They were trained at five centres in South Africa, Senegal, Ghana, Cameroon, and Tanzania (the latter four opened between 2011 and 2014). At least three-quarters of the graduates have now taken up jobs in research, innovation, and applications with academic, government, or private-sector organizations in Africa. New funding by a consortium of donors, led by the Government of Canada, is to enhance postgraduate opportunities for AIMS–NEI alumni by fostering industry–research linkages, and creating IDRC African Research Chairs in mathematics, physics, and astronomy (IDRC, 2015).

Still, as Holcombe underscores, bridging barriers also implies re-examining the curricula of development practitioners in the Global North, including critical self-appraisal. Approaches to measuring 'results' must change, providing for staggered outputs, outcomes, and impacts within the short, medium, and longer term, in order to track lasting change beyond the mere introduction of innovations. It must be recognized that the challenge of endogenous development rests also with organizations, structures, and systems that implement aid and change.

Overview of this book

Clearly, CSOs are only one of several communities of organizations active in the rapidly changing ecosystem of international development. And, as are others, this community is highly diverse. Putting knowledge to work for these CSOs to deliver on their mandate within the ecosystem requires them to pay increasing attention to how they manage knowledge in their relationships with other actors. Knowledge-relevant relationships are central to this book. Knowledge-relevant relationships are those that have bearing on what and how knowledge is produced and/or applied, for which these relationships are entertained in the first place. The kind of knowledge that will be accessed, created, shared, and used as the result of different actors interacting is conditioned by their respective culture and structure, mission and mandate, polices and processes (Hayman et al., 2016). Negotiating complementarity and synergies, as well as coordination and collaboration, is critical for the interplay of actors to deliver development outcomes beyond the reach of any of these individual actors.

This book examines the relationships that affect specifically how Global North CSOs define, produce, access, apply, reflect on, and learn from knowledge to support their work in international cooperation for positive change on human development. It focuses on critical issues, such as equity in agenda setting in North–South partnerships, research collaboration between contrasting cultures of academia and civil society, the use of research and knowledge by North-based CSOs collaborating with South-based counterparts to influence policies and practices in the Global South, and strategies for organizations to acknowledge, reflect, and learn from their own practices and those of others, for greater relevance and effectiveness in a rapidly changing arena. Quite distinctly, three of the contributions in this book examine the experience of Canadian organizations, while a fourth chapter reviews approaches tested by two OECD bilateral agencies with teachings for other donor countries.

Figure 1.1 schematizes the network which Global North CSOs must mobilize, involving major categories of actors at play (donors, recipients, partners, stakeholders, and communities that will benefit from CSO interventions) in the Global North and Global South, through relationships (funding CSO undertakings, collaboration for complementarity, influencing practices and policies, causing desirable impact, and learning from all the

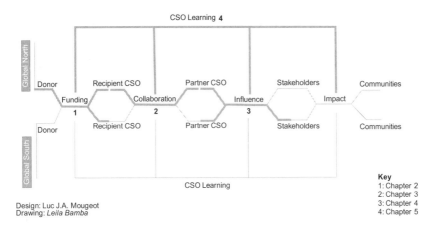

Design: Luc J.A. Mougeot
Drawing: *Leila Bamba*

Figure 1.1 Selected knowledge-relevant relationships between CSOs and other development actors

aforementioned) which are key to ensuring that their interventions bring about positive change for development.

The simplicity of Figure 1.1 should not dispel the complexity of interactions actually at work in any specific situation. Diverse types of organizations can play the role of 'donor' in any given situation (from governments and large NGOs to universities and corporate foundations), just as beneficiary 'communities' may include community-based organizations, institutions, enterprises, associations, local governments, or larger networks. Also, actual relationships that different categories of actors entertain with one another are not limited to those highlighted in the figure. Those featured in Figure1.1 are the prevailing ones, required by CSOs' strategies for development. Noteworthy in all relationships featured, knowledge potentially is being co-created and exchanged, used, and applied, and ideally informs reflection and learning by CSOs concerned with improving the way they engage with the various categories of actors as well as specific organizations within these categories, for more effective delivery on their end goals.

Figure 1.1 highlights four specific segments of this broad network that are addressed by the following four chapters in this book.

Struggling for equity in agenda setting for North–South research partnerships

In Chapter 2, Megan Bradley focuses on segment 1 in Figure 1.1: the funding relationship between Global North donors (official international development agencies) and recipients (development research CSOs) in North–South development research collaborations. She examines how bilateral donor strategies affect collaborative agenda-setting processes through a case study of novel partnership funding approaches experimented with in the first decade of this century by the Netherlands and the United Kingdom in an attempt to redress long decried power imbalances. Global North donor policies definitively shape agenda-setting processes, chiefly by requiring Southern organizations to partner with Northern counterparts in order to receive support, and for both of them to reach mutually productive agendas. The experiences of the Netherlands and the UK demonstrate that revamping bilateral donors' funding policies can potentially improve Southern researchers' ability to influence North–South research agendas, and diversify access to collaborative funding opportunities. However, Bradley's study concludes that even the most innovative partnership funding strategies cannot resolve all the tensions and inequalities that characterize collaborative agenda-setting processes. Bradley cautions donors and researchers alike to recognize the limitations of this approach and use it prudently: North–South partnerships are not necessarily the best way to advance research agendas rooted in Southern priorities.

The evolution of Global North donors' rapport with Global South research organizations in particular contexts, as documented by Bradley, in many ways complements that identified by Parks (2008) between donors and development NGOs in North–South cooperation. In both Bradley's and Parks' studies, a perfect alignment of vision and interests is rare and negotiations are heavily influenced by the relative power of the two actors. As with research organizations contacted by Bradley, Parks found that if NGOs are big fish in a small pond, they may hold an advantage for some time, while the sector develops in that country. But what Parks found was that over time, Global North donors tend to gain advantage vis-a-vis Global South NGO grantees, subjecting them to growing competition for less funding. It is not unlikely that the growing paradigm of global competition for research funding adopted by Global North bilateral donors could replicate in the Global South research community what Parks found to be a well-established phenomenon affecting Global South development NGOs. This 'process of convergence' may lead grantees to a growing upward accountability to their donor at the expense of downward responsiveness to their constituency. However, Bradley offers insights into factors enabling Global South organizations to walk away from unsatisfactory partnership prospects, as well as the trade-offs involved. Consistency and sustainability of funding through longer term grants or managed capital endowments would help grantees maintain their autonomy and buy time to find alternative funders. Donors can also support the development of a domestic funding environment through collaborating with prospective local donors. This is a strategy being pursued for instance by the Think Tank Initiative, co-funded and led by Canada's IDRC.

Bridging the divide in research collaboration between universities and other civil society organizations

In Chapter 3, Elena Chernikova explores primarily segment 2 in Figure 1.1: the collaborative relationship between different types of Global North CSOs (development NGOs and universities). Chernikova surveys the pros and cons of research collaboration between these two communities in the Canadian context, with an emphasis on strategies used to overcome some of the bigger challenges in this type of cross-sector collaboration. Although the body of literature on North–South partnerships for international development is growing rapidly, little has been written on this type of collaboration for research and knowledge on international development, particularly so in Canada. Chernikova collects and systematizes what so far has remained tacit, anecdotal knowledge on civil society–university collaboration between Canadian actors and we do not know of any similar study done as recently as hers in any other OECD country. She discovered a wide variety of types of collaboration at work and analysed four in particular, with attention to factors enabling such collaborations and benefits accruing to both academics and practitioners involved. Major challenges are addressed, as are some ideas in place to sustain these relationships. Several recommendations are formulated to encourage and nurture effective collaborations between universities and civil society.

Following Chernikova's original report from her research in 2011, the Development Studies Association of UK and Ireland funded a major study on university–NGO collaboration in international development. 'Cracking Collaboration' was implemented in 2012 by the International NGO Training and Research Center, the University of Bradford, and World Vision UK. The study echoes many of Chernikova's own findings (Stevens et al., 2013). For instance, as in other OECD countries (e.g. the Netherlands), academics and NGOs in the UK have been pressed by its Department for International Development (DFID) to collaborate more closely one with another in development research for greater impact on policy and practice. Also, in the UK and Ireland, there is a significant and growing number of academics and NGO staff experienced in both worlds (the 'pracademics'), who are well positioned to articulate and advocate closer collaboration (labelled as 'integrators' by Chernikova). What incentives do academic and non-academic organizations offer to encourage the advent of more of these 'pracademics', and how effective are such incentives? There is still little information on such practices and their results so far.

As in the Canadian study, the UK report recognizes the clash of contrasting institutional cultures and it cautions that different types of research require different types of partnerships. The report also recommends a flexible and clear division of labour, upfront investment in trust-building to address power imbalances, and staggered results over the course of the partnership. Published two years after Chernikova's study, the findings of Stevens et al. (2013) underscore the broader relevance of the Canadian findings.

In addition, since Chernikova's original research, at least a couple of initiatives supported by IDRC have reviewed trends and strategies for better collaboration between academia and development NGOs. The first one was the Global University Network on Innovation's 2013 Conference on 'Knowledge, engagement & higher education: contributing to social change' (Hall et al., 2014). This conference focused on universities' duty to proactively engage with civil society, particularly their immediate host communities. Co-organized by the UNESCO Chair in Community-Based Research and Social Responsibility, held by two such 'pracademics' (Budd Hall and Rajesh Tandon), the conference questioned the fact that universities usually rate their service mission as secondary to their teaching and research functions. It challenged a prevailing assumption that service is simply a derivative and basically equates with transfer to communities. Rather, community engagement itself should act as a catalyst for improving teaching and research. The conference pressed for policymakers and university leaders to rethink social responsibility, beyond how the university relates to the outside world as a service provider, and toward how the university can embed this social responsibility in its own pedagogical and investigative mission to nurture tomorrow's professionals and leaders. With this goal in mind, in 2012 the UNESCO Chair initiated a project supported by IDRC that surveyed over 50 countries and collected a dozen country case studies on various policy initiatives that have mainstreamed university–civil society collaboration for positive social change (Hall et al., 2015; Tandon et al., 2016).

A second initiative, in 2013, was the Coady International Institute–IDRC Learning Forum on 'Research for change: what is "research excellence" for civil society organizations and their academic partners?' The forum gathered some 25 participants, in addition to Coady and IDRC staff and others, equally distributed between Canadian civil society practitioners and Canadian university academics, most of them engaged in participatory action research for development in collaboration with organizations in the Global South. Ten case studies were commissioned prior to the forum and reviewed by participants. The forum focused on community-engaged research and identified four dimensions of what constitutes excellence in this type of research (Hogdson, 2014): participation, design, influence, and learning. Research purpose and context define the emphasis to be placed in specific instances on each of these dimensions to pursue excellence.

Noteworthy from these two initiatives is the fact that beyond NGOs or their collectives who usually engage with individual academics rather than with higher education institutions themselves, new arrangements are being experimented with, such as the one developed in Canada between Thompson River University and the British Columbia Council for International Cooperation, or between Managers Without Borders and Laval University's bachelors programme. These are worth following to assess to what extent such partnerships between academia and other CSOs might, over time, be more conducive to innovations in international cooperation for development.

Global North CSOs working with Global South counterparts to influence practice and policy for development

In Chapter 4, Stacie Travers tackles the challenging segment 3 in Figure 1.1: the collaboration between Global North (development NGOs) and Global South (development NGOs, community-based organizations, research institutions) CSOs to influence positive change in practices and policies of stakeholders for development in the Global South. How do North-based CSOs go about accessing and using knowledge when working with South-based partners to help them to influence local practice or policy for positive social change? As she found, much of what has been written on CSO engagement in the development policy process comes out of the UK, specifically the Research and Policy in Development programme of the Overseas Development Institute (ODI) (Court and Young, 2006). In Canada, IDRC did support a review of CSOs' strategies to influence policy and reviewed lessons from its own project portfolio on the research-to-policy link (Synergos, 2008; Carden, 2009). The role that CCSOs could play in influencing policy has long been of interest to the Canadian Council for International Cooperation (CCIC). Between 2003 and 2006, and with support from the former Canadian International Development Agency (CIDA), the CCIC carried out the project 'Building Knowledge and Capacity for Policy Influence'. This project was part of a larger initiative to strengthen civil society policy engagement with the Canadian federal government (CCIC, 2006). Out of this experience, in 2006, the CCIC published *Building Knowledge and Capacity for Policy Influence: Reflections and Resources* and organized a workshop to address challenges and develop strategies.

Travers' study has the merit of examining how the roles which CSOs play (the type of role and the number of roles) are linked to the use of research-centred strategies for influence. The changing relationships of CSOs with governments in both donor and beneficiary countries, as discussed earlier in this Introduction, clearly show that the (often different) political contexts in which partnering CSOs find themselves do affect their roles and, in turn, their potential for influencing policy and practice. As pointed out by Bradley (Chapter 2), the ability of partnerships to bolster Southern organizations' political clout and policy influence varies according to the partners' policy target. Leverage gained through partnerships often declines if Global North researchers seek to influence Southern policymakers, many of whom prefer 'home-grown' analyses, and may be hostile to Northern 'interference' in their sovereign political affairs. Politically prudent Northern researchers and NGOs who seek to influence Southern governments often team up with prominent Southern organizations to benefit from their specialized lobbying expertise and political connections. In some contexts, as Travers finds, achieving concrete and measurable goals may be less critical than affording space 'for citizen expression, experiment and participation in shaping their lives' (Tandon and Brown, 2013: 791).

Managing knowledge to learn for organizational self-improvement

Adding another degree of difficulty to this series, in Chapter 5 Eric Smith delves deep into segment 4 in Figure 1.1, perhaps the most critical to CSOs' ability to evolve their strategies: in this case, the learning relationship which Global North CSOs entertain with themselves and with other categories of actors with which they interact – for funding, collaboration, influence, and impact. As the figure shows, the learning focuses on working relationships with key categories of actors: how best to work with these categories, and individual actors within them, based on a constant reassessment of results and changes in the make-up of such groups of actors and the way they engage in relationships critical to CSOs' ability to deliver on their mandate. Learning for organizational improvement acquires renewed urgency for CSOs' positioning in the new ecosystem for international development.

Unfortunately, too little of ongoing learning gets recorded and even less is shared. Some 10 years ago, recognizing the critical link between knowledge management and organizational learning, ODI undertook to review knowledge management strategies in 13 development organizations of varying type and size (Ramalingam, 2005, cited by Powell, 2006). The study found that this was an enduring problem: the centrality of knowledge to development strategies was not being recognized, the common prioritization of internal issues often distracted from exchanges with Global South partners, and knowledge and learning work was often marginalized. And yet, nearly a decade after the ODI review, Whatley (2013: 964–65) concluded that, notwithstanding some exceptions, 'a strong learning posture is uncommon in the development sector', particularly among Global North NGOs. Past efforts that have emphasized organizational learning – namely through processes of interface between select practitioners and academics and on specific issues – have usually been short-lived and confined, and have had few transformative effects at an organizational level (for instance, van Klinken and Prinsen, 2007).

Smith's study helps to clarify some of the factors enabling effective organizational learning practices among Canadian development NGOs. It is one of the few available on organizational learning (OL) in the civil society sector engaged in development cooperation, and particularly so in the CCSO context. This is a difficult subject to tackle, as so much of the knowledge remains largely tacit in individuals' memory or in organizations' established practice, and is rarely recorded and shared in formal ways by NGOs themselves.

Smith's literature review found that studies about organizational improvement with a development focus examine large institutions and funders, rather than the common recipients of those funds – smaller not-for-profit institutions that work with their counterparts in developing countries. The Istanbul Principles call on CSOs to be knowledge creators and brokers (CCIC, 2010), but little work examines how they are doing so. His findings show that CCSOs are engaged in a variety of knowledge creation and knowledge-sharing activities to improve the work they do.

As in Sarah Parkinson's study of Uganda's National Agricultural Advisory Service (2010), the Canadian case studies reviewed by Smith point to the interaction between the concept of the learning organization and the role of reflective learning, and the organization's culture (allowing stakeholders to negotiate new roles) and its resilience in the face of external pressure (by legitimizing and normalizing organizational adjustment). Yet, and precisely because it remains challenging for most development NGOs to translate the concept of 'learning organization' into design and policy, Smith's study should be of particular interest to those anxious to do so.

Becoming more competent at putting knowledge to work for them is likely to become more vital to development NGOs' future, given a need to pay more attention to what Cavill and Sohail (2007) define as practical (use of inputs, methods, outputs) and strategic (performance relative to mission) accountability. In their review of some 20 international NGOs, Dr Sue Cavill, infrastructure engineer and expert in accountability of public service delivery at PublicWorld, and Dr M. Sohail, Director of Research and Enterprise at the Water, Engineering and Development Centre of Loughborough University, found several factors justifying greater attention to accountability on the part of these NGOs: a crisis of legitimacy and criticisms from press and international policymakers, concerns about the quality of development practice, growing professionalization of development practice, and the growth of the sector, as well as the rising political visibility of international NGOs.

Such good reasons for greater accountability undoubtedly should apply to a much larger circle of international development oriented CSOs. Smith's review of select CCSOs identified several learning mechanisms which they have adopted. These have helped them to also improve their accountability, including mission statement, board of trustees, self-regulation, consultation and participatory mechanisms, and monitoring and evaluation processes, even participation in sector-wide voluntary mechanisms. Smith's study also underscores tensions arising from CSOs' efforts to balance attention to both practical and strategic accountability, a challenge faced by even the larger international NGOs reviewed by Cavill and Sohail.

Although Smith's study focuses on CCSOs' own approaches to learning, there is an equal need for development partnerships between organizations in the Global North and the Global South to make room for mutual learning, as pointed out by Dr Robin Vincent, social anthropologist and Visiting Fellow at Durham University School of Applied Social Sciences, and by communications specialist Dr Ailish Byrne of the Communications for Social Change Consortium (2006). In their review of relationship aspects that foster or inhibit learning, they point to the impact of accountability demands, procedures, and processes.

Smith's recommendations buttress others issued by Vincent and Byrne (2006) as to the kinds of activities which should be promoted for better learning. These include building on existing opportunities and creating spaces for learning, designing projects to facilitate learning explicitly, and negotiating and clarifying purposes and principles of partnerships (expectations, rights, and responsibilities). CSOs should consider the longer term, should fund learning as a core activity, and should develop appropriate systems of evaluation, measurement, and accountability that make learning a key focus of evaluation.

They should also address internal factors of organizational culture and question deeply held assumptions, address power-related issues and other barriers to learning, and look beyond partnerships for networks and communities of practice (CoPs), as exemplified in Canada by AQOCI and the CCIC, both examined in Smith's study. Above all, funders should value CSOs' learning activities as an intrinsic part of the projects and programmes they fund.

Original fieldwork

It is worth emphasizing that, once informed by their reviews of relevant conceptual frameworks and methodological options, all studies involved original and extensive fieldwork by their authors, in Canada or abroad. In three contributions, Canada-wide surveys of academic and civil society communities were initially carried out, some were followed up, and case studies were selected for their potential to inspire larger communities in addressing the challenges identified through national e-surveys. In-person and remote interviews were carried out with actors involved in the case studies.

Megan Bradley's study on donor recipient dynamics in research agenda setting was originally informed by an analysis of contemporary donor policies, as well as an understanding of North–South partnerships and development research funding gained while working at IDRC's Canadian Partnerships Program. She also draws extensively on the results of 43 semi-structured personal interviews with donors, NGO representatives, academic officials, and researchers involved in North–South research partnerships. These interviews were carried out by her in person in the Netherlands, the United Kingdom, Botswana, South Africa, Jordan, Israel, and the Palestinian Territories. Other researchers have attempted to explore donor–recipient relations through a participatory action approach, with limited success, lessons from which are well worth reading (e.g. Eyben et al. 2007).

Elena Chernikova's examination of academic–practitioner research collaborations involved a Quick Survey to 98 international liaison officers at 94 Canadian universities (distributed with help from the Association of Universities and Colleges of Canada). The survey had a 24 per cent response rate. A similar survey was conducted with 87 CCSOs (response rate: 40 per cent) through the CCIC. Responses underwent qualitative analysis to reveal a typology of collaborations, and the variety and frequency of several dimensions of such collaborations. Both surveys were followed up with emails and phone calls to selected key informants. Field trips were made, focusing on areas in Canada where collaboration between universities and NGOs was deemed strong, based on survey responses and follow-ups. Field interviews were used to verify this and gain a more comprehensive understanding of context and conditions. Forty-five academics, practitioners, and beneficiaries were interviewed in person in Victoria, Nanaimo, and Vancouver on the west coast; Montreal in Quebec; Halifax and Antigonish on the east coast; and in the Ottawa–Gatineau area in Ontario and Quebec, plus 16 more by phone or Skype. The interviews were recorded for further analysis.

For her study on how CSOs use research to influence policy and/or practice, Travers initially surveyed 129 international development CCSOs (response rate: 53 per cent) across Canada in order to gauge their level of research use and address specific research questions. As with Elena Chernikova's survey, this afforded a broad overview of the CCSO landscape. Here, it helped identify CCSOs with ongoing projects or programmes where research played a role in their attempts to influence policy and/or practice. Four of these CCSOs were later chosen as case studies, since their projects were collectively located in the same geographic region but they represented various thematic areas and types of CCSOs. Information for the writing and analyses of these particular CCSO projects and programmes was collected through multi-country fieldwork (Argentina, Bolivia, Colombia, and Peru). This included interviews with CCSO and Global South partnering CSO staff, local government officials, and project beneficiaries. Focus group discussions, participation in workshops, visits to project sites, and conferences were carried out during this fieldwork. This combined-methods approach produced both quantitative and qualitative data on the links between CCSOs, research, and influence over policy and practice in the Global South.

Eric Smith is distinctive in that he initially reviews and integrates key concepts (learning organization, OL, knowledge management, organizational knowledge, and practice-based approach) into a single framework, enabling him to typify the various learning approaches used by the CCSOs that participated in the study. A first survey was sent to 126 CCSOs, addressed to senior managers (with approximately a 20 per cent response rate), while a second survey targeted a smaller community of 11 Canadian networking organizations (provincial councils, topical coalitions or CoPs). Responses to these surveys were complemented through interviews and email exchanges. Final results were used to design a semi-structured interview guide, later applied through visits to select organizations across the country. Four case studies were retained and are discussed individually, each exemplifying an effective learning strategy to deal with specific challenges; these are then cross-analysed for more generic lessons.

Conclusion

The ecosystem in which CSOs active in research and cooperation for international development operate has been transforming in dramatic ways over the last decade; this transformation will continue in the years ahead. As seen, the global geography of development has become multi-polar at the same time that dissatisfaction has been growing with assumptions buried in the prevailing development paradigm. The set of development actors has diversified and resource flows have changed in remarkable, even unprecedented ways. Reduced ODA budgets and a country programmable aid now redirected to middle-income countries, the rise of foreign direct investment to developing and transition economies, and the too often questionable contribution of ODA deployment to even a minimalist kind of development, have all led longstanding donor countries to revisit their approach to ODA. In the Global North, new development assistance strategies have been issued which seek a stronger alignment with other policy objectives (both foreign and domestic). These affect Global North CSOs' positioning in the arena of players.

As private and corporate foundations and private capital investors are becoming more prominent actors, governments favour public–private partnerships. CSOs are expected to be more accountable, generate larger impact, professionalize their staff, apply new business models, master knowledge systems for constant learning, and work more than before through partnerships with different actors. Complexity is growing and such shifts in Global North policies have had a domino effect on the Global South partners of Global North CSOs. Global North CSOs have been reviewing their experience with private-sector organizations to govern their future engagement with them, and ethical concerns have prompted actors in some fields to develop new codes of conduct. Global North CSOs are also required to collaborate more with academic institutions, a major source of volunteers for them. On this point, there is much need for comprehensive reviews of the impact of such programmes on both sending and hosting organizations, on contributions of student research placements to host organizations' agendas, and stronger links between engaged scholarship by faculty and service learning by students.

Global North CSOs' added value is also being challenged by development in the Global South: more non-OECD governments are funding CSOs at home, including development NGOs, and launching their own bilateral development agencies. Transnational corporations based in emerging economies are creating their own foundations, supporting a wide range of CSOs. More of these are also becoming important players in international coalitions. Global South scholars are taking a larger role in informing and influencing domestic policy, even assuming regional leadership, through research institutes, think tanks, and very large NGOs. This sophistication in capacity is challenging the Global North's fixation on developing-country fieldwork and pressing scholars and activists to acknowledge dysfunctions in the Global North and the connectedness of many challenges (and responses) across the Global North and South. This development calls for a revision of curricula for development practitioners in the Global North, for which CSO–academia collaboration should be critical.

Given these changes, more than ever before Global North CSOs must tap into knowledge to adjust their working relationships with long-time and new actors both in the Global North and the Global South. While the need for creative thinking and experimentation is greater than ever, there is still little research published on the challenges experienced and solutions found by CSOs as they adjust to changes in the larger international development ecosystem.

Having discussed changes in this ecosystem, this Introduction turned to the working relationships between CSOs, and between them and other actors in the Global North and Global South, with an emphasis on the use of (and impact on) knowledge in such relationships. The chapter proposed a chain of working relationships between different categories of actors, from donors to beneficiary communities (Figure 1.1); in this chain, it highlighted specific segments covered by the chapters in this book. Each of the subsequent chapters focuses on a particular section of the scheme (Figure 1.1), discussing the role of knowledge in donor–recipient interactions centred on funding, in collaborations between different types of civil society organizations (universities and development NGOs) centred on mutually building capacity and informing practice, in partnerships between CSOs in the Global North and the Global South focused on influencing practices and policies of local stakeholders, and finally in processes within and across CSOs centred on self and collective learning from experience with the aforementioned dynamics, so as to improve themselves as organizations.

Knowledge plays a critical role in tackling challenges such as redressing power imbalances between donors and recipients for more locally owned agendas; magnifying the impact of official development assistance and its coherence with other policy objectives; improving synergies between the missions of the academic, other civil society, and private-sector organizations involved; informing and influencing local dynamics for positive change at scale; systematizing and sharing results that can be meaningful to all those involved; and finally, learning from ground-level experience for organizations to remain relevant, effective, and efficient players within the new ecosystem. It is the hope of all contributors to this book that solutions to some of the challenges widely faced by mainstream CSO practice – and the central role played by knowledge – will inspire others in tackling their own challenges so as to remain significant players in international development.

Acknowledgements

I wish to thank Ann Weston, former director of IDRC's Special Initiatives Division and leader of its former Canadian Partnerships Program, who now leads IDRC's new Foundations for Innovation programme, for releasing time for me to work on this project. My appreciation also goes to the contributing authors for their comments on this and other chapters, as well as an anonymous reviewer for many constructive suggestions which greatly assisted us in enhancing the final version of the book as a whole. Finally, I wish to warmly thank IDRC's publisher Nola Haddadian for her guidance and support, as well as our summer student Leila Bamba for her assistance in final manuscript formatting. Views expressed in this and other chapters are the sole responsibility of the authors and do not necessarily reflect those of IDRC or its Board of Governors.

References

Alexander, Nick, Rowe, Sylvia, Brackett, Robert E., Burton-Freeman, Britt, Hentges, Eric J., Kretser, Alison, Klurfeld, David M., Meyers, Linda D., Mukherjea, Ratna, and Ohlhorst, Sara (2015) 'Achieving a transparent, actionable, framework for public–private partnerships for food and nutrition research', *American Journal of Clinical Nutrition* 101 (6): 1359–63 <http://ajcn.nutrition.org/content/101/6/1359.short> [accessed 29 July 2016].

Anderson, M., Brown, D., and Jean, I. (2012) *Time to Listen: Hearing People on the Receiving End of International Aid,* Cambridge: CDA Collaborative. <http://cdacollaborative.org/publication/time-to-listen-hearing-people-on-the-receiving-end-of-international-aid/> [accessed 29 July 2016].

Association of Universities and Colleges of Canada – AUCC (2014) *Canada's Universities in the World. AUCC Internationalization Survey 2014,* Ottawa: AUCC.

Association québécoise des organismes de coopération internationale (AQOCI) (2013) *Institutionalisation* [website] <http://www.aqoci.
qc.ca/spip.php?article2362> [accessed 29 July 2016].

Benmamoun, Mamoun, and Lehnert, Kevin (2013) 'Financing growth:
comparing the effects of FDI, ODA, and international remittances', *Journal
of Economic Development* 38 (2): 43–65.

Blais, André, and Loewen, Peter (2011) *Youth Electoral Engagement in Canada*,
Working Paper Series, Ottawa: Elections Canada <http://184.150.235.237/
res/rec/part/youeng/yeefr-2011-eng.pdf> [accessed 29 July 2016].

Bolden, Richard, and Kirk, Philip (2009) 'African leadership: surfacing new
understandings through leadership development', *International Journal of
Cross-Cultural Management* 9 (1): 69–86 <http://ccm.sagepub.com/content/
9/1/69.short> [accessed 29 July 2016].

Brown, Stephen, den Heyer, Molly, and Black, David R. (2016) *Rethinking
Canadian Aid*, 2nd edn, Ottawa: University of Ottawa <https://press.
uottawa.ca/rethinking-canadian-aid-2.html> [accessed 13 September 2016].

Bradley, M. (2016) 'Whose agenda? Power, policies, and priorities in North-
South research partnerships', in L.J.A. Mougeot (ed.), *Putting Knowledge to
Work: Collaborating, influencing and learning for international development*,
pp. 37–70, Rugby, UK and Ottawa: Practical Action Publishing and IDRC
<http://dx.doi.org/10.3362/9781780449685.002>.

Buckles, Daniel (ed.) (2013) *Innovations with Evaluation Methods: Lessons from
a Community of Practice in International Development*, Montreal: Canada
World Youth <http://canadaworldyouth.org/wp-content/uploads/2013/02/
Innovation-with-Evaluation-Methods.pdf> [accessed 29 July 2016].

CCGHR (Canadian Coalition for Global Health Research) (2014) *Partnership
Assessment Tool* [website] <http://www.ccghr.ca/resources/partnerships-and-
networking/partnership-assessment-tool/ > [accessed 29 July 2016].

CCIC (Canadian Council for International Cooperation) (2006) *Building
Knowledge and Capacity for Policy Influence: Reflections and Resources*, Ottawa:
CCIC <http://www.ccic.ca/what_we_do/capacity_building_reflections_e.
php> [accessed 29 July 2016].

CCIC (2010) *Open Forum for CSO Development Effectiveness* [website] <http://
www.ccic.ca/_files/en/what_we_do/2010_09_istanbul_principles.pdf>
[accessed 29 July 2016].

Carden, Fred (2009) *Knowledge to Policy: Making the Most of Development
Research*, New Delhi and Ottawa: Sage Publications and IDRC <http://idl-
bnc.idrc.ca/dspace/bitstream/10625/37706/1/IDL-37706.pdf>   [accessed
29 July 2016].

Carney, Jason (2014) *Promoting Ethics When Partnering with the Private Sector for
Development*, Ottawa: North-South Institute <http://www.nsi-ins.ca/wp-con-
tent/uploads/2014/09/Promoting-Ethics-when-Partnering-with-the-Private-
Sector-for-Development-August-2014.pdf> [accessed 29 July 2016].

Cavill, Sue, and Sohail, M. (2007) 'Increasing strategic accountability: a
framework for international NGOs', *Development in Practice* 17(2): 231–48.

Chandhoke, Neera (2007) 'Civil society', *Development in Practice* 17(4–5): 607–14.

Chandy, Laurence (2011) 'Reframing development cooperation', Washington,
DC: Brookings Institute <http://www.brookings.edu/wp-content/uploads/
2016/07/2011_blum_reframing_development_cooperation_chandy.pdf>
[accessed 27 October 2016].

Chernikova, E. (2016) 'Negotiating research collaboration between universities and other civil society organizations in Canada', in L.J.A. Mougeot (ed.), *Putting Knowledge to Work: Collaborating, influencing and learning for international development*, pp. 71–106, Rugby, UK and Ottawa: Practical Action Publishing and IDRC <http://dx.doi.org/10.3362/9781780449685.003>.

Coston, Jennifer (1998) 'A model and typology of government–NGO relationships', *Nonprofit and Volunteering Sector Quarterly* 27 (3): 358–82 <http://nvs.sagepub.com/content/27/3/358> [accessed 29 July 2016].

Court, Julius, and Young, John (2006) 'Bridging research and policy in international development: an analytical and practical framework', *Development in Practice* 16(1): 85–90.

Currie-Alder, B. (2016) 'The state of development studies', *Canadian Journal of Development Studies* (March) 37(1): 5–26.

Deneault, Alain (2014) *Paradis fiscaux: la filière canadienne*, Montréal: Ecosociété.

DFATD (Department of Foreign Affairs, Trade and Development) (2014) *Report on Plans and Priorities 2013–14 – Supplementary Information Tables*, Ottawa: DFATD, Government of Canada <http://www.international.gc.ca/gac-amc/publications/plans/rpp/rpp_1314_sup.aspx?lang=eng> [accessed 27 October 2016].

DFATD (2015) *International Development and Humanitarian Assistance Civil Society Partnership Policy*, Ottawa: DFATD, Government of Canada <http://www.international.gc.ca/development-developpement/cs-policy-politique-sc.aspx?lang=eng> [accessed 29 July 2016].

Do Carmo Guerra, Fátima Júnia, dos Santos De Sousa Teodósio, Armindo and Mswaka, Walter (2016) 'Knowledge and power of civil society: an empirical study of Brazilian professionals working in NGOs', *Cosmopolitan Civil Societies Journal* 8 (1): 64–85 <https://epress.lib.uts.edu.au/journals/index.php/mcs/article/viewFile/4259/5298> [accessed 29 July 2016].

Driffield, Nigel, and Jones, Chris (2013) 'Impact of FDI, ODA and migrant remittances on economic growth in developing countries: a systems approach', *European Journal of Development Research* 25 (2): 173–96 <http://www.palgrave-journals.com/ejdr/journal/v25/n2/full/ejdr20131a.html> [accessed 29 July 2016].

Dunlop, Judith M. (2006) 'Privatization: how government promotes market-based solutions to social problems', *Critical Social Work* 7(2) <http://www1.uwindsor.ca/criticalsocialwork/privatization-how-government-promotes-market-based-solutions-to-social-problems> [accessed 29 July 2016].

Entrepreneurcountry Global (2016) *Welcome to Entrepreneurcountry* [website] <http://www.entrepreneurcountryglobal.com/welcome-to-entrepreneur-country> [accessed 12 August 2016].

Eyben, Rosalind, Leon, Rosario, and Hossain, Naomi (2007) 'Participatory action research into donor–recipient relations: a case study', *Development in Practice* 17 (2): 167–78.

Favreau, Louis (2015) *La finance solidaire québécoise peut-elle server de levier dans des communautés du Sud?* [blog] 18 February, Enjeux et défis du développement international <http://www.defisdvm.com/blog/la-finance-solidaire-quebecoise-peut-elle-servir-de-levier-dans-des-communautes-du-ud> [accessed 29 July 2016].

George, Susan (2014) *Les usurpateurs. Comment les entreprises transnationales prennent le pouvoir*, Paris: Seuil.

GAC (Global Affairs Canada) (2014) *Report on Plans and Priorities 2013-14 Supplementary Information Tables* [website] <http://www.international.gc.ca/department-ministere/plans/rpp/dev_rpp_1314_sup.aspx?lang=eng> [accessed 29 July 2016].

GAC (2015) *Civil Society and Development* [website] <http://www.international.gc.ca/development-developpement/priorities-priorites/civil_society-societe-civile.aspx?lang=eng> [accessed 29 July 2016].

Grady, Heather (2014) 'Philanthropy as an emerging contributor to development cooperation', UNDP background paper for the *Conference International Development Cooperation: Trends and Emerging Opportunities – Perspectives of the New Actors*, Istanbul, June <http://www.undp.org/content/dam/undp/documents/partners/civil_society/UNDP-CSO-philanthropy.pdf> [accessed 29 July 2016].

Granados Sánchez, Jesús, and Gemma, Puig (2014) 'Community–university engagement initiatives: trends and progress', in GUNI, *Knowledge, Engagement & Higher Education: Contributing to Social Change*, pp. 113–26. London: Palgrave MacMillan.

Hall, Budd, Tandon, Rajesh, and Tremblay, Crystal (2015) *Strengthening Community University Research Partnerships: Global Perspectives*, Victoria and New Delhi: University of Victoria Press and PRIA Press.

Hayman R., King, Sophie, Kontinen, Tiina, and Narayanaswamy, Lata (eds) (2016) *Negotiating Knowledge: Evidence and Experience in Development NGOs*, Rugby, UK: Practical Action Publishing.

Heidrich, Pablo, Kindornay, Shannon, with Budell, Matthew (2013) *Economic Relations between Canada and Latin America and the Caribbean*, Ottawa: The North-South Institute <http://www.nsi-ins.ca/wp-content/uploads/2013/11/2013-Economic-Relations-Between-Canada-ALC.pdf> [accessed 29 July 2016].

Hobbins, Von Michael Andre, Bryant, Margi, Haggblom, Anna, Helmold, Peter, Balen, Julie, Miwa, Takeshi, Masengu, Chendela S., and Ehmer, Jochen (2015) *How to Overcome Inherent Gaps between NGOs and Research Institutions*, Basel: Medicus Mundi Schweiz <http://www.medicusmundi.ch/de/bulletin/mms-bulletin/implementation-research-the-way-forward/cases-from-the-field/case-report-from-a-collaboration-on-health-research-between-the-university-of-sheffield-uk-and-solidarmed-switzerland> [accessed 29 July 2016].

Hodgson, Wayne (2014) *Research for Change: What is 'research excellence' for civil society organizations and their academic partners?* A report on the 2013 IDRC/Coady Canadian Learning Forum, November 12–13, 2013, Ottawa: IDRC <http://idl-bnc.idrc.ca/dspace/bitstream/10625/52773/1/IDL-52773.pdf> [accessed 29 July 2016].

Holcombe, Susan H. (2014) 'Donors and exogenous versus endogenous development', *Development in Practice* 24 (5–6): 750–63.

Hulchanski, J. David (2010) *The Three Cities Within Toronto: Income polarization among Toronto's neighbourhoods, 1970–2005*, Toronto: Cities Centre Press <http://3cities.neighbourhoodchange.ca/wp-content/themes/3-Cities/pdfs/three-cities-in-toronto.pdf> [accessed 29 July 2016].

IDRC (International Development Research Centre) (2015) *Africa – home of the next Einstein? An IDRC-AIMS Hangout* [website] <https://www.youtube.com/watch?v=cIDs-1MXv_M> [accessed 29 July 2016].

Kindornay, Shannon, Tissot, Stephanie, and Sheiban, Nabeel (2014) *The Value of Cross-Sector Development Partnerships*, Ottawa: North-South Institute <http://www.nsi-ins.ca/wp-content/uploads/2014/01/The-Value-of-Cross-Sector-Development-Partnerships.pdf> [accessed 29 July 2016].

King, Sophie, Kontinen, Tiina, Narayanswamy, Kata, and Hayman, Rachel (eds) (2016) 'Introduction: why do NGOs need to negotiate knowledge?', in Hayman et al., *Negotiating Knowledge*, pp. 1–16, Rugby, UK: Practical Action Publishing.

Kiva (2016) [website] <https://www.kiva.org/> [accessed 29 July 2016].

Klassen, Jared, and Reilly-King, Fraser (2014) *Leveraging the Private Sector?*, Ottawa: Canadian Council for International Cooperation.

Lacalle-Calderón, Maricruz, Chasco, Coro, Alfonso-Gil, Javier, and Neira, Isabel (2015) 'A comparative analysis of the effect of aid and microfinance on growth', *Canadian Journal of Development Studies* 36 (1): 72–88 <http://dx.doi.org/10.1080/02255189.2015.984664>.

Laval University (2016) *International Development and Humanitarian Action* [website] <http://english.fsa.ulaval.ca/cms/site/fba/page41387.html;jsessionid=C6122C5463BE0F35F4F93F008F771311> [accessed 29 July 2016].

Malunga, Chiku, and Holcombe, Susan H. (2014) 'Endogenous development going forward: learning and action', *Development in Practice* 24 (5–6): 777–81.

Nandy, A. (1992) *Traditions, Tyranny and Utopias: Essays in the Politics of Awareness*, Delhi: Oxford University Press.

OECD (Organisation for Economic Co-operation and Development) (2011) *An Overview of Growing Income Inequalities in OECD Countries. Main Findings*, Paris: OECD <http://www.oecd.org/els/soc/49499779.pdf> [accessed 29 July 2016].

OECD (2016) *Aid to poor countries slips further as governments tighten budgets* [website] <http://www.oecd.org/dac/stats/aidtopoorcountriesslipsfurtherasgovernmentstightenbudgets.htm> [accessed 29 July 2016].

Parkinson, Sarah (2010) 'The learning organization as a model for rural development', *Development in Practice* 20 (3): 329–41.

Parks, Thomas (2008) 'The rise and fall of donor funding for advocacy NGOs: understanding the impact', *Development in Practice* 18 (2): 213–22.

Pickard, Miguel (2007) 'Reflections on relationships: the nature of partnerships according to five NGOs in southern Mexico', *Development in Practice* 17 (4–5): 575–81.

Powell, Mike (2006) 'Which knowledge? Whose reality? An overview of knowledge used in the development sector', *Development in Practice* 16 (6): 518–32.

Ramalingan, B. (2005) *Implementing Knowledge Strategies: Lessons from International Development Agencies*, ODI Working Paper 244, London: Overseas Development Institute.

Rashid, Ahmed K. (2014) 'Canada–Global South two-way student mobility: challenges and inspiring practices', Ottawa: IDRC (December 2014 draft).

Salamon, Lester (2014) *Leverage for Good: An Introduction to the New Frontiers of Philanthropy and Social Investment*, New York: Oxford University Press.

Salamon, Lester M., Sokolowski, S.W., and List, R. (2003) *Global Civil Society: An Overview*, Baltimore: Johns Hopkins Center for Civil Society Studies.

Schneider, Friedrich (2010) 'Turnover of organized crime and money laundering: Some preliminary empirical findings', *Public Choice* 144 (3): 473–86 <http://dx.doi.org/10.1007/s11127-010-9676-8>.

Sen, Amartya (1988) 'The concept of development', in H. Chenery and T.N. Srinivasan (eds), *Handbook of Development Economics*, pp. 9–26. <http://ivut.iut.ac.ir/content/300/5915.THE_CONCEPT_OF_DEVELOPMENT.pdf> [accessed 29 July 2016].

Smith, E. (2016) 'The learning needs and experiences of Canadian civil society organizations in international cooperation for development', in L.J.A. Mougeot (ed.), *Putting Knowledge to Work: Collaborating, influencing and learning for international development*, pp. 143–182, Rugby, UK and Ottawa: Practical Action Publishing and IDRC <http://dx.doi.org/10.3362/9781780449685.005>.

Stevens, Daniel, Hayman, Rachel, and Mdee, Anna (2013) '"Cracking collaboration" between NGOs and academics in development research', *Development in Practice* 23 (8): 1071–77.

Synergos (2008) *A practitioner's guide to influencing policy: Learning from the senior fellows annual global meeting*, New York: New York.

Tandon, Rajesh, and Brown, L. David (2013) 'Civil societies at crossroads: lessons and implications', *Development in Practice* 23 (5–6): 784–96.

Tandon, R., Hall, B., Lepore, W., and Singh, W. (2016) *Knowledge and Engagement: Building Capacity for the Next Generation of Community Based Researchers*. Victoria and New Delhi: University of Victoria and PRIA Press.

The Global Journal (23 January 2013) Special Feature: The Top 100 NGOs 2013 Edition <http://theglobaljournal.net/group/15-top-100-ngos-2013/article/986/> [accessed 4 November 2016].

The Global Journal (2015) *The new 2015 Top 500 NGOs is out* [website] <http://www.theglobaljournal.net/article/view/1171/> [accessed 29 July 2016].

Think Tank Initiative (2016) *Think Tank Directory* [website] <http://www.thinktankinitiative.org/think-tanks/map> [accessed 29 July 2016].

Tiessen, Rebecca, and Huish, Robert (eds) (2014) *Globetrotting or Global Citizenship? Perils and Potential of International Experiential Learning*, Toronto: University of Toronto Press.

Travers, S. (2016) 'Canadian civil society organizations using research to influence policy and practice in the Global South', in L.J.A. Mougeot (ed.), *Putting Knowledge to Work: Collaborating, influencing and learning for international development*, pp. 107–142, Rugby, UK and Ottawa: Practical Action Publishing and IDRC <http://dx.doi.org/10.3362/9781780449685.004>.

United Nations Conference on Trade and Development – UNCTAD (2014) *World Investment Report 2014: Investing in the SDGs: An Action Plan*, New York and Geneva: United Nations <http://unctad.org/en/PublicationsLibrary/wir2014_en.pdf> [accessed 29 July 2016].

University of Pennsylvania (2016) *Think Tanks and Civil Societies Program* [website] <http://gotothinktank.com/> [accessed 29 July 2016].

van Klinken, Rinus, and Prinsen, Gerard (2007) 'Practitioner-led research: experiences with learning platforms', *Development in Practice* 17 (3): 419–25.

Vincent, Robin, and Byrne, Ailish (2006) 'Enhancing learning in development partnerships', *Development in Practice* 16 (5): 385–99.

Volunteermatch (2016) *We bring good people & good causes together* [website] <https://www.volunteermatch.org/> [accessed 29 July 2016].

Wallace, T. with Bornstein, L., and Chapman, J. (2006) *The Aid Coercion: Commitment and Coercion in Development NGOs*, London: IT Publications.

Whatley, Barry (2013) 'Improved learning for greater effectiveness in development NGOs', *Development in Practice* 23 (8): 963–76.

Woods, Ngaire (2008) 'Whose aid? Whose influence? China, emerging donors and the silent revolution in development assistance', *International Affairs* 84(6): 1205–21 <http://dx.doi.org/10.1111/j.1468-2346.2008.00765.x>.

Ziai, Aram (2013) 'The discourse of "development", and why the concept should be abandoned', *Development in Practice* 23(1): 123–36.

About the author

Luc J.A. Mougeot is a Senior Program Specialist with the Technology and Innovation Division of Canada's International Development Research Centre (IDRC) in Ottawa. From 2004 to 2014, he worked with IDRC's former Canadian Partnerships Program, where contributing authors to this book held research awards. Luc has been managing research grants to Canadian universities and their national association, learned societies, and non-governmental organizations active in research and cooperation for international development. Luc led IDRC's Cities Feeding People Program (1996–2004) and was associate professor at the Federal University of Pará, in Belém, Brazil (1978–1989). He holds a doctorate in geography from Michigan State University. His latest publication reviews lessons from collaborative research by scholars, non-government organizations, and local governments for policy development, in *Integrated Urban Agriculture* (2016) edited by Robert France, Green Frigate Books.

CHAPTER 2

Whose agenda?
Power, policies, and priorities
in North–South research partnerships

Megan Bradley

Abstract

Research for development is often undertaken through partnerships between researchers working in the Global North and Global South. Continued domination of collaborative agendas by the interests of Northern donors and scholars is often lamented, almost invariably eliciting calls for more equitable Southern engagement in agenda-setting processes. Yet the implications of this and the obstacles to its realization are rarely examined. This chapter examines how bilateral donor strategies affect collaborative agenda-setting processes: donor policies definitively shape these by requiring Southern researchers to partner with Northern counterparts in order to receive support. Innovative experiences of the Netherlands and the UK in the first decade of the 21st century demonstrate that revamping funding policies can improve Southern researchers' ability to influence North–South research agendas, and diversify access to collaborative funding. But even the most innovative partnership funding strategies cannot resolve all tensions and inequalities inherent to collaborative agenda-setting processes.

The chapter also explores researchers' motivations for entering into North–South partnerships, the obstacles Southern researchers encounter in agenda-setting processes, and the strategies they employ to ensure that such partnerships respond to their concerns. North–South partnerships can augment individual and institutional resources and skills, but they are not a panacea for all the challenges associated with capacity building and the creation and use of knowledge for development. Donors and researchers alike are well advised to recognize the limitations of this approach and use it prudently: North–South partnerships are not necessarily the best way to advance research agendas rooted in Southern priorities.

Keywords: development research, donor–recipient partnerships, agenda setting, North–South collaboration, demand-driven approach, excellence-focused approach

Current relevance

Central to any discussion of what knowledge is created by whom and for which purpose in research and cooperation for development is the question

http://dx.doi.org/10.3362/9781780449586.002

of the power, politics, and priorities of those involved in donor–recipient partnerships. On this count, even if original research on which this chapter is based was completed in 2007, nearly a decade ago, this study remains more relevant than ever to the ongoing debate on this issue. Despite variations of degree in donor–recipient power imbalances, in Buffardi's words (2013) there is a persistent under-representation of recipient-country actors in such partnerships. And there is a real risk that such an imbalance will endure, if not worsen. Over the last decade, slow economic growth and a more conservative political climate have been affecting donor governments' revenues and priorities in most high-income and even in some emerging economies, thereby increasing domestic pressure everywhere for restraint on spending overseas and for shifting attention to widening domestic inequalities. As mentioned in the introductory chapter (Mougeot, 2016), official development assistance has stagnated or declined, becoming more selective and concerned with supporting trade to grow donor countries' own competitiveness. Control over knowledge is becoming paramount to trade and includes creating development agendas in new resource or consumer markets, recruiting the best talents from such countries to advance science and innovation at home, as well as expanding abroad the reach of one's own knowledge industry.

In this context, this scholarly examination of the inequity risks linked to power imbalances in donor–recipient research partnerships adds value to the debate in three ways. Firstly, it provides a unique review of innovative policy experiments from the first decade of this century by a couple of the more progressive and reflective OECD agencies that were trying to redress the power imbalance in partnerships involving Global North donors and research recipients in the Global North and Global South. Surprisingly, the Dutch 'demand-driven' and the British 'excellence-focused' approaches to development research partnerships garnered limited attention in the scholarly literature. Beyond their adoption to varying extents by most bilateral agencies, or at least they were said to have been adopted, the jury is still out on whether the adoption of these approaches significantly enhanced capacity; that is, turned nascent Global South institutions into strong national actors for the development of their society. But secondly, and more critically, although the broader literature on North–South research cooperation often laments the persistent domination of collaborative agendas by Northern donors and scholars – and perhaps more so when these tackle global challenges – and does call for more equitable Southern engagement in agenda setting, the implications of this and the obstacles to its realization are still rarely examined in detail. That is what this study does. Thirdly, beyond its scrutiny of institutional innovations in the Global North and the struggle of Northern and Southern researchers to agree on productive research agendas, the study quite distinctly explores Global South researchers' own motivations for entering into North–South partnerships. It looks, from their perspective, at the obstacles that they face in agenda-setting processes and the strategies they use to ensure that partnerships do respond to their own concerns. On this latter point, Southern researchers' emerging strategies are consistent with a growing availability of more flexible sources of funding to Global South researchers and organizations, as well as with growing pressure for local control over agendas, as noted in the introductory chapter. Overall, the study offers a well-rounded appreciation of the political economy at play in the Northern donor–Southern recipient relationship.

Introduction

In 1972, the Northern and Southern delegates to an OECD Conference of Directors of Research and Training Institutes identified two major trends in international research cooperation. First, they applauded a growing commitment to Southern self-reliance. Second, they noted increased interest in 'new forms' of North–South research collaboration, particularly interdisciplinary, mutually beneficial partnerships managed in the South, and based on Southern priorities (Amin et al., 1975: 790). More than 40 years later, North–South partnerships remain a prominent feature of the development research landscape, but donors and researchers are still struggling to come to terms with these 'new forms' of cooperation.

Partnership suffers from no lack of proponents. Among many donors and researchers, partnership is often seen as a good in and of itself, and arguing against partnership is akin to standing up against motherhood or friendship. Advocates of North–South research partnerships suggest that it is efficient, intellectually enriching, and conducive to capacity building. Above all, it is seen as mutually beneficial (Hatton and Schroeder, 2007: 157–58). However, veterans of North–South research partnerships describe a more complex reality, shaped first and foremost by the fact that 'partnering' is often the only way for Southern researchers to access funding. Alongside the benefits of partnership come a range of obstacles from language barriers and complex management structures to inequitable access to financial resources, libraries, conferences, training, and publishing opportunities. Mismatched expectations, lack of face-to-face interaction, and different levels of methodological sophistication can also throw a wrench into partnership plans.[1]

The agenda-setting process represents a particularly formidable obstacle for many development research partnerships. The literature on North–South research cooperation often laments the continued domination of collaborative agendas by the interests of Northern donors and scholars, and almost invariably calls for more equitable Southern engagement in agenda-setting processes. Yet the implications of this statement and the obstacles to its realization are rarely examined in detail. This gap between what is necessary and the reality is striking because the developmental impact of research initiatives is typically limited if they are divorced from the priorities that resonate among Southern actors. Furthermore, better integrating Southern perspectives into collaborative research agendas promises to diversify and enrich the quality and insightfulness of scholarship in fields from disaster management and urban planning to competition policy and conservation.

As a modest response to this gap, the first section of this chapter examines how bilateral donor strategies affect collaborative agenda-setting processes, focusing on approaches adopted by the Netherlands and the United Kingdom, in particular on policies in effect between 2000 and 2007. I argue that donor policies definitively shape agenda-setting processes, chiefly by prompting or even requiring Southern researchers to partner with Northern counterparts in order to receive support. The experiences of the Netherlands and the UK demonstrate that revamping bilateral donors' funding policies may improve Southern researchers' ability to influence North–South research agendas and diversify access to collaborative funding opportunities. However, even the most innovative funding strategies cannot resolve all the tensions and inequalities that characterize collaborative agenda-setting processes.

The second section explores researchers' motivations for entering into North–South partnerships, the obstacles Southern researchers encounter in agenda-setting processes, and some of the strategies they employ to attempt to ensure that research partnerships respond to their concerns. This analysis suggests that while North–South partnerships have the potential to significantly advance the production of knowledge for development, strong Southern research organizations are best placed to maximize the benefits of collaboration. However, many of the organizations entering into partnerships lack a clear sense of their own priorities and other institutional capacities critical to successful agenda negotiations. Although North–South partnerships can augment individual and institutional resources and skills, they are not a panacea for all the challenges associated with capacity building and the creation of knowledge to inform sustainable development policies. Donors and researchers alike are therefore well advised to recognize the limitations of this approach and use it prudently, as North–South partnerships are not necessarily the best way to advance agendas rooted in Southern priorities.

Before developing these arguments, the chapter introduces some of the key concepts that underpin this research and reviews the state of knowledge on North–South research partnerships, concentrating on the question of agenda setting. Next, the methodology used to execute this work is explained. Briefly, the arguments advanced in this chapter are informed by an analysis of contemporary donor policies, as well as by the understanding of North–South partnerships and development research funding gained while working with the Canadian Partnerships (CP) Program of the International Development Research Centre (IDRC), and subsequently as a university-based academic and as a policy researcher with the Brookings Institution in Washington, DC. The chapter also draws extensively on the results of 43 semi-structured interviews on North–South research partnerships that were conducted in Europe, the Middle East, and Southern Africa with donors, NGO representatives, academic officials, and migration and governance researchers (see the section on methodology for additional detail).

State of knowledge and key concepts

Before proceeding, the state of knowledge in this field and the slippery terms employed in it demand a word of clarification.

Slippery terminology

While the terms 'North' and 'South' usefully underscore how geography and colonial history have structured development and research opportunities, they are certainly not discrete concepts. In fact, the practice of partnership underlines the impossibility of using these terms as binary opposites, as many of the foremost actors in international research cooperation elude easy categorization as 'Northern' or 'Southern'. In some regions, 'North and South' is not the most relevant terminology of partnership. In the Middle East, for example, many researchers suggested to me that the key distinction structuring research partnerships was not North–South, but rather the distinction between western and predominantly Muslim states. Furthermore, countries like South Africa, Brazil, China, and India are home to well-financed, world-class research institutions, which operate alongside innumerable organizations struggling simply to pay their bills. International organizations, such as United Nations agencies, often play major roles in research cooperation, but cannot be neatly labelled 'Northern' or 'Southern'. Individual researchers also subvert the North–South 'divide', as many Southern citizens pursue their education and careers in the North. At the same time, in some fields a growing number of Northern researchers are joining Southern institutions.

This chapter is concerned with agenda-setting processes in North–South *development research* partnerships. Development research may be defined as 'applied research that has the objective of leading directly to sustainable improvement in the quality of human existence or basic research that results in an improved understanding of factors that affect development' (Pestieau et al., 1998). To be sure, there are no monolithic research agendas on any issue in the Global North and South. Rather, broad regional and national priorities are tempered by factors ranging from institutional mandates and community-level economic interests to individuals' political convictions and sociocultural allegiances. Development research agendas are increasingly enriched by the involvement in research partnerships of not only university-based academics, but also policymakers, practitioners, NGO representatives, and members of communities grappling directly with the causes and consequences of poverty.

Just as there are innumerable research agendas, there are myriad partnership modalities, including one-on-one co-authorship, training schemes, institutional twinning arrangements, networks, and the co-management of journals and other publications. Partnerships also vary remarkably in their duration, composition, budgets, and the extent to which they focus on capacity building. This study is principally concerned with partnerships linking teams of researchers in the Global North and South, which aim to produce new knowledge to support the development process. Although various authors have attributed different meanings to partnership, collaboration, and cooperation, throughout this chapter these terms are employed interchangeably, reflecting their practical usage by the participants in North–South exchanges. There are pitfalls to any set of terminology. An important shortcoming of my use of the term 'collaboration' was pointed out to me by Palestinian researchers who stressed that in their context, 'collaboration' denotes support for the Israeli occupation of the Palestinian Territories. This is of course not my meaning.

State of knowledge

Many professionals involved in North–South development research projects lament the lack of studies on these partnerships to support critical reflection and the refining of approaches to collaboration (Box, 2001). However, a review of the literature on North–South research partnerships suggests that studies and evaluations of collaborative research endeavours are more plentiful, and their findings more instructive, than often assumed (Bradley, 2007a).

Still, significant issues remain to be explored. Many scholars interested in the challenges of research partnerships appear to work in isolation, with little interdisciplinary dialogue. For example, while there are a considerable number of studies on North–South research partnerships in the fields of health and agriculture, opportunities have not been grasped to compare the experiences of each group. Furthermore, most of the literature on North–South research partnerships appears to have been produced by Northern or Northern-based researchers and institutions. Southern reflections on North–South research partnerships seem few and far between, although there may be studies by Southern scholars that are simply not available electronically or in Northern libraries. Major types of studies and reflections on North–South research partnerships include programme reports and evaluations (often produced by donors), discussions of policies and principles to guide effective partnerships, reports from conferences on North–South partnerships, and chapters in academic books and articles in peer-reviewed journals (Swiss Commission for Research Partnership with Developing Countries, (KFPE) 1998; RAWOO, 2001; AUCC, 2006). Most of these articles review the experiences of major research partnerships and suggest avenues for improving collaborative work. They are typically published in journals on research management and methodology.

The literature on North–South research partnerships identifies a wide range of partnership modalities. Ogden and Porter (2000) and Scholey (2006) provide detailed perspectives on the terminology of partnership. Ogden and Porter, for example, highlight the difference between individuals' goals and concerns, and institutional needs and agendas in the context of research cooperation. They call the relationship between individual researchers 'partnership', and use the term 'collaboration' to denote institutional relationships.

Major types (structures) of North–South partnerships relevant to research include:

- Partnerships between individual researchers / research teams brought together to carry out a specific project (ranging from one-off co-authorship of research papers to large-scale, long-term inter-institutional research partnerships);
- Capacity-building partnerships (no direct research component) (may be focused on individual or institutional levels, e.g. institutional twinning); and
- North–South research networks (formal and informal).

Beyond differences in the structure of North–South partnerships, collaborations also vary in terms of duration, sources of financial support, the degree of focus on advocacy and policymaking, and the frequency and intensity of interactions between Northern and Southern partners. Principal actors whose roles are examined in the literature on North–South research partnerships include individual researchers and research teams, research organizations (universities, NGOs, and think tanks), Southern communities, policymakers, international organizations, and donors. The literature on donor approaches to supporting research cooperation is plentiful, especially in terms of Canadian and Dutch experiences.

The literature on North–South research partnerships identifies a number of key trends that have emerged over time in the collaborative research landscape. As early as 1975, researchers argued that collaborative research frameworks were often inadequate and counterproductive. They called for a reorientation of North–South partnerships so that collaborations could strengthen Southern institutions while producing more policy-relevant, critical research. Early calls were also raised for the creation of mutually beneficial partnerships, supported with long-term, flexible, and diversified funding. In varying degrees, over the course of the past three decades, these prescriptions have matured into discernible trends. For example, the production of policy-oriented research has emerged as a virtually uncontested goal, and partnerships are increasingly seen as an opportunity for developing the capacity of Northern and Southern researchers alike. Sector-specific trends are also evident. For instance, the literature demonstrates significant and sustained interest in partnerships in the fields of health and agricultural research, and rising interest in the field of science and technology. Despite increased donor interest in multidisciplinary development research, the literature suggests that creating multidisciplinary North–South partnerships and promoting interdisciplinary dialogue remains a struggle.

A significant range of the literature in this field is devoted to examination of concepts and theories closely related to North–South partnerships, including innovation theory, demand-led research, and 'knowledge-based' approaches to development. However, there is much more limited research available on motivations for partnership. In contrast, there is more abundant work on the ethics and politics of partnership. Much of this literature suggests that asymmetry between partners remains the principal obstacle to productive research collaboration. This asymmetry manifests itself in the form of inequitable access to tangible and intangible goods, including information, training, funding, conferences, and publishing opportunities, as well as in the disproportionate influence of Northern partners in project administration and budget management. Structural inequalities also clearly impact the process of selecting partners and setting the research agenda. In this connection, the literature on the ethics and politics of partnership also discusses the continued impacts of neocolonialism and globalization on collaboration. Although these obstacles face researchers working in a wide range of fields, they are perhaps particularly pertinent in the context of North–South development research partnerships.

As with development research more broadly, it is difficult to evaluate the precise impacts of North–South research partnerships. However, the literature suggests that conceptions of the success and impact of research partnerships are broadening. While the literature reviewed for this study highlights the considerable body of research on co-authorship, it also acknowledges widespread scepticism regarding the utility of co-publication as a measure of the health of a research partnership or collaboration strategy. By the same token, it is increasingly well recognized that scientific advances are only one yardstick that can be used to measure the utility of a North–South partnership. Mutual capacity building and the translation of research results into policy interventions are increasingly seen as significant achievements and indicators of success.

A review of the literature on North–South development research partnerships identifies a range of knowledge gaps that deserve greater attention. For example, the literature on North–South research partnerships is predominantly produced by Northerners. More in-depth examinations by Southern researchers of the questions and challenges surrounding partnerships would be an invaluable complement to the state of knowledge on this issue. The literature review undertaken in advance of this work concluded that subjects that would benefit from further research include: the approaches of key donors, including the United States and Japan, whose experiences do not appear to be well-documented in the literature; the changing role of North–South partnerships in 'Southern' countries with increasingly robust national research communities (e.g. Brazil, India, China, South Africa); alternative and emerging partnership structures and activities; strategies to maximize the potential of North–South research partnerships to be mutually beneficial; and the challenge of designing collaborative research agendas that advance mutual interests, but are firmly rooted in Southern needs and priorities. The latter issue was chosen as the focus of this chapter.

Methodology

The study profiled in this chapter is an analysis of donor policies and a detailed review of the secondary literature, as well as a series of 43 in-depth, semi-structured interviews on North–South research partnerships that were conducted in Southern Africa, the Middle East, Europe, and Canada with researchers working in the fields of migration and governance, academic officials, NGO representatives, and donors. The distribution of the interviews across the relevant areas was as follows: the Netherlands (8), the United Kingdom (5), Botswana (4), South Africa (9), Jordan (8), and Israel and the Palestinian Territories (9). Interviewees in the initial participant pool were contacted largely on the basis of recommendations provided by programme officers at IDRC. The interview pool was expanded on the basis of independent research and suggestions from various interviewees. Participants' names and identifying details have been omitted to preserve confidentiality.

The interviews were carried out in English between October 2006 and March 2007, and each lasted from 45 minutes to two hours. (The analysis presented in this chapter draws on these interviews, but is also updated in light of more recent research and policy developments.) They focused on the fields of migration and governance because these are timely, contentious issues that place the question of setting equitable, locally appropriate research agendas in sharp relief. However, this chapter does not analyse the distinctive challenges facing migration and governance researchers involved in North–South partnerships, as these have been discussed elsewhere (Bradley, 2007a). Rather, it offers a more holistic discussion of agenda-setting challenges, given that these interviews underlined that many of the difficulties associated with agenda setting are common to different fields. Making accurate generalizations about researchers' experiences is a delicate task. Owing to the highly personalized nature of partnership experiences, there are exceptions to almost every trend.

In terms of focusing on the development research policies adopted by the Netherlands and the United Kingdom, these donors were selected on the basis of a purposive sampling strategy. These countries were selected because over the course of the past 30 years they have concertedly engaged in a process of reflecting upon and refining their policies on funding research for development, and supporting partnerships between researchers in the Global North and South. An examination of these deliberations and policies, and their implications, may therefore be informative for a broader discussion of the influence of donor strategies on collaborative research agendas.

More broadly, the arguments advanced in this chapter are informed by the understanding of North–South partnerships and development research funding gained while working with IDRC's CP Program, and in subsequent professional work as a researcher in the field of forced migration. As a university-based academic and as a policy researcher with the Brookings Institution, I have had the opportunity to participate in the development of North–South research partnerships, and have come to appreciate from a first-hand perspective the complexities surrounding the agenda-setting process that are explored in this chapter.

North–South partnerships: donor policies and the business of research cooperation

The pervasive influence of donors on North–South research partnerships is widely accepted as a foregone conclusion among many experienced researchers.

Indeed, according to many Southern researchers, it is a 'buyer's market' where partnerships and research agendas are concerned. One leading Southern researcher I interviewed used the term 'partnership' to convey the major role economic interests play in the creation of North–South research partnerships. Research funding opportunities are limited, particularly as development and research funding budgets have been cut in the aftermath of the 2008 financial crisis. Collaboration with Northern institutions is often a prerequisite for support; consequently, many Southern researchers enter into partnerships far removed from their own priorities simply to generate the income required to stay afloat. Some researchers object that this approach reduces research cooperation to a business, although many of its benefits (and harms) are not easily quantified or aggregated. While bilateral donors have received the lion's share of the blame for the continued Northern dominance of collaborative research agendas, these agencies operate under a wide range of different 'business models', some of which are more conducive than others to bolstering Southern priorities. To be sure, other members of the donor community, such as independent foundations, research councils, and the private sector, also shape the creation of collaborative research agendas. The strengths and shortcomings of these donors' approaches certainly merit further examination, but are largely beyond the scope of this study.

Assessing bilateral donors' influence on collaborative research agendas is a complex task, as donor priorities and researchers' interests are constantly interacting and evolving, and it cannot be assumed that donor policies affect all recipients in a uniform manner. Studies on donor influence typically concentrate on how funding policies affect advocacy efforts and field interventions, rather than research. This literature struggles to identify and account for the numerous variables that increase or decrease donors' influence, and the case studies used to explicate donors' influence are often anecdotal (Minear and Weiss, 1995; Vakil, 1997). At the general level, however, donors' impact on collaborative research agendas is best understood on a spectrum from direct to indirect influence.

While troubling, overt donor interference in shaping or restricting the dissemination of research results appears to be relatively rare. Instead, donors exert considerable indirect influence over agenda-setting processes by identifying their programming priorities and establishing the structure of the international research funding system. Many facets of donor influence are well-known and their merits hotly debated: for example, donors influence the development of research agendas by requiring the studies they support to be explicitly 'policy relevant'; by concertedly supporting multidisciplinary, multi-stakeholder projects; and by constantly revising or scuttling certain programmatic priorities, which can impede researchers' efforts to create coherent, long-term research plans. For instance, Bakewell (2008) has critiqued the conditioning of funding on the assumed 'policy relevance' of research results. Donors also affect agenda-setting efforts through their categorization of different countries in the Global South. Botswana, for instance, is defined by most bilateral donors as a middle-income country, rendering researchers in the country ineligible for many funding streams. Since domestic funding remains scarce, various research institutions in Botswana continue to pursue international support by repositioning themselves as brokers for regional and inter-regional collaborative work. This strategy underlines that, despite donors' considerable influence, researchers do not simply respond to donors' frameworks, but challenge their policies and priorities, as well as the assumptions that underpin them.

Perhaps most significantly, donors affect agenda-setting processes by making partnership a prerequisite for funding. Using North–South partnerships as a 'default' for funding not only adds an extra layer to agenda negotiations, but also creates a problematic starting point for articulating common research goals. As Hatton and Schroeder (2007: 157) argue, 'the funding context within which partnerships must exist … increasingly represents a significant barrier to genuine partnership among Northern and Southern organizations'. In a context in which partnership is all too often 'forced rather than volunteered' (Hatton and Schroeder, 2007: 158), to what extent can carefully honed donor strategies mitigate inequities in collaborative agenda-setting processes?

'Almost an ideology': Dutch support for demand-driven partnerships

In the early 1990s under the leadership of then Minister of International Development Jan Pronk, the Dutch government launched a programme of 'experiments' in demand-driven research. According to Nair and Menon (2002: 2), demand-led research refers to 'activities in which people are able to bring about their own development, with the objective of building up research systems to unleash the potential of the South'. Although experimental, the Netherlands' demand-driven approach was a comprehensive policy that aimed to make a 'novel' contribution to development research, in large part by reducing the influence of Dutch academics and policymakers and transferring managerial and substantive responsibility for Dutch-supported research programmes to Southern researchers and communities. The demand-driven policy was manifested in a handful of innovative projects including nine Multi-annual Multidisciplinary Research Programmes (MMRPs) and several 'symmetrical cooperation' projects, among them the Indo–Dutch Programme on Alternatives in Development (IDPAD), the South Africa–Netherlands Research Programme on Alternatives in Development (SANPAD), the Ghanaian–Dutch Programme of Health Research for Development, and the Philippine–Dutch Programme of Biodiversity Research for Development. While the Dutch Directorate General for Development Cooperation (DGIS) channelled direct support to Southern researchers through the MMRPs, some of the symmetrical cooperation projects were overseen by the Netherlands Development Assistance Research Council (RAWOO), an advisory body based in The Hague.

Although the demand-driven programmes absorbed a considerable proportion of DGIS research specialists' time and energy, the projects did not represent a significant percentage of the agency's budget for development research, much of which continued to be directed towards more traditional research partnerships. Rather than being managed by embassy staff in the South, the demand-driven projects were supervised by a dedicated group of staff at DGIS headquarters in The Hague, whom observers of the process have described as having an 'almost ideological' commitment to the demand-driven approach. The research agendas guiding these projects were determined through carefully crafted 'demand articulation' processes, often involving civil society advocates and community representatives, but the proponents of these projects nonetheless struggled to resolve what the Dutch refer to as the 'Ganuza dilemma'. The dilemma carries the name of Latin American sociologist Enrique Ganuza, who articulated the problem in 1989 at an influential conference on development research in Groningen, the Netherlands: when Southern stakeholders express competing demands, whose priorities should receive support? Dutch advocates of the demand-driven approach stressed that lack of Southern consensus was not an invitation for Northern donors and researchers to substitute their own priorities, nor could local priorities be trumped by appealing to the pressing nature of global problems of concern to Northern populations, such as environmental degradation or, in the more contemporary context, the fight against terrorism. However, champions of the demand-driven approach were also forced to recognize that Southern researchers were not always the best allies in advancing locally defined priorities as the basis for development research. Often, researchers in the South 'inhabited ivory towers at least as high as those of their counterparts in the North' (Van de Sande, 2006: 3).

The success of the Netherlands' demand-driven approach is a matter of debate – but while the construction of equitable development research agendas is little more than an obscure puzzle for academics and bureaucrats in most political constituencies, for 15 years debate on the demand-driven approach took place at remarkably high levels in the Netherlands, including in parliament. From its genesis, DGIS's demand-driven policy sparked contention as it challenged the historical dominance of Dutch scholars in the research process and undercut, albeit minimally, their preferential access to development research funding.

Although DGIS staff members were concerned to counteract the perception that demand-driven research and North–South collaboration were mutually exclusive, it proved difficult to meld the demand-driven approach with the notion of mutually beneficial partnership. To preclude the possibility of Northern domination of the research agenda, the Southern partners had considerable control over decision-making processes, which at times resulted in the adoption of research questions of little interest to the Dutch participants. Furthermore, the collaborative projects had cumbersome managerial and decision-making structures, prompting some Dutch researchers to conclude that the minimal amount of funding DGIS provided was not worth the trouble. Despite the government's professed commitment to supporting Southern demands, various observers pointed out that the projects' research agendas were remarkably relevant to the Netherlands' development priorities, thus generating scepticism regarding the independence of the demand articulation processes. Within DGIS, however, supporters of the demand-driven approach were confident that the policy resulted in innovative, locally relevant research agendas. It was suggested that a sign of the policy's significance was that it ruffled other bilateral donors, who regarded some DGIS-supported research as overly radical.

While the rhetoric of responding to local demands has been mainstreamed throughout the Dutch development architecture and is *au courant* in the broader donor community, by 2007 the Netherlands had adopted a strategy more firmly grounded in 'enlightened self-interest' and less focused on Southern-led research. This shift was prompted by a combination of factors including academic protest and the rise of a more conservative political climate in the Netherlands. This shift was foreshadowed in the title of DGIS's 2003 development policy statement: *Mutual interests, mutual responsibilities: Dutch development cooperation en route to 2015*. This policy emphasizes the role of North–South partnerships in the Netherlands' development assistance strategy, but downplays the provision of direct support to Southern researchers and the importance of supporting locally defined priorities. The 2005 DGIS policy memorandum *Research in development* also made several modifications to the demand-driven approach in effect since 1992. In 2006, the Netherlands announced its intention to enhance its support for development research partnerships through the Netherlands Foundation for the Advancement of Tropical Research (WOTRO), now known as WOTRO Science for Global Development. WOTRO is a branch of the national research council, the Netherlands Organization for Scientific Research (NWO). Soon after, in 2007, the government disbanded RAWOO, an organization historically outspoken in its support for demand-driven research.

WOTRO was committed to supporting research in accordance with both Southern and Northern priorities, as reflected in a 2006 strategy intended to guide the agency in this task (WOTRO, 2006); the 2006 strategy's thematic framework was based on the Millennium Development Goals (MDGs). In its 2011–2014 strategy plan *Science and development: mutual inspiration*, WOTRO indicated that 'Although the MDGs remain important as a collective focus of development efforts and markers of progress, there is a growing need for evidence-based knowledge into the interplay of global and contextual dimensions of development' (WOTRO, 2010: 26–27). The strategy indicates that:

> The core of the WOTRO approach to research funding lies in enhancing both scientific quality and the use of research results for development. To this effect, WOTRO puts emphasis on stakeholder consultation, inter- and trans-disciplinarity, and international partnerships in research collaboration. This approach, representing the flagship of the WOTRO programmes developed under the 2007–2010 strategy period, will continue to absorb most of the funding that WOTRO can leverage. (WOTRO, 2010: 39)

One can question whether the MDGs represented a legitimate Southern agenda, and WOTRO supported critical research on this very issue. Beyond the inevitably thorny problem of how to determine what constitutes a Southern agenda, WOTRO's institutional structure and mandate complicated its efforts to support collaborative research in tune with Southern priorities. The only research council in the Netherlands, the NWO functions as an umbrella organization under which agencies, including WOTRO, cooperated with one another while simultaneously competing for their share of the council's centralized pool of funding. Balancing the imperatives of intra-organizational cooperation and competition is a major challenge for all the bodies within the NWO, but is often particularly difficult for WOTRO as an organization concerned with development. For example, as part of the Dutch research council, WOTRO does not generally have the latitude to fund Southern researchers independently, but seeks to involve Southern scholars in partnerships with Dutch counterparts. Using Dutch money to support Southern researchers has not historically been uniformly accepted throughout NWO, nor has inter-disciplinary, policy-relevant development research necessarily been held in high esteem throughout the organization.

As part of the Netherlands' national research council, WOTRO typically awards funding on the basis of blind peer reviews that promote 'research excellence' first and foremost. WOTRO staff members interviewed for this study expressed strong support for the principle of peer review, arguing that it is unethical to fund development research that is not scientifically reliable. However, WOTRO recognizes the shortcomings of the peer-review process, particularly when applied to proposals for North–South development research partnerships. Because the members of peer-review panels are typically Northern academics with little development experience, the process often fails to value the developmental impact of the proposed work, focusing instead on questions of theoretical rigour. Further, Northern reviewers are sometimes suspicious of interdisciplinary research and start from the assumption that policy-relevant research is scientifically suboptimal. Reviewers charged with identifying the most academically 'excellent' proposals are also not necessarily in a position to consider how projects may advance development by strengthening the capacities of the partners and their institutions.

In response to these limitations, WOTRO introduced several innovations to its proposal-development and peer-review processes. For example, as of 2007, WOTRO has provided funds for teams to gather in the South to develop rigorous proposals that incorporate Southern perspectives from the outset and are more likely to survive the peer-review process. Proponents are given the opportunity to sharpen their proposals in response to feedback raised through an initial review. Proposals must be accompanied by support letters from NGOs or other stakeholders, and community advisory boards including NGO representatives and policymakers weigh in on partnership proposals, focusing in particular on the developmental relevance of the proposed research.

However, because of the risk of polarized discussions, the organization's practice as of 2007 was that community advisory boards and the scientific panels would not generally sit down to review proposals together, and the scientific committees make the final decisions on whether proposals are accepted.

WOTRO's efforts demonstrate how a Northern funding agency facing significant institutional constraints can endeavour to create conditions more amenable to the expression and validation of Southern research priorities. Whether these innovations actually translate into the increased approval of North–South partnerships grounded in equitable, mutually beneficial research agendas remains a matter of some debate. Reflecting on its shift towards more immediately 'policy relevant' research and the growing influence of DGIS on its own funding activities, WOTRO itself asks, 'Could it be that this alignment of research funding with the priorities of the Dutch Ministry of Development Cooperation has led to important research falling between two stools? Are we missing out on possible revolutionary research findings resulting from an individual scientist's pure curiosity?' (WOTRO, 2014: 9) WOTRO recognizes the critiques of researchers such as Hebert Prins: beyond the challenges associated with setting priorities in the context of North–South partnerships, Prins argues that 'When civil servants rule the research agenda, ground-breaking science goes down the drain. Civil servants will not fund "risky" research. They will always play it safe. And that will not lead to innovation' (WOTRO, 2014: 9).

Although the symmetrical research partnerships' agenda-setting processes were far from smooth, DGIS's 'experiments' in demand-driven research placed the Netherlands in a leadership role among bilateral donors, challenging preconceived notions of how development research should be done and supported. In comparison to this approach, Dutch policies in effect over the past 10 years appear predominantly to return to an earlier way of doing business, in which Northern researchers' contributions and concerns are centre stage, or at least close by.[2]

The prevalence of this approach among bilateral donors is reflected in the Report of the Danish Commission on Development-Related Research, which was convened to examine 'Denmark's future role as a provider of development research', and frankly admitted that 'the development of indigenous research capacity in developing countries, in itself much to be welcomed, [poses] new challenges for the Danish development research sector' (DANIDA, 2001).

Taken in total, the Dutch experience demonstrates how an ambitious commitment to supporting Southern research agendas is dependent on the political climate in donor countries, and that even the most ambitious or ideological commitment to advancing Southern agendas cannot fully resolve the challenges presented by agenda setting in the context of North–South research partnerships. At best, donor policies can attempt to mitigate any disadvantages to Southern researchers as the parties navigate the agenda-setting process.

Beyond North and South? British partnership funding strategies

In contrast to the Dutch funding strategies adopted in the first decade of the 21st century, which saw a retreat from the Netherlands' ambitious experiments of the 1990s in Southern-led, 'demand-driven' research partnerships, the British approach to financing research for development in this period was less explicitly based on North–South partnership models. In this period, by some estimates, the British emerged as one of the more progressive and reflective of the bilateral agencies involved in funding research for development. To be sure, all progress is relative; despite improvements in some bilateral agencies' strategies, many Southern researchers interviewed for this study indicated that they still preferred to work with independent funders, such as the Ford Foundation, which often have greater flexibility than bilateral agencies obliged to advance Northern foreign policies.

Two events stand out as having significantly shaped the approach to research partnerships embraced by the UK Department for International Development (DFID) in the first decade of the 21st century. The first was the UK government's affirmation of the key role of science in the achievement of the MDGs, and its subsequent decision to dramatically increase funding for development research, doubling its 2005–06 budget of £110 million to £220 million in 2010. With this increased budget, DFID provided direct support to national research teams, as well as to international partnerships.

The second key event had direct bearing on how DFID supported these partnerships: the passage of the *2002 Development Act* officially untied all British development aid, with the result that DFID-sponsored research partnerships could no longer *require* the involvement of British researchers. Rather, grants were to be awarded on the basis of open competition between researchers worldwide. While the British academic community was initially hostile to this policy, DFID's efforts to untie development aid gradually garnered broader support. DFID officials attribute this change to researchers' recognition that tying aid is morally dubious, and their awareness that they need to be prepared to compete in a 'global market of ideas', without relying on the British government for preferential treatment. (As discussed later, British researchers' opposition to this policy was also arguably tempered by the fact that, by drawing on their close networks with the British government, many were able to continue to meet with success in obtaining nationally funded research grants.)

At the same time as it banned partnerships that formally required the participation of British researchers, DFID questioned the very significance of the terms 'North' and 'South' to development research cooperation. Although DFID broadly supported the view that collaborative research agendas should respond to Southern concerns, the salience of North and South as categories to structure international research cooperation has been called into doubt by the emergence of countries such as Brazil and China as new research powerhouses, and the transboundary nature of development challenges such as climate change and migration. The propensity to question the relevance and timeliness of traditional North–South research partnerships was shared by scholars at various leading UK development research institutes. For example, Haddad underlines that the:

> North does not have a monopoly on solutions nor does the South have a monopoly on problems ... A research model that looks at an issue across a wide range of contexts, unencumbered by labels of North and South, that can connect chains of events across the world and that can see an issue from multiple perspectives ... has to be more independent, legitimate, rounded and integrated than current models. (Haddad, 2006: 11–12)

It is difficult to determine precisely the full implications of these changes and debates in terms of ensuring that Southern voices are heard in collaborative agenda-setting processes. Although many applauded the move away from privileging domestic researchers' access to partnership opportunities, others expressed scepticism about the sincerity and sustainability of the policy, noting that UK institutions were not, for the most part, actually edged out of DIFD-funded partnership opportunities. While this may be a testament to the quality of development research in Britain, various researchers and donors questioned whether this policy change would significantly affect *practice*, given the close connections between DFID and certain British development research institutions. Indeed, various observers in the academic and donor communities suggested that domestic opposition to the policy would likely increase if British institutions' access to partnership funding and control over DFID-supported research agendas significantly diminished.

Just as DFID grant-makers may not always recognize when Southern institutions are better placed than their British counterparts to take on the leadership of international research projects, there are also Southern organizations (just as there are Northern organizations) that are simply not yet ready to take on this type of work. It was and remains unclear how 'excellence-focused' research strategies such as those embraced by DFID may surmount this problem, to support not only cutting-edge, practical research, but also nascent Southern institutions' ability to carry out such work.

While reflecting on the relevance of 'North' and 'South' to contemporary development research partnerships added nuance to DFID's approach, the drive to 'globalize' collaborative agendas may in fact detract from efforts to advance Southern priorities and enable timely, evidence-based policymaking in the poorest countries and communities. Making links between conditions in far-flung communities may result in more sophisticated interpretations of development problems and policy imperatives. However, it may also overshadow local research agendas, which are arguably more likely to make direct contributions to resolving the challenges faced by the poorest countries. IDRC's extensive experience of supporting development research in a variety of fields suggests that while Southern researchers are certainly interested in international-level debates and analyses, many are often sceptical about the practical importance of this work, and are particularly driven to carry out specific, ground-level analyses that can have direct and immediate impact in their own contexts. When programmes such as IDRC's former Peace, Conflict, and Development initiative have operated in a wholly responsive manner, the proposals submitted by Southern scholars have tended to focus on specific, pressing, local concerns, and almost never concentrate on 'trendy' issues occupying Northern scholars (Scholey, 2006: 185). This experience may serve as a reminder of the importance of recognizing the qualitatively different nature of many research agendas in the Global North and South, and as a rejoinder to the suggestion that internationalized, comparative studies are the most fruitful direction for donor-funded development research in the future.

The persistent face of business as usual

Taken in total, the experiences of the Netherlands and the UK in the first years of the 21st century demonstrate that revised bilateral donor policies have the potential to improve Southern researchers' ability to influence collaborative research agendas while broadening access to partnership opportunities. However, even the most innovative partnership funding strategies cannot resolve all the tensions and inequalities that characterize collaborative agenda-setting processes. The impact of changes in donors' funding strategies are tempered by factors including changes in political climate, the attitudes of domestic researchers, and the mandate and structure of institutions responsible for implementing collaborative funding programmes. The experiences of the UK and the Netherlands also illustrate the difficulty of translating policy innovations into improved practice. As weighty bureaucracies accustomed to using Northern-directed partnerships as a primary modus operandi, bilateral donor agencies may be slow to internalize and act on new policy initiatives, even those that promise to advance widely accepted principles, such as the importance of ensuring that research partnerships are grounded in, or at least attuned to, Southern priorities.

Many of the seasoned researchers interviewed suggested that Southern partners often have more leverage in agenda negotiations than is commonly assumed. This is due in large part to the popularization of donor policies that require North–South partnerships to be headquartered at Southern institutions. Various Northern researchers underlined the importance of this shift, pointing out that responsibility for the management of partnerships often translates into increased influence in substantive agenda-setting processes. However, this policy is not uniformly popular among Southern researchers, some of whom argue that it reflects the unfounded assumption that all Southern institutions are weak and require more experience in project management. When proficient but under-resourced Southern organizations work with longstanding, trusted Northern partners, it can be beneficial to base partnerships in the North, as this relieves the administrative burden on the

Southern side. These researchers maintain that flexible donor policies that can account for the nuances of each partnership situation are preferable to blanket policies uniformly requiring partnerships to be based in the North or in the South.

My interviews with both researchers and bilateral donor representatives also highlighted pervasive confusion and unresolved tensions surrounding the rationale for bilateral donors' support for North–South research partnerships. On one hand, most donors have, to varying degrees, adopted the rhetoric of the demand-driven approach, suggesting that their goal is to support Southern priorities, as defined by Southern researchers, leaders, and community members themselves. On the other hand, there is strong support among donors, and Southern researchers in particular, for the idea that partnerships should be mutually, and even *equally*, beneficial. Indeed, many of the Southern researchers interviewed objected to the notion that their views should automatically dominate those of their Northern counterparts and donor representatives. Integrating the concerns of all partners and donors is, they argued, an essential part of productive research cooperation, and demonstrates respect for the Northern citizens who provide the bilateral agencies' money.

As these researchers stress, demand-driven partnerships and mutually beneficial partnerships are not necessarily mutually exclusive. Yet, balancing the interests of Northern and Southern researchers, institutions, communities, and governments is rarely a simple task. While the prevention and resolution of poverty is surely in the general interest of both the North and South, there is clearly heated debate over the best route to take to achieve this goal, and it would be a grave oversimplification to suggest that Southern priorities can always be met without a cost to the interests of Northern actors at numerous levels.

Recognizing the potential dissonance between the concept of equally or mutually beneficial partnerships and the commitment to prioritizing Southern demands, is an important first step towards ensuring that donor strategies and North–South partnerships are based on coherent, viable principles. Some funders have made more progress than others in reflecting on and refining their approaches to supporting development research, including North–South partnerships. Numerous interviewees emphasized the need for these 'progressive donors' to take on a leadership role, challenging the face of 'business as usual' in the donor community. First and foremost, this entails a judicious approach to the use of North–South partnerships as a funding modality. Donor financing should be prefaced by detailed institutional assessments and open discussions with Southern researchers and governments. These discussions should identify when alternative funding modalities, such as direct support to Southern institutions, are more timely and appropriate approaches to advancing critical development research agendas than North–South partnerships. Second, while many welcome the drive towards donor coordination, experienced researchers caution that this can stifle the emergence of innovative collaborative agendas. When donors overly focused on coordination go 'to the field', they are, as some interviewees suggested, more keen to talk to their fellow funders than to prioritize the opportunity to speak to Southern researchers and community members about their priorities and concerns. This risks muting Southern perspectives in favour of consensuses rooted in the North.

Individual donor representatives can make invaluable contributions to facilitating the development of equitable collaborative research agendas and prompting change from within the donor establishment. Yet numerous researchers stressed that individual donor representatives could also do serious harm by establishing cliques of Southern contacts, over-empowering certain researchers and their agendas. Rather than simply relying on leadership from donor institutions and representatives, interviewees emphasized the need for complementary leadership from researchers as well as from Southern governments. While the governments of emerging research powerhouses, such as India and South Africa, are well placed to pressure donors to retune their policies in accordance with Southern agendas, convincing these governments to take a stand on the issue is a difficult proposition. The question of research collaboration and equitable agenda setting typically remains a low priority for national governments, despite the impact it has on efforts to understand and respond to development challenges from environmental management to political reform.

Advancing agendas: Southern motivations and strategies

Given the perpetual elusiveness of 'genuine' partnerships and the limited role donor policies play in facilitating equitable agenda-setting processes, why do Southern researchers and institutions continue to pursue partnerships? How do Southern researchers advance their agendas, in spite of restrictive cooperation frameworks and often crippling institutional contexts? The abundant literature on North–South research partnerships illuminates some of the goals and strategies guiding Northern researchers involved in international research cooperation, but is virtually silent on the subject of Southern aims and approaches to agenda setting. In response to this dearth in the literature, concerted efforts were made during the design and execution of this study to draw out the perspectives of Southern researchers from a wide variety of professional and institutional backgrounds. Naturally, this does not mitigate the need for more research and reflection on the partnership process from Southern researchers themselves.

Although this study focuses on substantive agenda-setting processes, discussions with Southern researchers highlighted the multitude of interconnected, often competing agendas at stake in North–South partnerships. Much like substantive research agendas, capacity-building activities are subject to competing interests, and must be negotiated alongside management and research dissemination strategies. Prior to identifying shared research questions, diverse personal and institutional interests determine who gets involved in partnerships in the first place. In both the North and South, access to cooperation opportunities is shaped by factors such as age, gender, professional seniority, social class, religious convictions, and political affiliations. Indeed, researchers' drive to find 'like-minded' partners can preclude cooperation with those best-placed to provide insight into particular research questions. For example, as some interviewees in the Middle East pointed out, Islamist scholars are almost universally shut out of North–South research partnerships examining the rise of political Islam.

Time and again, discussions with Southern researchers underlined that partners' motivations and agenda-setting strategies cannot be understood through uni-dimensional analyses that focus only on the interests of researchers, institutions, governments, or community groups. Rather, these different levels of interest constantly intersect, both enriching and confounding agenda-setting processes.

Why partner?

'Received wisdom' in the donor community suggests that Northern researchers seek out North–South partnerships principally to gain access to data and fieldwork opportunities, while Southern researchers are primarily looking for funding and the chance to publish in Northern peer-reviewed journals. The interviews affirmed that access to data, funding, and publishing opportunities are major motivators for prospective partners, but that they are mediated by a range of other interests, depending on the partners' mandate and strengths.

While the opportunity to travel and the desire to contribute to development and poverty alleviation are important incentives for Northern and Southern researchers alike, among the researchers interviewed, almost without exception, access to funding stood out as a principal impetus to partner. This is partially a reaction to the structure of the international research funding system, in which most Southern governments have insufficient resources available to support domestic researchers, resulting in reliance on international donors who use North–South partnerships as a dominant funding modality. Although some donors certainly accept independent proposals from both Northern and Southern proponents, even prominent Southern institutions often struggle to secure support when they compete against well-connected, accomplished Northern organizations. Consequently, partnerships are a key source of funding for many Southern institutions, despite the fact that direct donor support remains their preference. Partnerships may be particularly appealing as a funding avenue for Southern institutions because their Northern counterparts are often better placed to secure large grants covering salaries and infrastructure. Furthermore, pairing up with influential Northern organizations may improve Southern institutions' ability to attract independent support in the future. However, many Southern researchers emphasized that preserving their scholarly reputation and personal and institutional integrity was more important than funding, and they highlighted instances when they turned down or withdrew from partnerships that could have endangered either.

Discussions with Southern researchers confirmed that the desire to publish, like the drive to secure funding, is subject to a number of provisos. The opportunity to publish in elite, peer-reviewed journals was simply not a top concern for various civil society research organizations primarily dedicated to channelling research into local and national policymaking processes. Although staff working with these organizations did not covet publications in top-tier Northern journals, they welcomed occasions to share their work with wider audiences, and appreciated the opportunity to collaborate with Northern academics who had the time and commitment necessary to shepherd their joint research through the peer-review process. On the downside, when collaborative research papers were unable to weather the peer-review process, Northern partners occasionally stymied the dissemination of the work through grey literature publications or other channels as they were unwilling to be associated with research that did not meet the top standards of western scholarship.

Access to data proved to be a significant impetus to partner for Southern researchers as well as their Northern colleagues. North–South research partnerships often provide Southern researchers with access to electronic libraries and extensive statistical databases held at Northern universities. At the same time as interviewees stressed the fallacy of viewing North–South research partnerships as exercises in Southern capacity building, access to professional opportunities such as conferences and tailored training programmes for junior staff represented important motivations to partner. Equally, for national-level Southern organizations seeking to expand to the regional or international scene, North–South partnerships are also a valuable source of contacts and advice. Indeed, partnerships can serve as a laboratory for the development and refinement of globalized institutional visions. For example, at Birzeit University in the West Bank, North–South research partnerships prompted new thinking on the 'internationalization' of the university, broadening horizons that might otherwise have been foreclosed by lack of resources and the pressure of the occupation. In return for these benefits, Southern researchers contribute their own contacts, linguistic abilities, methodological expertise, and knowledge of local conditions, which often translates into nuanced theoretical insight.

Beyond funding, publishing, access to data, and capacity-building benefits, Southern researchers confirmed that North–South cooperation holds out the possibility of richer learning and scholarly output, particularly when considering truly global issues such as climate change and the spread of pandemics. Partnerships allow researchers to gain direct insight into the diverse manifestations of particular phenomena and open up opportunities for scholars to refine their theoretical approaches. The opportunities partnerships present for international interaction and collegial debate are especially valuable when domestic research communities are isolated or small.

Particularly in conflict and post-conflict contexts, the decision to engage in international research cooperation is often a carefully considered political statement. In dangerous locales, affiliation with a prominent Northern organization can lend a degree of added protection to Southern researchers undertaking sensitive work, while in volatile political environments, trusted Northern partners can provide valuable outside advice and play a critical role in removing barriers to the research process by rallying political and diplomatic pressure against officials obstructing fieldwork activities (Brookings, 2007: 8). Notably, interviewees pointed out that in countries such as Iraq and Iran, affiliation with a Northern organization can have the opposite effect, drastically heightening the risks faced by local partners.

In some cases, partnerships are pursued because they bolster Southern researchers' political clout and policy influence. This varies according to the partners' policy target. For example, if Southern organizations aim to amend the policies of Northern governments or United Nations agencies, North–South cooperation often augments Southern researchers' perceived credibility and access to decision-makers. Northern researchers may also convey their Southern partners' concerns directly to their political representatives in capitals from Washington to London. However, the leverage gained through partnerships often declines if researchers seek to influence Southern policymakers, many of whom prefer 'home-grown' analyses and may be hostile to Northern 'interference' in their sovereign political affairs. Indeed, politically prudent Northern researchers and NGOs seeking to influence Southern governments often team up with prominent Southern organizations to benefit from their specialized lobbying expertise and political connections.

Many of the motivations for partnership receive almost universal approval. For example, donors, researchers, and politicians alike are pleased to support partnerships as a means to attract and retain talented researchers at Southern institutions. Partnerships are also heartily welcomed as an opportunity for Northern and Southern counterparts to affirm the strategies developed in their respective communities. Yet, it would be a mistake to assume that the motivations for partnership are all equally benign. For example, in highly competitive milieus, interviewees pointed out, researchers may cooperate with their foreign counterparts simply in order to undercut other potential partners. Numerous researchers in the South suggested that, for better or worse, many Northern researchers simply do not know what they are looking for when they approach potential Southern partners, confusing muddle-headedness for open-mindedness to Southern ideas and agendas. To be sure, many Southern researchers in the 'partnership market' are equally blurry about their own priorities, despite the fact that experienced partners recognize that balancing a clear set of strategic motivations with readiness to learn and adapt is the best preparation for the many obstacles that complicate negotiations on the collaborative research agenda.

Parachuting partners and mercenary researchers: agenda-setting obstacles and strategies

Obstacles and responses to the challenges of equitable agenda setting are intertwined as reactions to the issue often raise problems of their own. My discussions with researchers in the Middle East and Southern Africa underscored that the difficulties associated with creating equitable, locally appropriate collaborative agendas are inseparable from a number of cross-cutting systemic challenges. As these problems elude easy and prompt resolution, astute Southern agenda-setting strategies often aim to limit risks and hedge bets, with some 'flag bearers' challenging the system at a deeper level, either by structuring innovative cooperative relationships in spite of marked structural constraints or by 'opting out' of North–South research partnerships altogether.

First and foremost, many Southern researchers' approaches to collaborative agenda setting are shaped by the structure of the development research funding system, in which partnerships are the primary funding modality; financing is devoted to short-term projects, rather than long-term core support; and donors have predefined substantive interests, which change often enough to be labelled 'flavours of the month' by jaded Southern researchers. While the vast majority of researchers hope their work makes a real contribution to improving wellbeing and combating disparity, many of the researchers interviewed stressed the difficulty of crafting agendas that could meet donors' demands for concrete and ideally immediate results in terms of poverty alleviation.

Many researchers emphasized the difficulty of trying to anticipate the policy relevance of their work at the proposal stage, rather than once their results were clear, and underscored the need for more independent, theoretically demanding research. This is essential to the evolution of a strong research base in the South. As various interviewees stressed, sustainability in the research sector comes from the ability to make well-argued intellectual contributions to national and international debates, not just to churn out studies to match prescribed terms of reference.

In the most extreme cases, donors completely preclude collaborative agenda negotiations by granting money to a Northern institution for collaborative research on a particular set of questions before a Southern partner is even identified. When the research agenda is a *fait accompli*, Southern researchers are sought out as 'mercenaries', a problem that is particularly severe in the case of consultancies, where the terms of reference are set by the contracting agency, with researchers given only minimal time and flexibility to react. While some researchers stoically accept this type of work as an inevitable part of making a living in cash-strapped Southern organizations, others rail against it as a cardinal example of the presumptuousness that makes collaborative research so draining.[3]

The second major structural factor that frequently affects Southern agenda-setting strategies is the existence of pervasive inequalities between prospective partners in the North and South. To be sure, Southern researchers do not necessarily enter agenda negotiations disadvantaged in terms of their scholarly and managerial skills. Many elite Southern researchers are not only intellectual leaders, but are also deft negotiators who use their role as gatekeepers to local research subjects to increase their leverage in the agenda-setting process.

Yet organizations' internal constraints inevitably limit the research agenda as the scope of researchers' investigations is foreshortened by lack of time, staff, and money. These organizational constraints are often particularly severe for Southern organizations, and hamper Southern partners' ability to respond to new issues that arise over the course of the partnership. Particularly well-planned partnerships budget extra funds to allow researchers to adapt or expand the research agenda to ensure its continued relevance in light of unforeseen events, discoveries, or political changes. However, the amount of work that can be accomplished on a particular collaborative agenda is limited by the fact that in the vast majority of cases Northern researchers' time and efforts are extremely costly. On certain agendas, Southern researchers working independently or in cooperation with other Southerners could arguably make more progress than they are able to when arbitrarily tied to a collaborative model.

On the other hand, collaboration has been instrumental to the introduction of entirely new fields of research in Southern countries. For example, cooperation between Norwegian and South African universities was instrumental to the establishment of African research programmes dedicated to the study of fisheries, a longstanding area of specialization in the Nordic countries. In cases such as this, the inequalities that must always be dealt with in a collaborative research endeavour are particularly stark. Experienced researchers suggest that these inequalities should be frankly acknowledged by all sides with the understanding that, as the partners develop new views and expertise, the agenda will be revisited and adjusted accordingly.

The third systemic factor that must be accounted for in Southern agenda-setting strategies is the fact that good partnership practice is rarely rewarded by the academic system. Tenure review committees are prone to take a disparaging view of the policy-relevant, multi-stakeholder, applied research that emerges from donor-funded North–South research partnerships (RAWOO, 2001). Moreover, managing diverse research teams and facilitating equitable, culturally sensitive, yet rigorous agenda-setting processes are specific skills that are under-emphasized in traditional academic training (Ettorre, 2000). Because there is little structured incentive to or expectation that academics will engage in respectful partnerships, harmful collaborative practices persist and are passed down to new generations of researchers.

Beyond these structural challenges, Southern researchers highlighted a number of other factors that both enrich and complicate the agenda-setting process. For example, even when partners agree on the broad content of their research agenda, pinning down viable research questions may be difficult as many partners have been schooled in different academic traditions and theoretical frameworks, depending on linguistic, cultural, geographic, and religious backgrounds. Agenda-setting processes are often smoother if researchers have comparable educational backgrounds, professional roles, and political views. However, a growing number of partnerships strive to bring together diverse Northern and Southern actors, betting that cooperation between diverse actors will result in richer research questions and more perceptive findings. Researchers involved in these multi-stakeholder initiatives suggest that rocky agenda-setting experiences are attributable not so much to the challenge of melding Northern and Southern interests, but to the difficulty of enabling cooperation between different actors, including academics, grassroots activists, policymakers, and corporate leaders.

Agenda-setting processes can be frankly gruelling in partnerships that aim to advance volatile political processes, such as the Palestinian–Israeli peace negotiations. Changes in the political situation often necessitate revision of the collaborative agenda. Preparing for agenda negotiations by getting each side up to speed on one another's views and reactions to current events is a valuable process, but a cumbersome one that can drastically cut into the time available for actually negotiating the agenda and moving research forward. Some architects of cooperative projects in the Middle East try to take a proactive approach to this problem by circulating detailed information on partners' reactions to changes in the political landscape ahead of face-to-face meetings. Even when the researchers are in agreement, negotiations can be protracted due to slow-moving university and donor bureaucracies, which exacerbate the challenge of maintaining a timely, mutually acceptable research agenda.

As many of the Southern researchers suggested, interpersonal chemistry and strong character judgement are essential to sidestepping or resolving these agenda-setting obstacles. Almost unanimously, researchers stressed that partnerships sink or swim on the character and commitment of the individuals involved in them. While many researchers value having shared political views with their partners, even more critical are the attributes of flexibility, modesty, and willingness to learn. Beyond the stated goals of collaborative initiatives, individual partners also strive to move forward 'silent agendas', from padding their publication list in advance of a promotion, to increasing the partnership's advocacy role and theoretical richness. Astute partners recognize one another's informal interests, and are able to distance themselves from individuals and initiatives burdened by silent agendas they do not support.

Although strong interpersonal relationships are essential, researchers also stressed the importance of 'institutional chemistry' to successful agenda-setting processes. While various guides provide extensive criteria for choosing appropriate partners, there is no strict recipe for effective institutional cooperation (KFPE, 2005). Similar management and accounting styles are often beneficial. Various Southern researchers suggest that institutional cooperation is easier when the Northern partner's country does not have an 'imperial past'. Institutional compatibility ensures that the partnership provides room for organizational growth, and is critical given that the individual members of collaborative teams often change over a project's lifetime. Strong institutional compatibility can smooth these transitions. Researchers increase their institutional stake in research partnerships by ensuring that the collaborative agendas are negotiated by organization-wide teams, rather than only by senior management. This approach recognizes and responds to the fact that competing agendas may exist even among members of the same organization, and ensures that the collaborative agenda is backed not only by the institutional director, but also by the junior staff with responsibility for the day-to-day implementation of the project.

Individuals and institutions who gain the most from North–South partnerships do not tend to describe their partners in terms of specific, short-term projects. Rather, they have nurtured long-term interpersonal and inter-organizational relationships that often span multiple projects, and remain a source of insight and support even in the absence of donor funding. The development of long-term partnerships is an investment with considerable returns when it comes to agenda setting, as negotiations benefit from the trust partners have built up as well as their ability to be candid with one another and draw on past lessons to iron out present difficulties. Creating long-term partnerships requires dedication and ingenuity as neither donor funding systems nor academic promotional frameworks are set up to reward sustained commitment between Northern and Southern partners. Long-term commitment is especially fundamental in unstable conflict and post-conflict locations where 'parachuting partners' typically do not remain on the ground long enough to earn the trust necessary for locals to share their views. In fact, parachuting partners can erode local actors' willingness to trust those Northerners who are committed to the long haul. Even between longstanding partners, difficulties can emerge if Southern researchers remain committed to a particular line of research while the Northern partners' interests change. If Northern researchers decide to move on to new issues, they often 'take the money with them', limiting their former partners' ability to advance the research agenda independently.

Strong Southern institutions: the lynchpin of successful agenda-setting processes

In light of the abundant obstacles to equitable agenda setting, the strength of the Southern institution in a North–South partnership emerges as the foremost factor affecting the successful negotiation of a research agenda that is both mutually beneficial and rooted in Southern concerns. Currently, many partnerships are premised on the assumption that all those involved are well-intended, informed, culturally sensitive people, and that these qualities, in combination with due regard for 'good partnership principles', are sufficient conditions for equitable, effective agenda-setting processes. While good intentions and respect for Southern concerns on the Northern side can facilitate smooth agenda-setting processes, they cannot substitute for the advantages enjoyed by strong Southern organizations in partnership negotiations.

In the context of North–South research partnerships, strong organizations are characterized by a realistic awareness of their own strengths and weaknesses, sound administrative systems, and relatively stable finances. Most importantly, they have a clear institutional mandate and agenda.

Albeit critical, the question of how strong Southern research organizations emerge and evolve is largely outside the scope of this paper. Preliminary discussions with Southern researchers suggest that, in certain cases, North–South partnerships aimed at capacity building have supported the development of strong Southern research centres, but this is certainly not the only contributing factor. Concerted leadership from driven, well-trained, and well-connected Southern researchers is typically essential to the creation and maturation of Southern institutions. IDRC's experience confirms that cooperation between Southern institutions can be instrumental to the emergence of strong research centres and, in turn, vibrant national research communities.

Strong organizations exist in both the North and South, but articulating and sticking to clear institutional goals is often a serious challenge for Southern institutions struggling to withstand economic and political instability or stagnation. Northern institutions and coalitions are also often unsure of their own agendas. Support for North–North cooperation is in some fields even scarcer than funding for North–South interactions, despite the fact that interaction between diverse Northern communities and institutions is essential to establishing and refining solid advocacy and research agendas. Consequently, Northern researchers from large and heterogeneous countries such as Canada may struggle to fully appreciate the scope of national experiences with issues such as indigenous self-governance and resource management. This limits Northern partners' ability to contribute to the development of rigorous North–South research agendas.

In some cases, interviewees pointed out that Southern organizations may appear to have clear agendas, but upon closer examination the 'organizations' are only individuals whose agendas have not been enhanced through collegial debate, and who do not necessarily enjoy the support of community members.

Even where Southern organizations have clearly defined agendas, they may be pressured by donors and local actors to disregard their chosen mandates. Many strong Southern organizations receive regular invitations to participate in a variety of partnerships unrelated to their goals. While these invitations may represent valuable opportunities for Southern organizations to expand their scope and skills, they may also detract from their focus and efficacy. Some specialized, driven Southern organizations perceive as an affront persistent pressure from donors and other actors to take on activities outside their carefully defined remits, reflecting a lack of respect for the decisions the organization has made for itself. As the frustrated director of a prominent Middle Eastern research centre expressed it, 'It should matter what [our Institute] *does*. We should be able to say, "This is what we do."'

Armed with a clear conception of their own motivations and agendas, strong Southern organizations also have a cluster of tools and strategies they can apply to increase the likelihood that their partnerships yield the desired benefits. Where organizations are unclear about their own institutional strengths and goals, capacity assessment exercises can play an important clarifying role, both for donors and for the research institutions. These exercises can help determine whether partnerships should focus primarily on capacity building, in-depth research, or a mixture of the two. Open and honest assessment exercises may well conclude that North–South partnerships are not as relevant to the Southern organization's institutional and scholarly goals as other funding modalities, such as core funding or South–South cooperation.

For example, many robust Southern organizations cultivate close connections with grassroots groups, which help them ensure that their agendas retain local relevance. Locally connected Southern research institutions then serve as gatekeepers to grassroots populations, a role they use to increase their leverage in agenda negotiations. Close grassroots connections can also alert Southern researchers to ethical concerns associated with particular lines of research that could escape the attention of foreign review boards. By carefully establishing their credibility beforehand, strong Southern organizations may have the latitude to challenge assumptions and attitudes prevalent at the grassroots level and among policymakers, taking on agendas that are unpopular because they are seen to be donors' 'turf'. Equally, researchers working within reputable Southern institutions may be well placed to advance agendas critical of donor governments because their institutional clout can mitigate the risk of funding being withdrawn in reaction to researchers' criticisms.

In many cases, the senior staff of savvy Southern organizations prepare their colleagues for the challenges associated with collaborative agenda negotiations, and mentor them throughout the process. This has often proven more effective than the default approach of learning in the saddle. The leaders of robust Southern institutions also ensure that their researchers enter into collaborative negotiations with clear minimum criteria that they expect the partnership to meet, which serve as a guide throughout the agenda-setting process.

To be sure, innovative, reputable Southern organizations face challenges of their own in collaborative research. These include the need to balance the desire for equity among partners with the pragmatic recognition that leadership is required if partnerships are to move forward. Some participants in this study suggested to me that even leading Southern organizations tend to operate in responsive modes where the creation of new partnerships is concerned, waiting for invitations from Northern parties rather than initiating collaborations themselves. Taken in total, however, the attributes discussed earlier strengthen Southern parties' hands in agenda negotiations, and limit the cost to the Southern organization if a partnership does not materialize. Indeed, many researchers are proud of their ability to be selective in their partnerships, pursuing their own priorities even when they did not meet with outside support. Among leading Southern research organizations, walking away from unsatisfactory partnerships is virtually a rite of passage. However, the researchers interviewed did not underestimate the difficulty of turning down partnership opportunities for struggling Southern institutions. The price of refusing or pulling out of North–South research partnerships is often not only financial, but also reputational, as organizations that step out of troubling partnerships may be labelled as belligerent or uncooperative, thus hindering their ability to secure new collaboration opportunities and influence decision-makers in the future. While recognizing the validity of these concerns, interviewees questioned whether nascent institutions could ever transform into successful, locally relevant organizations by simply going along with agendas forged in the North and divorced from local priorities.

Conclusion

Although strong Southern organizations are instrumental to successful, equitable North–South agenda-setting processes, in many fields of development research there is only a limited number of organizations involved, with strikingly different levels of capacity. North–South collaboration can certainly strengthen partnering institutions, and exciting research questions often emerge through the training and capacity-building exercises that are part of many North–South partnerships. However, even the most successful partnerships have their limits; it is virtually impossible for a partnership to develop the capacity of an institution that lacks key resources and a firm set of priorities while also pursuing a cutting-edge, collaboratively developed research agenda.

The challenges associated with collaborative agenda setting are deeply rooted in academic politics, intercultural misunderstandings, and the structure of the international donor system, wedded as it is to a model of short-term, project-based collaborative financing. While bilateral donors such as the Netherlands and the UK have met with modest success in challenging the strictures of this model, their endeavours have inadvertently underscored researchers' and bureaucracies' resistance to change, even change which they rhetorically and morally support.

Strong Southern organizations are best placed to navigate the numerous obstacles associated with collaborative agenda setting, but the magnitude of these obstacles is illustrated by the fact that some of the most reputable and well-skilled Southern organizations simply sidestep the issue, eschewing North–South research partnerships altogether. For the minority of organizations that can rely on the more flexible, direct funding offered by independent donors, the benefits of partnership often cannot outweigh the management burden and complex agenda negotiations that partnerships almost invariably entail. This calls into question the salience of the wide range of guidelines and principles that aim to reform the partnership experience (KFPE, 1998; 2005).

It is perhaps overly optimistic to hope that careful planning and laudable ideals can neatly avoid the entrenched problems that have complicated international research collaboration for decades.

The cross-cutting, structural nature of barriers to equitable agenda setting and successful partnership should not dissuade researchers, donors, and policymakers from tackling these issues. Partnerships make an essential contribution to understanding and responding to transboundary development challenges. For this reason, it is critical that the practice of partnership improves. This is an inescapably long-term endeavour, however. In the meantime, donors and researchers alike are well- advised to candidly recognize the limitations of partnership and ensure that a broader range of funding modalities are applied in support of the creation and application of knowledge for development. Before settling on North–South partnership as a funding modality, detailed organizational assessments and negotiations between donors and researchers are in order. In these discussions, donors and Northern researchers should be willing to heed Southern researchers' calls for different forms of support, including greater levels of direct, core support. While this undoubtedly poses a challenge for those donor agencies formally obliged to exclusively support North–South partnerships, a commitment to respecting Southern perspectives and priorities must encompass not only the substantive research agenda, but also the modalities through which development research funding is distributed. This type of flexibility is critical to ensuring that struggling Southern institutions can evolve into strong organizations well equipped to hold their own in North–South agenda negotiations and to assist in strengthening other Southern organizations.

Northern researchers' critical reflections on partnership often stop short of this conclusion, focusing instead on how partnerships may be modified or improved, while retaining Northern researchers' place at the table. This may be in Northern researchers' short-term interests, but the goal of equitable collaborative agenda setting would be better served if North–South research partnerships were initiated and financed more judiciously, alongside other approaches to supporting the creation of knowledge for development, including significantly increased core funding for Southern organizations and South–South partnerships. This is not to suggest that South–South research partnerships are immune from agenda-setting debates. As several Southern researchers suggested, all too often these partnerships mimic and even amplify the negative power dynamics associated with North–South research partnerships.

Acknowledgements

Portions of this chapter appear in the following publication, and are reprinted by permission of the publisher, Taylor & Francis Ltd (www.tandfonline.com): Megan Bradley (2008) 'On the agenda: North–South research partnerships and agenda-setting processes', *Development in Practice* 18(6): 673–85 <http://dx.doi.org/10.1080/09614520802386314>.

Notes

1. Recommended discussions of North–South research partnerships in a variety of fields include Barrett et al., 2011; Muldoon et al., 2012; Hynie et al., 2014; Carbonnier and Kontinen, 2015.
2. For further discussion of WOTRO's role and evolution over the past 50 years, see WOTRO, 2014.
3. For a lively debate on partnering practices in the field of forced migration, see Landau, 2012, and the responses to Landau: Banerjee, 2012; Castles, 2012; and Ferris, 2012 in *Journal of Refugee Studies* 25(4).

References

Amin, S., Fossi, G., Jolly, R., Oteiza, E., and Wignaraja, P. (1975) 'New forms of collaboration in development research and training', *International Social Science Journal* 27(4): 761–76.

AUCC (Association of Universities and Colleges of Canada) (2006) *Highlighting the Impacts of North–South Research Collaboration among Canadian and Southern Higher Education Partners*, Ottawa: AUCC.

Bakewell, O. (2008) 'Research beyond the categories: the importance of policy irrelevant research into forced migration', *Journal of Refugee Studies* 21(4): 432–53.

Banerjee, P. (2012) 'Response to Landau', *Journal of Refugee Studies* 25(4): 570–73.

Barrett, A., Crossley, M., and Dachi, H. (2011) 'International collaboration and research capacity building: learning from the EdQual experience', *Comparative Education* 47(1): 25–43.

Box, L. (2001) *To and fro: international cooperation in research and research on international cooperation*, Maastricht: University of Maastricht.

Bradley, M. (2007a) *North–South Research Partnerships: Challenges, Responses and Trends*, Canadian Partnerships Working Paper 1, Ottawa: IDRC.

Bradley, M. (2007b) 'Refugee research agendas: the influence of donors and North–South partnerships', *Refugee Survey Quarterly* 26(3): 119–35.

Bradley, M. (2008) 'On the agenda: North–South research partnerships and agenda-setting processes', *Development in Practice* 18(6): 673–85 <http://dx.doi.org/10.1080/09614520802386314>.

Brookings-Bern Project on Internal Displacement (2007) *Researching Internal Displacement: State of the Art and an Agenda for the Future*, Washington, DC: Brookings-Bern Project on Internal Displacement.

Buffardi, A.L. (2013) 'Configuring "country ownership" patterns of donor–recipient relations', *Development in Practice* 23(8): 977–90 <http://dx.doi.org/10.1080/09614524.2013.841862>.

Carbonnier, G. and Kontinen, T. (2015) 'Institutional learning in North–South research partnerships', *Revue Tiers Monde* 221(1): 149–62.

Castles, S. (2012) 'Response to Landau', *Journal of Refugee Studies* 25(4): 573–76.

DANIDA (2001) *Partnerships at the Leading Edge: A Danish Vision for Knowledge, Research and Development: Report of the Commission on Development-Related Research*, Copenhagen: DANIDA.

Ettorre, E. (2000) 'Recognizing diversity and group processes in international, collaborative research work', *Social Policy and Administration* 34(4): 392–407.

Ferris, E. (2012) 'Response to Landau: On partnerships, power and policy in researching displacement', *Journal of Refugee Studies* 25(4): 576–80.

Hatton, M. and Schroeder, K. (2007) 'Partnership theory and practice: time for a new paradigm', *Canadian Journal of Development Studies* 28(1): 157–62.

Haddad, L. (2006) 'Reinventing development research: listening to the IDS40 roundtables', <https://www.researchgate.net/publication/48139853_Reinventing_development_research> [accessed 29 July 2016].

Hynie, M., McGrath, S., Young, J., and Banerjee, P. (2014) 'Negotiation of engaged scholarship and equity through a global network of refugee scholars', *Scholarship and Research Communication* 5(3), 0301164 <http://www.src-online.ca/index.php/src/article/view/164>.

KFPE (1998) *Guidelines for Research in Partnership with Developing Countries*, Bern: Swiss Academy of Sciences.

KFPE (2005) *Choosing the Right Projects: Designing Selection Processes for North–South Research Partnership Programmes*, Bern: KFPE.

Landau, L. (2012) 'Communities of knowledge or tyrannies of partnership: reflections on North–South research networks and the dual imperative', *Journal of Refugee Studies* 25(4): 555–70.

Minear, L. and Weiss, T. (1995) *Mercy Under Fire: War and the Global Humanitarian Community*, Boulder, CO: Westview.

Mougeot, L.J.A. (2016) 'Introduction: Knowledge for civil society in the rapidly changing ecosystem for international development', in L.J.A. Mougeot (ed.), *Putting Knowledge to Work: Collaborating, influencing and learning for international development,* pp. 1–36, Rugby, UK and Ottawa: Practical Action Publishing and IDRC <http://dx.doi.org/10.3362/9781780449685.001>.

Muldoon, K., Birungi, J., Berry, N., Ngolobe, M., Mwesigwa, R., Shannon, K., and Moore, D. (2012) 'Supporting southern-led research: implications for North–South research partnerships', *Canadian Journal of Public Health* 103(2): 128–31.

Nair, K.N. and Menon, V. (2002) 'Capacity building for demand-led research: issues and priorities', Maastricht: European Centre for Development Policy Management.

Ogden, J. and Porter, J. (2000) 'Politics of partnership in tropical health', *Social Policy and Administration* 34(4): 377–91.

Pestieau, J., Foley, J., Ramalingaswami, V., and Slaymaker, O. (1998) *The Nature of Research at IDRC: Report of Research Ad Hoc Committee of the IDRC Board*, Ottawa: IDRC.

RAWOO (Netherlands Development Assistance Research Council) (2001) *North–South Research Partnerships: Issues and Challenges*, The Hague: RAWOO.

Scholey, P. (2006) 'Peacebuilding research and North–South research relationships: perspectives, opportunities and challenges', in S. MacLean, D. Black, and T. Shaw (eds), *A Decade of Human Security: Global Governance and New Multilateralisms*, London: Ashgate.

Vakil, A. (1997) 'Confronting a classification problem: toward a taxonomy of NGOs', *World Development* 25(12): 2057–70.

Van de Sande, T. (2006) 'Priority setting in research for development: a donor's perspective', in L. Box and R. Engelhard (eds), *Science and Technology Policy for Development: Dialogues at the Interface*, London: Anthem Press.

WOTRO (Netherlands Foundation for the Advancement of Tropical Research) (2006) *Science for International Development: Strategy Plan 2007–2010*, The Hague: WOTRO.

WOTRO (2010) *Science and Development: Mutual Inspiration – WOTRO Strategy Plan 2011–2014*, The Hague: WOTRO.

WOTRO (2014) *WOTRO 50 Years – Forward Thinking*, The Hague: WOTRO. <http://www.nwo.nl/en/about-nwo/organisation/nwo-divisions/wotro/wotro+50+years> [accessed 29 July 2016].

About the author

Megan Bradley is Assistant Professor of Political Science and International Development Studies at McGill University. She is the author of *Refugee Repatriation: Justice, Responsibility and Redress* (Cambridge University Press, 2013) and the editor of *Forced Migration, Reconciliation and Justice* (McGill–Queen's University Press, 2015). She holds a doctorate in International Relations from St Antony's College, University of Oxford.

CHAPTER 3

Negotiating research collaboration between universities and other civil society organizations in Canada

Elena Chernikova

Abstract

This study is a first attempt to systematize tacit knowledge on Canadian university–civil society collaboration in research and cooperation for international development. This chapter identifies and documents a wide variety of ongoing relationships. Relationships between Canadian universities and other civil society organizations (CSOs) can be differentiated as interactions, collaborations, or partnerships, according to the reciprocity, intensity, and formality involved. Four types of collaborations are discussed: on research projects, study placements, training programmes, and university fellowships for practitioners. Collaborations may take place at different stages of a project cycle. While more formalized partnerships are less frequent, most likely struck by larger institutions, they build on a history of collaborative work and resources for conducting research.

This chapter further examines their enabling factors, including the agency of activist scholars, as well as the benefits accruing to academics and practitioners. Major challenges are addressed, as are measures already in place to sustain collaborations. Although trust, reciprocity, and a long history of relationships are important, the most critical factors were found to be: a joint engagement in the initial stage of conceiving the idea for the research or project, a clear understanding and open discussion of each other's goals, and the realization and acceptance of the challenges to be addressed. Recommendations are submitted to encourage and nurture more effective collaboration between universities and other CSOs active in international development.

Keywords: civil society organizations, university–NGO collaboration, study placements, research fellowships, training programmes

Current relevance

The sociopolitical context in Canada and the world today is such that in the international development arena it calls for collaborative research to be more

http://dx.doi.org/10.3362/9781780449586.003

relevant and efficient in supporting actions for positive change in the lives of people. The original research on which this chapter is based was completed in 2011, and since then funding for international development has become more competitive, and in some cases has been reduced, so civil society organizations (CSOs) have grown even more pressed to rethink institutional boundaries and continue their quest for innovative approaches to cross-sector collaboration. While this study was completed five years ago, there are still only a few empirical studies specifically focused on collaborations between non-governmental organizations (NGOs) and research institutions (Olivier et al., 2016).

As this study finds, universities and other civil society entities can and do work together in multiple ways to meet this challenge. They have tended to do so in an incremental and risk-aware fashion, for good reasons, and should be supported to continue to do so in a way that is respectful of their differences (Hall et al., 2014). This chapter identifies the various ways in which universities and NGOs collaborate and qualifies such relationships as potentially evolving from simple interactions to more formal partnerships, if the parties involved so wish. Also, cross-sectional data on the types of joint activities in which a particular university or NGO is involved indicate that these vary in diversity from organization to organization, with more of them engaged in casual and low-risk activities, while a few have added other elements that require more sustained and comprehensive commitments. In working together, universities and NGOs tend to proceed with care, developing mutual trust and only taking their relationship to the next level when it is for mutual benefit. Given a lack of similar and more recent studies, the findings remain relevant as they offer guidance to the growing rapprochement between academia and CSOs advocated by donor governments in the field of international development. Could a progression over time by NGOs in particular of more and higher forms of engagement with universities be a function of growing levels of trust and commitment to reciprocity as identified by Olivier et al. (2016)? In order to inform policies for more comprehensive collaborations between the two communities, more evidence is needed on the genesis of more advanced or multi-pronged relationships between specific universities and NGOs. In addition, both communities probably need to better reward professionals (as well as nurture emerging talents) in both academia and civil society who are willing to play a critical role in bridging agendas and learning between the two communities for mutual benefit (Stevens et al., 2013).

Introduction

This chapter is based on a research project carried out in 2010–2011 and informed by the work of the Canadian Partnerships (CP) programme within the Special Initiatives Division (SID) of the International Development Research Centre (IDRC) in Ottawa, Canada. Unlike other programming units at IDRC, which primarily support international development research initiatives proposed and carried out by organizations in the Global

South, the CP programme worked for 20 years with two major categories of Canadian actors – higher education institutions and other CSOs – to support research and knowledge-oriented initiatives for international development.

A growing number of Canadian CSOs (CCSOs) have been recognizing the value of research to support their international work. According to the 2007–08 SID Annual Report, 'increasingly they are forming networks to address issues of common concern, combining forces to define and undertake the research required to inform the positions and policy recommendations to be put forward' (SID, 2008: 7). Many CSOs in Canada are linked to universities through collaborative research and learning initiatives. The CP Strategy for 2010–2015 called for 'further support of capacity building in research, knowledge building and evaluation methods ... in particular for some newer CSOs' (SID, 2008: 2). Over the course of their work, CP officers have come across a small number of collaborations for international development between Canadian universities and other CSOs. This study was a first effort at documenting the range of such collaborations at work in Canada, as well as reviewing their effectiveness so far, with a view to hopefully assisting future collaborative efforts.

The *Macmillan Dictionary* provides a basic definition of collaboration: 'the process of working with someone to produce something'. In their attempt to define research collaboration, Katz and Martin concluded that it had

> a very 'fuzzy' or ill-defined border. Exactly where that border is drawn is a matter of social convention and is open to negotiation. Perceptions regarding the precise location of the 'boundary' of the collaboration may vary considerably across institutions, fields, sectors, and countries as well as over time. (Katz and Martin, 1997: 13)

For this research, I use the word 'collaboration' inclusively to identify a range of engagements between universities and CSOs in Canada for international development research and knowledge activities. Apart from research, these activities include creating tools and methods, evaluating, reflecting, and developing a programme/project together – everything with the focus of learning together and from each other.

Specifically this study aimed to:

- identify and document the typology of civil society–university collaborations for knowledge-oriented activities on international development;
- analyse examples of different collaborations, in terms of drivers, challenges, and benefits to parties involved;
- use selected examples to identify factors and conditions which have been responsible for making collaborations effective; and
- suggest ways to encourage knowledge-oriented collaborations between Canadian academic institutions and CSOs which are addressing international development issues.

The chapter begins with a review of the state of knowledge on cross-sector collaborations for international development, including events and conferences underlining the importance of developing and supporting such collaborations in Canada.

The methodological approach for this study consisted of a search of IDRC's internal project information system, as well as methods for conducting surveys, collecting interviews, and organizing various types of data. The steps followed to analyse current and recent collaborations are discussed, as well as the researcher's bias and the dissemination of results. The discussion of results includes examples of promising practices identified through the interviews. The conclusion outlines lessons from conducting this research and suggestions for supporting university–CSO collaboration for international development research.

Literature review

There is a growing body of literature on evidence-based partnerships for change between universities and communities. Fitzgerald and Zientek (2015) argue that community engagement scholarship is being established as a result of higher education slowly reconnecting with society over the last decades. There is an increasing recognition that co-creative and blended knowledge collaborations with community partners increase the asset-driven change. Those academics who work with communities soon realize the benefits of such collaborations for producing sustainable change. 'Today's challenge is to build upon the historical research successes of higher education while seeking contemporary solutions to such problem areas as renewable and green energy, quality of air and water [...] and health and well-being' (Fitzgerald and Zientek, 2015: 27). Thus, conceptualizing the structure, typology, and mechanics of such partnerships, ideally founded in the community engagement scholarship, remains the focus for the actors of change.

In their 2009 extensive in-depth review of the literature on partnerships and other closely related forms of collaboration, a team from the International Potato Centre in Peru discovered that studies of partnerships tend to reflect the concepts, methods, and priority issues of their authors' home disciplines; however, a number of cross-cutting themes were identified. Apart from definitions and success factors, aspects such as partnership dynamics, drivers, trust and mutuality, power, and equity – as well as evaluations of partnerships – were found to be recurring themes (Horton et al., 2009: 77).

The major knowledge gap identified by the authors concerned 'the lack of empirical studies and systematic evaluations of partnerships' (Horton et al., 2009: 94). At the level of specific partnerships, the lack of literature concerned with 'the factors that influence the performance of different types of partnerships in different contexts' was identified (Horton et al., 2009: 96). This research attempts to contribute to the body of literature on partnerships and collaborations.

Bradley (2016; see Chapter 2) found that much scholarly literature covers various challenges and trends in North–South collaboration for international development. A review of studies and evaluations of North–South research collaborations points to some knowledge gaps (i.e. issues that would benefit from further research). Among those are: alternative and emerging structures of partnerships, institutions' motivations for entering into partnerships, the challenge to design collaborative research agendas that advance mutual interest and address Southern needs and research priorities, and outputs and outcomes of North–South research partnerships (Chapter 2: 44).

Typologies of partnerships feature different interactions between the principal actors, which can include individual researchers, research teams, research organizations, universities, and think tanks as well as civil society communities, NGOs, policymakers, international organizations, and donors (Bradley, 2016: 1). Interest in building and strengthening such partnerships continues to grow globally, both from an academic and a practitioner standpoint. Such partnerships have been a recurring theme in international conferences for the last five to seven years.

The 5th Australian Council for International Development University Network Conference was hosted by Monash University in June 2015 and provided a unique opportunity to bring together researchers and practitioners to discuss growing inequality and its implications for policy and practice. The goal of the organizers was to promote knowledge sharing, collaboration, and partnerships among NGOs and universities within the development community (Monash University, 2015).

Hosted collaboratively by the Aalborg University's Center for Design, Innovation and Sustainable Transitions in Copenhagen and the international science shop network Living Knowledge, the 2014 Living Knowledge Conference, 'An Innovative Civil Society: Impact through Co-creation and Participation', focused on the role of CSOs as producers of knowledge and equal partners in research and innovation. The conference also called for civil society's own activities to be recognized as research and innovation (Living Knowledge, 2014). It raised awareness regarding the ways of integrating societal actors into university curricula and engaging them through partnerships into research, including research planning. At the same time, the need to develop research capacities in civil society actors was identified.

In early February 2010, Canada's leading higher education organization, the Association of Universities and Colleges of Canada (now known as Universities Canada), with support from IDRC, held an international Leaders' Symposium entitled 'Cardinal Points: How North–South Partnerships Support Internationalization Strategies' in Ottawa, Canada. The two organizations have a longstanding partnership to examine 'international research collaboration for development through research, communications, and outreach activities' (Universities Canada, 2010). In their reading list for the symposium, Universities Canada gave a statement on the changing character of internationalization, where Canadian universities are reconsidered as agents of change. Research that would capture the collective wisdom on why and how universities decide to develop (or not) narrowly defined partnerships into more encompassing ones over time, could help improve the ways in which they identify, manage, and develop such partnerships.[1] After this symposium, IDRC supported a number of other initiatives to further the relationships between research institutions and civil society actors; these are referenced in the introduction (Mougeot, 2016).

Indeed, the past three decades have witnessed a shift in universities' role in order to benefit society. This first manifested itself in the signing of the Magna Charta Universitatum Europaeum in 1988 in Europe, the Wingspread Declaration on Renewing the Civic Mission of the American Research University in 1998, and the University Presidents' Declaration on the Civic Responsibility of Higher Education in 1999 in the US,[2] as well as in the publication of several books on university–community partnerships and collaborations (Pezzoli, 2008). On 23 September 2010, eight international networks supporting community–university engagement across the world gathered to participate in the first Global Video Dialogue on Community–University Engagement. These networks were both university-led and community-led: the Centro Boliviano de Estudios Multidisciplinarios, Commonwealth Universities Extension and Engagement Network, Global Alliance on Community Engaged Research, Global Universities Network for Innovation, Living Knowledge Network, PASCAL International Observatory, Participatory Research in Asia, and the Talloires Network. Facilitated by the Canada-based Global Alliance for Community-Engaged Research, the dialogue resulted in the international 'Call to Action on North–South Collaboration in Community–University Research and Engagement' (Hall, 2010).

Similarly, according to Uma Kothari, editor of the book *A Radical History of Development Studies: Individuals, Institutions and Ideologies*, there has been a resurgence of the *non-governmental* within development studies, spurred by publications of books and articles since the late 1980s, especially in the United States and the UK (Kothari, 2005: 203). This tendency was noted also in Canada (Haslam et al., 2008). In her historical overview, Kothari traces the emergence of the 'non-governmental' in development studies research and she analyses the reasons for this growing interest.

The outcome of the first academic conference on NGOs in the UK in 1992 was the volume *Making a Difference: NGOs and Development in a Changing World*, edited by Mike Edwards and David Hume. It set the basis for a number of policy-like documents, placing NGOs under the spotlight in the field of international development research (Edwards and Hume, 1992: 204–05). However, as 'hidden histories', the traces of 'the non-governmental theme had always been marginally present within development studies research: but it had rarely if ever become explicit' (Edwards and Hume, 1992: 209).

Civil society is a very inclusive term, often including universities, but in this study it will refer mostly to NGOs, particularly development NGOs or, as they are called in French-speaking Canada, international cooperation organizations. According to Dr Lester Salamon, director of the Center for Civil Society Studies at Johns Hopkins University, civil society is

> a broad array of organizations that are essentially private, i.e. outside the institutional structures of government, that are not primarily commercial and do not exist primarily to distribute profits to their directors or 'owners', that are self-governing, and that people are free to join or support voluntarily. (Salamon, 2003: 3)

This definition embraces faith-based as well as secular organizations.

Both the desire and the necessity for academics and civil society to collaborate take the extreme degree of convergence in a novel form of a 'civil society university'. The idea emerged in 2005 at a Prime Timers conference and has been explored with cross-section organizations in the UK and academics. It represents a vision for a new institution that connects the diversity of knowledge interests in the third sector, and empowers civil society actors by overcoming the fragmented nature of knowledge and providing connectivity both nationally and internationally (Albrow et al., 2007).

In Canada, IDRC's support of collaborations between universities and CSOs on international development research has resulted in several initiatives. IDRC launched the CP programme in 1992 and this ran until 2015, one of the longest lasting programmes at IDRC. According to the 1996 memorandum *Canadian Collaboration*, 'Canadian collaboration is no longer seen as anchored principally on a university-based researcher collaborator' (Smart, 1996: 5). Smart suggested revisiting the CP programme's priorities because it gave IDRC 'a chance to enable some Canadian groups to do work on issues that are as much of concern to Canadians as to partners in the South, suggesting a shift from collaborative research on problems of the South to collaborative research on more global problems' (Smart 1996: 7). CP aimed at strengthening relationships with Canadian organizations. In order to support Canadian perspectives on international development that could complement IDRC's work, CP started issuing small grants for collaborative research between academic and other civil society collaborations.

The Social Sciences and Humanities Research Council (SSHRC) and IDRC have been collaborating since 2007 to test an International Community–University Research Alliances (ICURAs) programme between community organizations and academic institutions (IDRC, 2008). This collaboration fosters comparative research, training, and the creation of new knowledge in areas of shared importance for the social, cultural or economic development of communities in Canada and in low- and middle-income countries (LMICs).

Three other initiatives at IDRC also indirectly supported similar types of collaboration. They deal with inclusive research networks, under the

International Research Initiative on Adaptation to Climate Change, and with Centres of Excellence under The International Partnerships Initiative. The Canadian International Food Security Research Fund, a joint programme of the Department of Foreign Affairs, Trade and Development (now Global Affairs Canada) and IDRC, was launched in 2009 to fund a wide variety of applied research projects that aim to solve immediate and concrete food security challenges in LMICs. This programme funds inclusive research partnerships between organizations in Canada and in those countries.

Canada is home to many diverse organizations involved in international development research and North–South research partnerships. Every international development NGO and large community organization, as well as major universities, can demonstrate their connection one way or another with organizations or individual researchers from the Global South. However, as noticed in the course of work of IDRC's CP programme, there was little research available taking stock of knowledge-related collaborations between Canadian academics and Canadian practitioners on international development issues. This is particularly true of Canadian universities' engagement with Canadian NGOs and vice versa.

That being said, research by Science, Technology and Civil Society – actors in the European system of research and innovation – pointed to Canada as the 'country where participatory-type research enjoys the widest recognition and the strongest support from both the government and universities' (Gall et al., 2009: 13). This research compared SSHRC's Community–University Research Alliances programme with a smaller programme in France, demonstrating the efficiency of the Canadian programme and a history of community engagement with universities in Canada.

This history can also be traced to another research programme commissioned by SSHRC and executed by the Office of Community Based Research (OCBR) at the University of Victoria. The resulting research paper described various arrangements by Canadian research councils to fund community–university research and knowledge mobilization partnerships (Hall et al., 2009). It called for strengthening arrangements for community-based research led by indigenous peoples to generate knowledge for action by their governments and CSOs. The authors also recommended that Canada ensures it is learning from, and exchanging knowledge about, community–university research and civic engagement with partners across the globe 'to strengthen the relevance of higher education to sustainable development through community engagement' (Hall et al., 2009: 48).

Professor Budd Hall, the founding director of OCBR, now the Institute for Studies & Innovation in Community–University Engagement, calls for support of university–community research partnerships in the broad area of indigenous studies. Given the emergence of very strong currents of indigenous research in Canada, the country has a unique opportunity to build linkages and research partnerships with indigenous scholars and practitioners in other parts of the world, including Latin America, Africa, and Oceania. The First

Nations Council on Heritage Language and Culture in Canada is establishing international contacts and attention is growing for these activities.[3]

A Canadian author who, with her team, consistently writes on collaborations and partnerships in the field of global health and social work is Dr Gillian King, a professor at Western University. In the team's article on features and impacts of five community–university research partnerships in health and social services, it is noted that little is known about the characteristics of these partnerships, their ways of operating, and their outputs (King et al., 2010: 60). This team of researchers described three partnership models based on their findings: infrastructure-based, project-based, and participatory action-based (King et al., 2010: 63) to guide comprehensive evaluations of partnerships. Their analysis of relationships was based on the frequency of interactions within partnerships, which is challenging to capture. In conclusion, King called for more research on a greater range of characteristics and models of community–university research partnerships, so as to understand the effects of particular methods of operation and partnership structures on their outcomes and impacts in the community.

The concerns raised in the literature over the engagement of the university with the community are centred on a 'non-reciprocal, colonial relationship in which the former has tended to appropriate material and intellectual resources from the latter' (Kassam and Tettey, 2003: 56). The authors criticized the traditional paradigm of exploitative and asymmetrical relationships, driven solely by institutional criteria used to measure success. They noticed that universities' interest in studying serious problems in communities is often motivated primarily by their desire to secure grants and produce academic publications. Instances where communities are actually involved in the research process have been rather marginal, whereby those communities' involvement has been limited by the requirements of granting agencies (Kassam and Tettey, 2003: 157). Thus, universities often appear as dominating institutions, unable to recognize the need to work closely with civil society to genuinely serve its interests.

The 2008 workshop 'Strengthening the Contribution of Higher Education and NGOs in Education for All' argued that 'NGOs use urgent intervention while universities favour longer term projects' (IFUW, 2008: 2). A counter-argument was that some university research aims to produce papers, with little regard for sustainability, while many NGOs do work on short-term activities, albeit with a long-term perspective. The workshop confirmed that NGOs work closely with local institutions, whereas universities privilege larger audiences. Strategies were drawn out for building stronger partnerships, where each side has its role in order to meet the expectations of the other partners. Thus, institutions of higher education expect NGOs to serve a monitoring role and to bring local needs to the attention of universities. Universities in turn are expected to provide support in the areas of conceptualization, evaluation, forums for debate, publications, and colloquiums (IFUW, 2008: 3).

However, the literature suggests that there are expectations from modern universities to revisit these habitual ways. Traditional ways of transmitting and disseminating knowledge, through vertical and horizontal discourses (Bernstein, 1999), are now expanding into complex knowledge networks – often transcending not only disciplinary, but national, geographic, cultural, and institutional boundaries. In his essay, Bernstein refers to institutionalized, specialized, organized knowledge as vertical discourse and everyday local knowledge as horizontal discourse. Higher education worldwide is therefore undergoing a profound transformation. Multi-stakeholder initiatives using virtual learning platforms have been emerging to create and share new knowledge on development issues of common interest. Over a number of years the Centro Boliviano de Estudios Multidisciplinarios co-developed and offered, in collaboration with several Canadian and Latin American universities, other CSOs, and networks, a series of online courses for professionals from different sectors in Canada and Latin America, as well as a portal for information sharing, electronic forums, and collaboration. Universities are under pressure to create and distribute new types of knowledge in order to play 'a proactive and committed role in the transformation and positive change of societies' (GUNI, 2009).

Striving to meet the demands of rapidly changing labour markets and to keep pace with technologies and innovations, Canadian universities are also challenged to include and operate with other types of knowledge, beyond the one generated by academia, in order to be relevant to society. They are re-emphasizing community involvement and are experimenting with participatory and action research.

Methodology

Readers less interested in the methodology may skip to Findings on page 86.

Despite a large volume of literature on cross-sector collaborations and North–South partnerships, those that are the focus of this study do not appear to be well documented. This study emerged from a number of official consultations, formal interviews, and informal ad hoc conversations in a variety of settings. The methodology for this research has evolved, based on the information collected and the responses from participants. Because few sources on Canadian collaborations were found, a grounded-theory approach, where data is collected using a variety of methods, became the first stage of the research.

First, internal CP data sources were used to identify collaborations.[4] The CP programme issues grants to both Canadian universities and CCSOs, aimed specifically at fostering closer collaboration between these two sectors. The majority of the 2005–2010 projects funded were small grants. The reports containing short abstracts for 526 small grants, describing the projects supported, were reviewed. CP's corporate memory is documented and stored in annual reports, project approval documents, and evaluation and strategy documents. This information appeared to be the best resource for this search, in addition to corporate knowledge held by CP team members. These suggested possible collaboration models and helped to define the methodology for identifying existing collaborations in Canada.

Second, a short survey of IDRC programme officers, informal interviews at IDRC, and the electronic project database were used to add to the list of collaborations. The exercise revealed the drawbacks of IDRC's electronic system when it comes to the search for collaborations. These are not obvious in project descriptions. Knowledge and information move faster through networking and interaction with people. Only seven additional projects were identified outside CP. However, projects containing research collaborations between Canadian universities and NGOs in Canada may simply have been overlooked due to the current limitations of corporate project record systems.

Finally, examples of collaborations outside of IDRC were sourced. Among IDRC's core partners were Universities Canada and the Canadian Council for International Cooperation (CCIC). These two organizations were suggested by the CP team as central to the Canadian academic community and to Canadian civil society working in international development, respectively. A brainstorming session with the CP team members yielded the suggestion of sending out the survey to members of both organizations to find out about projects of interest beyond those supported by IDRC.

Organizational 'Quick Survey'

Internationalization of research is one field of activity of Canadian universities of particular interest to Universities Canada, and so is the incorporation of a university's social responsibility into its daily activities. As this research exists at the intersection of these two interests, it was viewed by Universities Canada as potentially lending useful information to the organization.

Universities Canada offered to send the survey to the international liaison officers (ILOs) on its contact lists. The conditions were that the survey have no more than three questions and that it be sent out as an attachment to a bilingual letter, as this is the habitual way Universities Canada works with ILOs. The Quick Survey and covering letter were sent to 98 ILOs at 94 Canadian universities. Some institutions had two ILOs, as in the case of Memorial University, whose Marine Institute operates as a separate entity.

The survey asked whether or not the university had any collaboration with Canadian NGOs for international development activities, what type of collaborations they were, and what the outcomes (benefits, challenges) of the collaborations had been so far. The participation of the ILOs in the Quick Survey was voluntary. Of 98 ILOs at 94 Canadian universities, 23 responded. Although 24 per cent participation does not seem very high, one needs to take into account that not all universities are research institutions and not all of them had an interest in international development. As well, it may be that at some universities ILOs are not aware of any examples of collaboration with CSOs, particularly if there is no current project that is explicitly defined as being collaborative. The results of the Universities Canada survey underwent quantitative analysis to reveal the typology of collaborations experienced, and the diversity and frequency of learning outcomes mentioned.

A similar survey was conducted with NGOs through the CCIC. In 2010, Canadian NGOs working internationally faced major budget cuts and so they have been redefining their operations as non-profit organizations, putting much stress on their personnel. In her informal interview, the deputy director of CCIC mentioned that she could name very few NGOs that worked with universities on the institutional level (these names were the same as those suggested by the CP team).

The invitation to participate in the survey was posted in the July 2010 CCIC electronic bulletin, *Flash*. The NGOs did not respond, so personalized emails were sent out to all CCIC members (with the exception of those who had already been interviewed). The personalized emails resulted in a higher participation rate: 35 responses (circa 40 per cent) were received from the 87 surveys sent.

The limitations of this survey are defined by the ways institutions operate. The system of higher education in Canada is decentralized and international development research at universities is not always captured and easily available. In order to remedy this problem, a few universities as of late have been introducing surveys of faculty, new databases, and software to capture the size and range of disciplinary and geographic expertise on campus for international activities. Perhaps the survey ought to have been sent not only to the ILOs but also to the offices that work with community projects.

The CCIC survey thus was more effective because the structure of most NGOs is less complex. However, this survey excluded some representatives of civil society, giving priority to NGOs who could afford to be CCIC members.

Snowball approach

The initial organization officials identified by the CP team and obtained from the project database were contacted in an informal way, by email or telephone. The informants were given an explanation of the research and were asked about their interest in participating. Initially, some participants did not consider their work to be relevant to the research. However, following our discussion and some time for reflection, many of these participants saw that their work did indeed fit within the parameters of the research. Thus, these early conversations proved to be useful because they gave the participant time to reflect on the purpose of the research and on their work, as observed by an outsider.

In the course of collecting information outside of IDRC, the snowball method grew. Those that were contacted provided the names of other people engaged in university–civil society collaborations. The names of some individuals and organizations kept coming up in the conversations. This created an impression that these were active and influential individuals, very often in the academic community, who had organized centres / university units and were directly connected to the activity of interest. Therefore, for any given area of work or issue, most academic informants would consider only a couple of individuals as the ones actually leading university–CSO intellectual collaborations in Canada on this or that issue. Those working on community engagement in research knew Budd Hall and Peter Boothroyd in British Columbia, those interested in co-construction of knowledge referred me to Margie Mendel and Nancy Neamtan in Quebec, and when it came to university learning from CSO practice, the names of Bonnie Campbell at Université du Québec à Montréal (UQAM) and Pierre Beaudet at University of Ottawa were mentioned.

Finally, potential types of collaboration were identified and interviews with their initiators were scheduled. Previously arranged fieldwork did not change but, on the contrary, was confirmed by the information collected. The snowball method continued throughout the interviews, as participants willingly shared information on other known collaborations in the field.

The majority of interviewees were those recommended initially by the CP team and they had been involved in initiatives supported by IDRC. This is not surprising: international research requires financial support and IDRC's primary interest is to support research initiatives in international development. The snowball method proved to be the most effective technique to identify the collaborations of interest to this research, an example of how networks developed by collaborative work are the sources for tacit knowledge which all too often ends up not being captured in reports.

Towards typology

The exploratory stage of the project helped me recognize a variety of collaborations. While my survey was ongoing, I could not confirm a definitive typology. The specific collaborations identified were of varying nature and intensity, and more information was necessary to visualize how they might relate one with another, under possibly more robust types. The research's evolving methodology called for more in-depth study of collaborations and personal interviews were necessary.

Field trips

As stated earlier, field trips had been planned early in the research. Geographic areas in Canada where collaboration between universities and civil society is strong were confirmed by further data collection. Victoria, Nanaimo, and Vancouver on the West Coast; Montréal in Québec; Halifax and Antigonish on the East Coast; and the Ottawa–Gatineau area in Ontario and Québec were identified as the places to visit. Field trips were the second step in data collection for this project. Apart from visiting the academics and practitioners involved in the collaborations that I identified, I used each visit to meet and interview participants in the same metropolitan area that had been recommended by key informants or by the CP team. The interviews were conducted to understand what makes working together efficient, what the enablers are, and what the benefits and challenges posed by these relationships are.

Interviews

The field trips were centred on personal, semi-structured interviews with university researchers and civil society activists. Because the goal of this research was to understand the collaborations primarily from the participants' perspective, qualitative in-depth interviews were selected as the method of data collection (Hancock and Algozzine, 2006). Open-ended responses were gathered to avoid predetermined points of view.

The participants had a variety of backgrounds, interests, and work settings. They included a representative of the homeless community, the director of a research laboratory, and an officer of a large international NGO. The interviews were held to reveal the story behind the formal project report, to understand what led to the achieved results, and what was learned in the process. Semi-structured interviews allowed for a better understanding of the enablers and drivers of collaborations and how the relationships are built. The in-depth interview approach was very useful in understanding the collaborative work of organizations over time. Forty-five people were personally interviewed in British Columbia, Nova Scotia, Montréal, and Ottawa, and 16 more people were interviewed by phone or on Skype.

With an evolving methodology, some interview questions were revised based on an analysis of the first set of interviews, and included in later interviews. For example, the first interviewees reflected on their projects, which had a discrete beginning and end as defined by the duration of financial support to them. By revising the question, future interviewees were prompted to reflect more on the relationship itself, beyond a specific project, when speaking about collaboration. With the subsequent focus emphasizing relationships over projects, the beginning and end of the collaboration became blurred, making it difficult to understand how these relationships had developed in the first place. The questions were again revised for the next interviews to enquire more specifically about the nature of collaborations. Another tendency which the participants exhibited was to build their story mostly around IDRC support, as the researcher was seen as an intern representing IDRC rather than as an independent professional.

Interviewees were asked about the importance of this study and what outcomes they hoped to see. They were advised that further follow-up was possible. Participants were also asked to provide an example of a successful practice from their own activities, to encourage them to do more than just talk about all the projects they were doing in the field. This helped to create an ongoing dialogue and build relationships with the interviewees, providing a space for future communication, for example, confirming details later that possibly had been omitted during the interviews.

Logistically, it was a challenge to meet the representatives from both the academic and practitioner sides of a collaboration during the trips. In some cases, interviews were conducted later by phone. Often the collaboration is not just a two-way street, but takes place within a larger network where the Canadian civil society representative, for instance, may not play a significant role. There were also cases when the collaboration was not particularly relevant to the research; however, interesting themes and ideas still came out of such interviews.

All the interviews, except one, were recorded for further analysis upon consent.

Outline of the analysis

The analysis covered the data collected through surveys, the materials produced by the participants in the collaborations, and the information collected during the interviews.

The surveys were arranged in two groups (universities and other CSOs) using NVivo software.[5] The analysis of the surveys followed the sequence of questions asked in the surveys. Some data were arranged in a table and presented in numbers and percentages (Creswell, 2003). Qualitative data derived from open-ended questions were described and compared between universities and CSOs. Conclusions were drawn about the variety of types of relationships which universities and CSOs entertained. Depending on the percentage of participation, generalizations were drawn on the degree and types of relationships that Canadian universities have with civil society in international development research. All information presented in this analysis originated from the two sets of survey data. Information on individual survey respondents was kept anonymous.

The analysis of in-depth interview data began after the first interview was finished and continued as the research moved forward (Maxwell, 2005). The interviews were reviewed shortly after they were held to capture the major points made by the interviewees and to revise the questions where necessary. Notes were made after the interviews to help identify major ideas and the categories discussed. All interviews were recorded and transcribed for processing with NVivo software. A research assistant helped in transcribing the interviews and verifying the coding. Recording allowed the earlier interviews to be reviewed while the analysis was carried out. Thus, more themes could be extracted from the interviews and, at the same time, the questions for future interviews could be refined.

Once all the interviews were transcribed and common themes had emerged around university–civil society collaborations, the data analysis went through several steps (Foss and Waters, 2007: 146–56).

1. The transcripts were arranged in the Sources section of NVivo and organized in three groups: university participants, CSO participants, and others (there were interviewees from granting agencies, a think tank, and a for-profit planners' organization).

2. The data from the transcripts were 'meshed' with the corresponding data from the surveys and coded around the questions asked. The information pertinent to the structure of the collaboration, drivers, obstacles, lessons learned, and positive and negative experiences from all sources was labelled accordingly and arranged in the NVivo Nodes section. The information not relevant to the questions was also coded with such labels as 'curious observations', 'comments about IDRC', or 'irrelevant' in order to be analysed for unexpected findings and possible directions for future research.

3. The coded categories and subcategories were verified by the research assistant in order to allow second opinion validation. This was especially necessary for the 'types of collaborations'. Categories and subcategories in this node underwent significant revisions in the course of data analysis.

4. The links between the categories were established; they were arrived at by comparing different sources of information and laid the foundation for the narrative of the corresponding parts of this chapter.

After the interviews were analysed and the findings were described, the participants were asked to validate their words selected for citations. The printed and online materials produced by the participants were used to support their stories of collaborations where necessary. A few anecdotes were featured regarding particularly interesting practices and the materials received from participants served as the sources in those cases.

Researcher bias

A major challenge stemmed from the fact that as part of the IDRC team, the researcher's ideas, opinions, assumptions, and points of view were influenced by the granting institution, especially prior to the interview phase, and may have differed from those held by certain universities, CSOs, and/or small grassroots organizations. Indeed, working with the granting agency affected the questions underlying the analysis. The researcher remained aware of the influence the IDRC team's perspective had on the shape of this inquiry.

The literature review for this project was biased toward English-language documents. It could benefit from a review of research published in other languages, especially publications in French regarding experiences in Québec.

Findings

Who are the actors in collaborations?

The concepts of academics and practitioners are very inclusive. In the course of data collection, a range of actors or stakeholders was identified from the university and civil society responses. The surveys polled universities (through the ILOs) and internationally oriented CSOs in Canada. For the purposes of this research, civil society actors who were interviewed represented:

- community-based organizations: generally service-oriented small organizations with no research agenda, but having ready access to a large clientele of interest to researchers;
- smaller NGOs: generally with little structure and few resources in place to do research but interested in engaging in it;
- small research NGOs with a few staff (some holding advanced degrees) and considerable engagement in research; and
- large Canadian NGOs: with structure and capacity for research, accountability mechanisms, and connections with universities in place.

Academic actors were grouped into three categories:

- university units: a department, a school, an office for civic engagement or a centre for community-based research;
- individual academics: lecturers and researchers; and
- students (undergraduate and graduate students).

There was a small category of participants that could be considered as belonging to both academia and civil society. This includes a university extension department listed among CSOs on the CCIC membership list and an NGO that provides training courses and issues certificates at a university.

It is important to keep in mind the different perspectives of the respondents, although this distinction was not consistently maintained throughout the study. Different actors identified different challenges, benefits, and incentives to engaging in collaboration. Depending on the actor's potential, the type of engagement varied.

Why collaborate?

During the interview process, it was noted that some academic respondents immediately understood what was being asked and gave examples off the top of their head. Others had difficulty comprehending the purpose of this research and provided examples that did not feature any Canadian collaboration. Sometimes the respondents from academia did not recognize the value of including CSOs in Canada in their international development work. Thus, when describing their project in the South one respondent said that they wanted first to build their relationships in the country of interest to figure out the local agenda, where the players were, and what role they played because they were helping to build capacity in that country to deal with crises faced by the people of that country. Bringing a CCSO into the picture was not a priority for them.

However, there was ample evidence from the vast majority of interviewees and survey respondents of the considerable benefits derived from university–CSO collaborations in international development research.

Both universities and CSOs benefited from complementary expertise and enhanced projects. CSOs were the most appreciative of access to the different kinds of knowledge gained through their collaboration with universities, be it theoretical expertise, research skills, integration of contemporary technology or the ability to evaluate their work. Most responses stressed the importance of academic expertise in research methodology. According to three sources, the demonstration, teaching, and sharing of research methodology were very useful for CSOs to learn from their work. Another source said their organization benefited from bringing academic rigour to their research.

Evaluation and assessment techniques helped CSOs reflect better on their work. Evaluation is often required to gain access to funding. With the help of faculty and graduate students, monitoring and evaluation become feasible and practitioners enjoy learning from it. It also enhances the capacity of CSOs and their partners on the ground and it raises the profile of CSOs. This affords a greater level of impact, greater recognition, and potentially a greater ability to influence policy. One CSO noted that they themselves were able to see their own impact based on a scholarly evaluation of their work. Another noted that research, advice, and consultations with academics had assisted them with their strategic planning and decision-making.

Apart from knowledge and skills, CSOs working with universities could gain access to networks, which in turn could result in business development, as well as access to human resources often in short supply. Durable networks that sometimes resulted from collaborative work were also considered a benefit by CSOs. These networks allowed for the mentoring of interns and staff and for expanding the human resources base beyond geographical borders by providing access to the best specialists in the field. At the same time, CSOs could share their own expertise through collaborations.

Youth engagement through collaborations with universities was cited as a benefit by three sources. Internships and work placements in CSOs provided students with an opportunity to perform research that otherwise might not have been undertaken; research that empowered youth by enabling them to apply findings to address real problems. Funding for research was often allocated through the university. Collaborative work with universities allowed CSOs to explore new ways of accessing funding for their projects.

Similar benefits were noted in the responses from universities. Most asserted that collaboration with CSOs advanced different aspects of academic research. For example, collaboration increased and enhanced academic researchers' knowledge about global issues, and provided complementary expertise and experience. It exposed them to different perspectives on international development. The inclusion of CSOs benefited different aspects of academia, such as enriching students' training, increasing the international expertise of professors, strengthening their practical work in the South, and enhancing the overall internationalization of a university by making CSOs' international knowledge available on campus.

Access to networks of experts within their region of interest and internationally was another major positive outcome, from the academics' viewpoint. These networks led to opportunities for collaborative research and 'on-the-ground' connections to people with whom field researchers might work. Networks thus enabled extensive knowledge transfer and the sharing of best practices.

University participants commented on the impact of collaborative work at different stages of the research project. Engagement with CSOs helped initially to define key questions and priorities in the research projects and made these more relevant. It provided access to communities and led to higher quality field-based projects. It also helped to understand the failures and successes of developing policy. Finally, collaborative projects left academics better equipped for future projects. Similar to CSOs, universities benefited from profiling their programmes and projects to a wider community and from raising the profile of the university internationally.

Since the majority of collaborations involved student internships and volunteer work through CSOs, the resulting benefits were abundant. These practices enhanced students' education, made their learning more relevant, motivated them through the practical application of their knowledge, and, finally, provided direction and opportunities for their future career.

The concept of cost sharing was viewed as both a challenge and a benefit. In one response from a CSO, it was noted that if clearly negotiated from the very beginning of a project, cost sharing could be a significant monetary incentive for working together.

A particular category of actors who benefited from these relationships was students. Both universities and CSOs testified that, as a result of collaborative work, students obtained a better understanding of cultures and issues related to development. They also learned to better appreciate Canadian values, and gain a broader perspective on global issues and how interrelated the world had become. Students also obtained concrete, hands-on experience, and a real understanding of international development as a field of work. Several responses from CSOs revealed that they considered relationships that resulted in clear benefits to students to be advantageous, even if there were no obvious benefits to the hosting CSO itself.

Factors enabling collaborations

Apart from the various benefits of collaborative work, other factors enabled cross-institutional relationships. Among them were: leadership of integrators, availability of spaces where the synergy of ideas happened, and priorities of funding agencies.

Championing integrators. The collected data revealed that the majority of university–CSO collaborations were driven by strong individuals based on their personal interests and convictions regarding how international development research should be done. The international development community in Canada is not large, and the work of certain champions is recognized by both academics and practitioners working around a common theme. These key people most often have many years of experience and act as a connection between the two worlds. It was a challenge to find an all-encompassing term for these experts.[6] In 2014, a new term was coined for this profile of actors by the writers of *Devex Newswire,* Neil Ghosh and Kate Warren – the 'integrator': someone 'who understands multiple specialties and how they impact each other and excels in fostering collaboration between various stakeholders who may not be accustomed to working together, like government, private sector, and civil society' (Warren, 2014).

For example, a professor of economics who started a small NGO in Nova Scotia was doing research and publishing papers. He was referred to in university textbooks, based on his research on the ground in Nova Scotia and Bhutan. He noted in the interview: 'Sometimes professors are frustrated with their work being too confined within scholarly journals and not being dispersed into the public arena.' Now, through collaboration with other academics, he is interested in working with particular individuals within universities who understand and value social engagement.

In another case, a social activist taught a course on community-based co-management at a university to bring the wealth of his life experience to the classroom. According to him, he was more connected with the community than he was with the university:

> Although my connections to the university are through CURA, through adjunct positions, and through ad hoc collaboration with the professors where I do some publishing, where I am rooted is at the community level. Not even with NGOs, but community-based organizations.

This was a particularly rare case, when a professor sacrificed tenure promotion for the passion of being part of a social movement.

At the University of Ottawa, one such integrator brought his academic credentials (PhD) and 25 years of experience as an international development practitioner to participate in the creation of a new programme in international development studies. The programme has a civil society component at its core. The respondent noted: 'Because of the way the programme was structured from the beginning, because of the kind of people that came to work there, most research projects are conducted in extensive collaboration with CSOs of different kinds.' These types of academics are generally critical of research engagements that do not involve an extensive partnership with a CSO.

For a professor at UQAM who is heading a research coalition of academics and NGOs, close research collaboration with civil society is the norm. Before her first international development project even began, she had already been very closely associated with NGOs in her research and teaching, long before IDRC provided support to formalize such collaboration. She received practitioners in the classroom as guest speakers and participated in the practitioners' meetings.

Throughout the 1980s and the 1990s, she held positions on NGO boards and participated in public consultations on Canadian aid policy through a series of roundtables. She believes that her own work was enriched through these give-and-take collaborations, even before they were formalized.

Spaces. Spaces can also serve as factors enabling collaboration, as they provide a place for dialogue and learning. From the data collected, networks, forums, and events were identified as cognitive spaces, while special institutional arrangements (an office, a centre, a cluster of actors) were identified as structural spaces.

Sometimes, a structural/physical space is created on the premises of a university to enable collaboration with civil society. For example, the Institute for Studies & Innovation in Community–University Engagement at the University of Victoria is a new initiative that builds on the work of the Office of Community Based Research (OCBR), which emerged as an idea from a forum of community-based researchers in 2005 and was created in 2007. OCBR grew into a community–university partnership. Now, the Institute for Studies & Innovation in Community–University Engagement continues to bring the university and community together using an innovative structure of joint collaboration. The institute provides a space for the study and practice of engaged scholarship and interdisciplinary innovation at the university.

Much evidence from the interviews pointed to theme-specific spaces – conferences, workshops, symposiums – as birthplaces for collaborations of variable nature. Thus, OCBR organized the 2008 Community University Expo Conference in Victoria, BC, which led to the creation of the Global Alliance for Community Engaged Research (GACER). GACER advocated for community-based research to meet the needs of communities both globally and locally. It comprised community–university partnerships built around a variety of themes.[7] This initial network eventually gained support through a UNESCO Chair, co-held by Budd Hall (University of Victoria) and Rajesh Tandon (Participatory Research in Asia – PRIA), that is still active.

Several extension programmes and departments at Canadian universities offered interesting examples of collaboration with civil society. The Embedded Graduate Credit Certificate in Community-Based Research and Evaluation was developed in partnership with community organizations and launched at the University of Alberta's Faculty of Extension in 2010. The Coady International Institute at St Francis Xavier University began as an Extension Department in the late 1920s and later became the cradle of the Antigonish Movement.

One university in the sample was found to host an NGO on campus. Based at Dalhousie University in Halifax, the International Ocean Institute's flagship interdisciplinary training programme is at the core of this NGO's work. It provides summer training to professionals working on oceans from all over the world.

Priorities of funding agencies. Data confirmed a finding from the literature review: in Canada, SSHRC, with its CURA programme, had been the leader in funding large community–university research partnership projects (OCBR, 2009: 19). Two respondents recognized that the availability of an international component for CURA funding – targeting international community–university collaboration (ICURA) – served as a considerable motivation for them to combine forces. Both researchers had worked with CSOs prior to applying for funding and understood the need and value of collaborative work. However, in both cases the applications were not funded, which led to their collaboration being suspended for some time.

In one of the interviews, a researcher suggested that, in light of public funding cuts for CCSOs, these had 'less autonomous resources to produce research and do lobbying, and so CSOs turn to the academic community for the research'. An interviewee from one CSO disagreed, however, saying that this situation put CSOs in survival mode and that research was downgraded on their list of priorities. Following the initial research on collaborations in this chapter, even tougher funding cuts were introduced.

Types of collaboration between universities and other CSOs

In the university survey, the ILOs were asked three questions regarding the existence of collaborations at their universities with civil society in Canada on international development activities, the types of collaboration experienced, and the outcomes of such collaborations.

Based on IDRC corporate knowledge, the following typology of collaborations was outlined:

- university–CSO collaboration on research projects;
- CSOs commissioning studies by academics;
- recruitment of CSO experts by universities;
- CSO input into training offered by universities;
- volunteering by academics in the Global South via CCSOs;
- visiting lectureships, research fellowships of CSO experts in universities;
- student study placements/internships with CSOs; and
- others.

In the Quick Survey, ILOs at Canadian universities were asked to select the modalities of engagement which they were aware of and to describe any modalities they might list under the category 'others'.

Of the 23 ILOs who responded, five did not identify any collaboration with Canadian civil society on international development knowledge-oriented activities, and one did not know whether there were any at their university. However, some noted that there were collaborations with civil society in developing countries or that there were projects with CCSOs that did not have an international component. The other 17 ILOs answered that their universities indeed had examples of such collaborations, ranging from a lesser variety (under three types) for four universities, to more engaged

(3–4 types of collaboration) for eight universities, to the most engaged group of five universities, each with five or more of the suggested types of collaboration.

All the types of collaboration suggested were found at the 17 universities that claimed collaborations with CSOs. The most common types were student study placements and internships, which was not surprising. With growing internationalization activities in Canadian universities, there is much emphasis on study and work abroad. Moreover, the management of these activities at universities is often centralized: there are study-abroad offices and students in most cases can receive credits for their international experience. Apart from international placements via CCSOs, students have the opportunity to get an internship with an organization in Canada working on international development projects.

One category that was not expected to be so popular was volunteering by academics in the Global South via CCSOs: 11 out of 17 universities reported this type of collaboration. University–CSO collaboration on research projects was also quite common: 10 out of 17 universities have it. It is not possible to determine the nature or degree of involvement of CSOs in this type of collaboration due to the quite general definition provided in the survey.

In eight cases, universities used CSO input in the training which they themselves offered. Commissioning studies from academics by CSOs arose four times, while recruitment of CSO experts by universities, visiting lectureships, and fellowships of CSO experts at universities were mentioned in the survey five times each.

Some correlations were noted in the analysis process. In every case where studies commissioned from academics by CSOs was reported, there were examples of collaborations on research projects as well. Given that some survey respondents specified their examples of collaboration on research projects as 'working on a proposal', 'university providing training to CSO' or 'collaboration on publication', could it be that CSOs' satisfactory experience with such research collaboration set the stage for their commissioning studies by the university later on, or vice versa? Quite possibly, but finer data would be needed to verify this. Similarly, in all cases where CSO input was incorporated by a university into its training, that university also did internship placements and conducted joint research with CSOs.

More categories under 'others' were revealed by the five participating institutions. Among these, two respondents identified the participation of faculty on CSOs' boards of directors. They also mentioned university input into CSOs' activities, co-sponsorship, and promotion of public events, as well as joint international development initiatives, including programmes during International Development Week. The university with the broadest range of collaborations indicated its long-term involvement in the implementation, monitoring, and evaluation of international development projects in partnership with local CSOs.

Fourteen out of 35 CSOs reported no examples of collaboration with Canadian universities. A number of CSO respondents asked additional questions; email and phone communication was notably active with this sector. As in the case of universities, there was a range of engagement for CSOs, and the most engaged group comprised six CSOs. All types of collaboration suggested were found in CSOs' responses. Similarly, the most common were student study placements and internships (16 of 21 respondents) and collaboration on research projects was identified in 11 of 21 responses.

The correlation between CSOs commissioning studies by academics and collaborations on research projects was not as strong as it was in the university survey. However, visiting lectureships by CSO experts at universities (which occurred for the most engaged CSOs) happened when these CSOs also practised internships. CSO experts also provided input into study programmes run by universities.

Comparison of university and CSO survey results

Figure 3.1 compares university and CSO responses on a variety of collaborations which they engage in, often more than one at the same time. CSOs' input into the training offered by universities yielded similar results to those from universities: about 47 per cent of respondents on both sides were engaged this way. Similar responses from both categories of participants (slightly less than 30 per cent) were received about recruitment of CSO experts by universities. The examples of visiting lectureships of CSO experts did not differ significantly between the two categories (24 to 29 per cent).

The two remaining categories received significantly different reactions from universities and CSOs. CSOs reported commissioning studies by academics twice as often as the universities themselves. The difference was

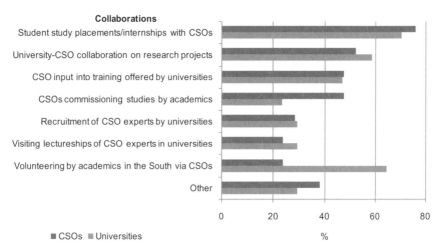

Figure 3.1 Comparison of collaborations reported by Canadian CSOs and Canadian universities

even more marked when it was noted that the responses from civil society were mostly from NGOs, whereas universities were responding about their collaboration with civil society broadly, which included communities, diasporas, and citizens in addition to NGOs. It was difficult to say whether this gap spoke to the lack of centralized knowledge in universities on this type of activity or whether it reflected a deeper issue of knowledge hierarchy and academia's domination in knowledge creation. The rate of participation in the survey of universities was not high enough to allow for generalized conclusions.

The number of participating universities that reported volunteering by academics in the Global South via CCSOs was almost three times higher than that of the participating CSOs. Keeping in mind the lower participation rate of universities, the higher awareness of CSO respondents about collaborative research activities with universities, and that many large CSOs engaged with volunteering in the Global South did participate in the survey, this finding was very surprising. Could it be that volunteering was understood differently in collaborative cases? It might be that CSOs did not consider placing an academic as a volunteer in the Global South to be an actual collaboration with Canadian universities unless the CSO's own research interests were addressed by the academic.

An attempt to draw a typology

Many respondents found it difficult to describe their cross-sector collaborative activities in a linear manner. Often they were puzzled about what exactly they should refer to: a project, a programme, or a relationship. Some referred to collaborations as multidimensional, complex, and fluid relationships that defy description. Other respondents found it easier to list their activities: organized conferences, asked for advice, shared findings, etc. In order to identify typology, the information on interactions occurring between universities and CSOs from the aggregated data was sorted into categories using the NVivo software. The 274 references about engagements appeared to answer two questions: (1) What collaborative activities did universities and CSOs engage in? and (2) How did they do it? The 'What' category reflected the types of collaboration. The major types derived were:

- university–CSO collaboration on research projects;
- (study) placements in (by) CSOs;
- research fellowship of CSO expert at a university; and
- collaboration on training programmes.

The original typology described by IDRC's Canadian Partnerships programme corresponded quite closely to the one derived from the aggregate data. In reality, there was often more than one form of collaboration that occurred in a given situation between CSOs and universities, and these appeared to be mutually reinforcing.

University–CSO collaboration on the research project

The interactions found in this category occurred at any given stage of the research project cycle. For example, a small CSO in Nova Scotia commissioned university doctoral students to do a survey of recent literature to inform research projects initiated by their CSO. On two occasions, academics helped CSOs to develop a research proposal. Academics used CSOs to access and collect data. In turn, CSOs interested in research and publication benefited from the university's ethics procedures.

The academic in charge of an ICURA project on youth resilience in stressful environments was approached by a First Nations community going through a spate of teen suicides. The community wanted this issue to be researched. Funding permitting, the ICURA team included the community and engaged them in participatory research (as a component of the bigger research project). In this way, the community was connected with other communities that deal with the issue of teen suicides nationally and globally.

Academics helped CSOs to draw lessons from their projects, and to document best cases and worst cases in order to strategize how best to inform policy or to design future grant applications. CSOs realize the importance of documenting their practices and communicating their findings through publications. A small NGO in Nova Scotia shared its draft with academic experts for their review. As a result, the practitioners published in certain journals and their work was widely cited in university textbooks. More commonly CSOs commissioned graduate students to document their practices or collect case studies.

Finally, there were some examples where academics and practitioners had produced joint publications. In the vast majority of cases, these academics are those described earlier as integrators.

Study placements

The data from interviews confirmed that this modality was an overwhelmingly popular way for universities and CSOs to collaborate. This type of activity was sometimes institutionalized in the form of a longstanding partnership. It included internships, volunteer placements, and work placements where students and, in some cases, academics were placed to learn from the work on the ground in Canada or in the Global South. They in turn made their competencies and skills available to assist CSOs. The placements in this category are those structured strictly around research and knowledge-creation activities.

Most of the examples of such placements reveal that the predominant arrangement was quite conventional: a university wanted to formalize its internships and make sure there was a consistent flow of students working with CSOs to 'apply their knowledge to local social issues' (from an interview with a university academic). This approach was criticized by the integrators as often bringing limited positive outcomes for CSOs and being mainly used as research platforms.

Still, one initiative that took NGO–university placement programmes to a higher level was launched in 2010 but was brought to an end a couple of years ago. An informal arrangement for research placements between Oxfam-Québec and three universities in Québec was turned into a formalized agreement: GRIOT (Groupe de recherche pour l'innovation, l'organisation et le transfert d'Oxfam-Québec) was expected to move a pre-existing relationship to a new level, whereby the NGO's own research needs would directly steer the research internship of interested students. The purpose of the memorandum of understanding between Oxfam-Québec and individual universities, besides formalizing the partnership, was to protect the university in terms of author rights, commercial benefit, and ownership of research or commercial results. It also guaranteed to Oxfam-Québec that the research placements would truly contribute to the work of their organization. Academics and the NGO held discussions to identify possible areas of research. The respondents from GRIOT agreed: 'this is a main challenge, to have such a common understanding about what the research will cover, how it will be conducted, and how the results of the research will be transferred and applied to the practices of Oxfam-Québec as a learning organization.' Much could be learned from a post-mortem of this experiment for universities and CSOs looking to set up similar partnerships.

Collaboration in training programmes

Many examples of university–CSO collaborations focused on developing and implementing training programmes. Relationships were not always equally balanced in this modality. The group of academics usually designed the programme, and then they invited practitioners to teach or to study. However, in cases where this worked, the organizing academics were integrators who had had long relationships and built trust with CSOs. It is noteworthy that the actors involved in this type of collaboration were either a university unit that had CSOs' interests on its agenda or a group of cluster-collaborators. Hosting units were an extension department, an institute for community development, or an office of community-engaged research.

An outstanding example was the undergraduate programme Certificate of International Cooperation at the University of Montréal, created and produced with the help of eight Québec CSOs directly involved in international cooperation. It was the university's idea to involve them. Specific individual practitioners were approached to help academics to design and manage this programme. From the beginning it was a partnership between the university and the CSOs, formalized through a jointly signed contract. Many instructors in the programme were CSO practitioners with either a Master's or a PhD degree.

Other interactions and modalities were entertained under the certificate programme: participants took part in the colloquium, published together, and collaborated on the internships and student placements. The idea was to create a hands-on educational basis for this programme. The director said, 'Cooperation is how you apply development', thus pointing out that a cooperative effort should be at the core of development strategies.

The major challenges identified for this method in general were: the inflexible structure of the university, language barriers (outcome of difference in institutional cultures), and the amount of time required to produce high-quality papers. Even so, the programmes tried to cope with such challenges as they forged ahead.

Research fellowships for CSO actors

Although there was only one example of this method, it stood out as an innovative form of engagement that will be promoted under a new partnership between the Canadian Council for International Cooperation and international development studies programmes at Canadian universities over the coming years. In this study, the director of a CSO spent one year researching and teaching at a university. This happened because the professor who made the invitation had some funding available and saw the opportunity.

The relationship started at a conference where both were presenters. At one point, the professor asked if the practitioner knew any people in Africa who would be interested in a research project that she was doing on globalization. After giving her some contacts, the interviewee said that she herself was interested. So the professor invited her to come to the university as her research assistant. She was granted the status of adjunct professor so that she could lecture and be a teaching assistant.

It was a very beneficial experience both for the practitioner and her CSO. When she returned to the CSO, her new knowledge helped strengthen the research dimension of its work. The experience was also shared with other CSOs. At the university, this practitioner had researched the political economy of aid and how it affects international solidarity as pursued by CSOs and development agencies.

The main challenge that this respondent identified was the unavailability of funds to support similar initiatives. The ripple effect from one person, who had time to reflect on the work of CSOs and to document it in a publication, was significant. The respondent suggested this should be practised more regularly and conference discussions should be held at the end of such fellowships to disseminate the learning widely to CSOs.

Summary of challenges

According to the literature on cross-sector partnerships, differences in institutional structure and culture often present an underlying obstacle to successful collaboration. The participants talked about a hierarchy of knowledge, where the learning process was predominantly top-down, about the red tape in academia, and the scarcity of time and resources in CSOs. As expected, limited funding appeared to be another major challenge. Both CSOs and some universities pointed out the tension that arises when sharing the costs of a project. This challenge was more strongly felt by smaller CSOs and community organizations than by large, internationally oriented NGOs. With recent public funding redirections, this may become a challenge for the latter as well.

Some participants confirmed that challenges also included different mindsets, goals, and visions for organizations. Some CSO participants pointed out that when it came to academics evaluating projects or programmes run by them, CSOs were sometimes resentful of critical academic research. Academics noticed that it was often difficult to capture information on what individual academics were doing in international development research. Some recognized that the field was competitive and, in some cases, researchers had a tendency to keep their contacts and ideas to themselves. The other reason was the lack of a centralized effort to coordinate collaborative activities on campus. Most Canadian universities request that professors report on three aspects of their work – teaching, research, and community work; however, they do not emphasize the importance of reporting on the latter aspect as much as on the former two. Academics engaged in collaborations lamented the lack of recognition of such efforts by their university.

The time factor was also confirmed as a major barrier. Some of the critical functions of many CSOs were fundraising and advocacy: very little time was left for research. The timeframe for academic research was much longer than that for implementing a practical project. The time factor was also identified as a challenge when it comes to building trust. This factor was more relevant for smaller CSOs and community organizations that did not necessarily have the capacity, but did have an interest in research.

Thus, the majority of challenges were mutual for academics and practitioners involved in research collaborations. Failure to link research to concrete results and to informing policy is one of the critiques that caused a disconnect in relationships. This disconnect is aggravated by the inaccessibility of academic language for the effective dissemination of research results. Both communities lamented the lack of knowledge and expertise of their counterparts, which sometimes interfered with successful collaboration. In both cases, this identifies the deeper problem of a lack of exposure to each other's work.

How are relationships structured?

Based on the data from the interviews, three stages that relationships between universities and CSOs could go through were identified. This is not a stepwise model through which all relationships would evolve. Also, the model does not imply that the quality of research necessarily improves from one stage to the next. It was noticed, however, that 'collaborations' were less sustainable than 'partnerships' and more sustainable than 'interactions'. Partnerships demonstrated the highest level of engagement or commitment by parties involved.

Stage 1 – Interactions. A majority of relationships between universities and civil society in Canada could be identified as interactions. These were ad hoc, spontaneous contacts, when one party needed the assistance of the other, but not necessarily vice versa. The actors who had benefited would go back and repeat the exercise within another project. Through these interactions mutual trust could be built over time; both sides realized potential benefits. At this stage, interactions were more likely to happen around research projects, at different stages of the research. Based on the data collected, most initial meetings happen at the dissemination stage of a project cycle, during conferences, symposiums, workshops, etc.

Stage 2 – Collaborations. Sometimes, under certain conditions, these interactions could grow into collaborations (of particular interest to this research). These collaborations varied from loosely structured to more formalized, but they were always characterized by reciprocity and mutual interest. The goals often stayed different and, at this stage, the university and the CSO learned to use each other's strengths in a complementary fashion. A majority of respondents enjoyed flexibility when the relationships were mature enough to be formalized. At this stage, some realized the benefits of simply staying in this collaborative stage, given the flexibility it allowed for creating space for innovation.

Stage 3 – Partnerships. This stage led to strategizing together. There was clear vision of everybody's roles and benefits, and assurance in funding. The collaboration could be taken a step further to an institutionalized and formalized partnership. This was most likely to happen between well-established larger NGOs or groupings of CSOs and universities.

I avoided addressing the question of success, realizing that its meaning was not the same for universities, CSOs, and funding agencies. Instead, I decided to address the depth of engagement and its sustainability. Based on the responses from integrators as those with extensive experience, major factors that make engagements more involved and relationships more sustainable were identified. All factors identified were significant; however, experts specifically underlined understanding each other's goals, realizing challenges early, and developing the idea together as crucial components for progression towards deeper and more sustainable collaborations.

Conclusions

This research can be refreshing for professors: university people need to start working horizontally. Knowledge is implicitly hierarchic, and we need to de-construct expertise. The longer you work at the university, the stronger you believe in yourself being an expert. We need to get out.

From an interview with an academic at UQAM

The sociopolitical context in Canada and the world today is such that it calls for more relevant and efficient collaborative research for international development. Given reduced and more competitive funding for international development, Canadian organizations are forced to rethink institutional boundaries and continue their quest for innovative solutions in cross-sector collaboration.

This study and its process point to clear lessons and suggest specific ways to encourage and strengthen university–CSO collaborations in Canada on research and cooperation for international development.

Lessons

Methodologically, the expert knowledge on CCSO–university collaborations available in-house (IDRC/CP) proved to be the most accessible source of background information to move this project forward. The snowball method proved to be the most effective in identifying collaborations of interest. The relationship side of collaborative work includes tacit knowledge, which is often not well captured in project reports.

Collaborative work between universities and CSOs in Canada on research-related activities for international development is being pursued in a range of different ways, given its benefits, and despite the challenges recognized by both communities. It was in fact a modus operandi for many professionals and organizations in both communities. It has penetrated the structure of Canadian universities and some consider that collaboration is essential in the field of international development research. Thus, university–CSO collaborations are here to stay and institutions face the task of making these effective.

The different types of collaboration in which a given university or CSO is involved vary greatly across the country. Even on the basis of small samples, the survey was able to clearly identify three groups of organizations in each of the two communities, ranging from those involved in very few to others engaged in many types of collaboration. Further research should help explain these differences, as well as identify processes by which a particular organization might move from one group to another. On their part, the interviews, which focused on the relationships and their evolution beyond discrete activities, greatly assisted in developing a gradation of relationships (from interactions to collaborations to partnerships). Future case studies should help to elicit the processes by which a given organization decides to move (or not) from one level of relationship to another.

The ingredients needed for effective collaborations, as identified from the interviews, point to the following essentials: supporting individual champions, providing space for dialogue, and allocating funding strategically.

The challenges can be divided into structural and ongoing. Structural challenges are relevant to the way institutions are organized and will take a long time to change; however, ongoing challenges refer to practices and these can be addressed, thus encouraging the behavioural change in institutions that is needed to confront issues of a more structural nature. Those engaged in collaborations found ways to overcome particular challenges and it is important for the larger community to capitalize on their experience.

The literature often points to a lack of mutual goals being a problem. Yet often in the collaborative arrangements examined it was not a shared goal but a commitment to find a fit for different goals pursued by different partners that was essential for effective work. Participants pointed out the challenge of converging interests and finding ways to achieve different goals. When this challenge was hard to overcome, they were opposed to formalizing collaboration and preferred occasional interactions in familiar ways. An 'integrator' could help to address this challenge. Mechanisms of training, honing, and supporting integrators' skills should be developed.

Suggestions

The role of funding agencies in nurturing research collaborations is absolutely critical. As sources of support, they have the capacity to affect the national dynamics of the entire international development research community.

First, building a stronger capacity to monitor national collaborative activity is essential, as locating and funding critical initiatives becomes more and more necessary. Certainly, the process of creating such capacity (building databases, using mapping capabilities, regularly surveying actors, etc.) is somewhat time- and resource-consuming. However, the benefits of such a capability should not be underestimated. Likewise, encouraging innovative approaches by funding case-study collaborations and by developing a library of best practices may prove quite important to a learning strategy for all parties involved. One such series of examples may be derived from the SSHRC–IDRC International Community–University Research Alliance Programme. This requires reflecting on partnership-building processes beyond the dissemination of reports on completed projects.

In the course of this research, both academics and practitioners expressed concern about the amount of paperwork and expertise required to apply for a grant. It appears that many opportunities for collaboration never materialize because of administrative hurdles and the lack of institutional and human resources on the part of potential partners. Grant applications and reporting requirements could be adapted for situations in which small CSOs and community organizations wish to work with universities for research-related activities.

To further encourage practitioner–academic interaction, reciprocity, and knowledge exchange, annual fellowships could be offered for a small number of CSO activists to be seconded to academic institutions where they could participate in teaching and research for a period of time. The academics playing host to such placements should benefit from the experience of practitioners, especially the opportunity to adjust their research and to make it more context-relevant. For practitioners, the experience would afford them an opportunity for self-reflection and knowledge sharing.

The factors that enable collaborations, such as interactive spaces in which actors from different sectors come together for a dynamic exchange, certainly deserve further and continuous support. The existing examples of organizational and institutional partnerships (e.g. GACER), created in the wake of specific events (conferences forums or roundtables), underscore the importance of strategic planning for such events (purpose, participants, programme, timing) and the value of small grants to make these possible.

Canadian universities' growing interest in research partnerships with indigenous communities gives them a leading advantage in valuing indigenous knowledge. Emerging linkages with similar partnerships led by indigenous scholars and organisations in the Global South deserve more attention.

Another avenue for innovative forms of collaboration attracting government interest is social entrepreneurship, including social impact bonds. Reviewing current experience in social impact investment and exploring opportunities for novel ways of financing cross-sector research partnerships for social impact could open up new forms of university–CSO engagement in Canada.

Notes

1. Communication from Dr Luc J.A. Mougeot, Senior Program Specialist, Canadian Partnerships, 2010, IDRC, Ottawa.
2. Retrieved June 19, 2015, from Campus Compact, a national coalition of more than 1,100 college and university presidents who are committed to fulfilling the civic purposes of higher education in the US. <http://compact.org/resources-for-presidents/presidents-declaration-on-the-civic-responsibility-of-higher-education/> [accessed 19 June 2015].
3. B. Hall and L.Williams, personal communication, 3 February 2011.
4. More detailed methodology and reflections on the search for collaborations within IDRC can be found in the original report. <https://idl-bnc.idrc.ca/dspace/bitstream/10625/46120/1/132609.pdf> [accessed 31 October 2016].
5. NVivo is a software designed for computer-aided qualitative and quantitative analysis of data. In this research Version 0.8 of NVivo was employed for data organization, sorting, categorizing, and analysing.
6. The importance of these leaders was underscored in many interviews conducted during this research. Different terms were used for these champions of collaboration: they were referred to as 'knowledge brokers', 'network weavers', and 'bridging experts'. The latter was the term was adopted from an interviewee in the original report on this research.
7. Read about GACER at University of Victoria (2016). <https://www.uvic.ca/research/centres/cue/collaborations%20gacer/index.php> [accessed 6 December 2016].

References

Albrow, M., Chadwick, M., and Thomas, B. (2007) *The Case for a Civil Society University: A Prime Timers Inquiry*, Preliminary report <http://www.civilsocietyuniversity.org/idea.htm> [accessed 3 March 2010].

Bernstein, B. (1999) 'Vertical and horizontal discourse: An essay', *British Journal of Sociology of Education* 20(2): 157–73.

Bradley, M. (2007) 'North–South research partnerships: literature review and annotated bibliography', Ottawa: IDRC.

Bradley, M. (2016) 'Whose agenda? Power, policies, and priorities in North -South research partnerships', in L.J.A. Mougeot (ed.), *Putting Knowledge to Work: Collaborating, influencing and learning for international development*, pp. 37–70, Rugby, UK and Ottawa: Practical Action Publishing and IDRC <http://dx.doi.org/10.3362/9781780449685.002>.

Creswell, J.W. (2003) *Research design: Qualitative, quantitative, and mixed methods approach* (2nd edn), Thousand Oaks, CA: Sage Publications.

Edwards, M. and Hume, D. (eds) (1992) *Making a Difference: NGOs and Development in a Changing World*, London: Earthscan.

Fitzgerald, H.E. and Zientek, R. (2015) 'Learning cities, systems change, and community engagement scholarship', *New Directions for Adult and Continuing Education*, 2015(145): 21–33 <http://dx.doi.org/10.1002/ace.20120>.

Foss, S. and Waters, W. (2007) *Destination Dissertation. A Traveler's Guide to a Done Dissertation*, Lanham, MD: Rowman & Littlefield Publishers.

Gall, E., Millot, G., and Neubauer, C. (2009) *Participation of Civil Society Organisations in Research*, STACS <http://www.livingknowledge.org/fileadmin/Dateien-Living-Knowledge/Library/Project_reports/STACS_Final_Report-Partic.research_2009.pdf> [accessed 29 July 2016].

GUNI (Global University Network for Innovation) (2009) *Higher education at a time of transformation: New dynamics for social responsibility*, Hampshire, UK: Palgrave Macmillan.

Hall, B. (2010 *Global Community University Networks, Call for North–South Cooperation*, Proceedings of the Global Video dialogue amongst eight global or regional networks in Community Engagement and Community Based Research, 25 October, London, UK.

Hall, B., Tandon, R., and Escrigas, C. (eds) (2014) *Knowledge, Transformation and Social Change in Higher Education*, GUNI Series on the Social Commitment of Universities 5, Basingstoke, Palgrave Macmillan.

Hall, B., Tremblay, C., and Downing, R. (2009) *The Funding and Development of Community University Research Partnerships in Canada: Evidence-based investment in knowledge, engaged scholarship, innovation and action for Canada's future*, Victoria, British Columbia: University of Victoria.

Hancock, D.R. and Algozzine, B. (2006) *Doing case study research: A practical guide for beginning researchers*, New York, NY: Teachers College Press.

Haslam, P.A., Schafer, J., and Beaudet, P. (2008) (eds) *Introduction to International Development: Approaches, Actors and Issues*, Don Mills, Ontario: Oxford University Press.

Horton, D., Prain, G., and Thiele, G. (2009) *Perspectives on partnership: A literature review*, Working Paper 2009–3, Lima: International Potato Center (CIP).

IDRC (2008) *International Development Research Centre 2007–2008 Annual Report*, Ottawa: IDRC.

IFUW (International Federation of University Women), (2008) 'Strengthening the Contribution of Higher Education and NGOs in Education for All (EFA)', <http://www.graduatewomen.org/what-we-do/policy-advocacy/

advocacy-news/strengthening-the-contribution-of-higher-education-ngos-in-efa/> [accessed 29 July 2016].

Kassam, K.A. and Tettey, W.J. (2003) 'Academics as citizens: collaborative applied interdisciplinary research in the service of communities', *Canadian Journal of Development Studies* 24(1): 155–74.

Katz, J.S. and Martin, B.R. (1997) 'What is research collaboration?', *Research Policy*, 26: 1–18.

King, G., Servais, M., Forchuk, C., Chalmers, H., Currie, M., Law, M., Specht, J., Rosenbaum, P., Willoughby, T., and Kertoy, M. (2010) 'The features and impacts of five multidisciplinary community–university research partnerships', *Health and Social Care in the Community*, 18: 59–69.

Kothari, U. (2005) *A Radical History of Development Studies: Individuals, Institutions and Ideologies*, London: Zed.

Living Knowledge (2014) *6th Living Knowledge Conference 2014*, 9–11 April, Copenhagen <http://www.livingknowledge.org/lk6/> [accessed 29 July 2016].

Maxwell, J.A. (2005) *Qualitative Research Design: An interactive approach* (2nd edn), Thousand Oaks, CA: Sage Publications.

Monash University (2015) 5th ACFID University Network Conference, *Evidence and Practice in an Age of Inequality*, 4–5 June, Melbourne, Australia <http://artsonline.monash.edu.au/acfid/> [accessed 29 October 2016].

OCBR (2009) 'The Funding and Development of Community University Research Partnerships in Canada, Evidence-Based Investment in Knowledge, Engaged Scholarship, Innovation and Action for Canada's Future', Victoria, British Columbia: University of Victoria.

Olivier, C., Hunt, M.R., and Ridde, V. (2016) 'NGO–researcher partnerships in global health research: benefits, challenges, and approaches that promote success' *Development in Practice* 26(4): 444–455 <http://dx.doi.org/10.1080/09614524.2016.1164122> [accessed 6 December 2016].

Pezzoli, K. (2008) 'Enabling excellence in higher education through civically-engaged research and service learning', Instructional Improvement Grant Proposal, UC San Diego: Urban Studies and Planning Program & Superfund Basic Research Program.

RAWOO (Netherlands Development Assistance Research Council) (2001) *North–South Research Partnerships: Issues and Challenges*, The Hague: RAWOO.

Salamon, L.M., Sokolowski, S.W., and List, R. (2003) *Global Civil Society: An Overview*, Baltimore: Johns Hopkins Center for Civil Society Studies.

SID (Special Initiatives Division) (2008) 'Special Initiatives Division 2007–2008 Internal Annual Report', Ottawa: IDRC.

Smart, C. (1996) 'Canadian Collaboration', internal IDRC memorandum, 18 March (From 'History' box).

Stevens, D., Hayman, R., and Mdee, A. (2013) 'Cracking collaboration between NGOs and academics in development research', *Development in Practice* 23(8): 1071–77 <http://dx.doi.org/10.1080/09614524.2013.840266>.

Universities Canada (2010) 'Cardinal Points: How North-South Partnerships Support Internationalization Strategies', Promising Practices Guide and Case Studies, Ottawa: Universities Canada.

University of Victoria (2016) Institute for Studies & Innovation in Community–University Engagement <http://www.uvic.ca/research/centres/cue/> [accessed 29 July 2016].

Warren, K. (2014) 'Career matters. Move over generalists, make way for integrators' *Devex Doing Good*, 7 October <https://www.devex.com/news/move-over-generalists-make-way-for-integrators-84498> [accessed 29 October 2016].

About the author

Elena Chernikova is an analyst at Indigenous and Northern Affairs Canada in Ottawa. She previously worked with Statistics Canada, Graybridge Malkam, Citizenship and Immigration Canada, and Human Resources and Skills Development Canada, in Ottawa. She holds an MA in globalization and international development from the University of Ottawa and a PhD in comparative languages and cultures from Moscow State Linguistics University. Her postgraduate fellowship at Kent State University, USA, focused on the internationalization of higher education. Elena immigrated from Yakutia, Russian Siberia.

CHAPTER 4

Canadian civil society organizations using research to influence policy and practice in the Global South

Stacie Travers

Abstract

Just how civil society organizations (CSOs) engage in research and use both the research process and the resulting information to influence policy and practice is still not well understood by many in the ecosystem of international development. There is a need to better understand such strategies in order to strengthen cooperation between CSOs and other actors for better development outcomes. Based on a nationwide survey of CSOs, plus multi-country fieldwork in South America, this chapter investigates how Canadian CSOs (CCSOs), in their work with Global South partners, produce and use research and knowledge to influence positive change in the Global South.

CCSOs use research extensively to influence policy and/or practice in the Global South. Furthermore, they retain considerable control over the research agenda, process, dissemination, and use of the results. The large majority use their own staff, interns, and volunteers to conduct this research. They also draw on research by other actors, both in Canada and the Global South. CCSOs rely more on research produced by or with Southern CSOs than on research by or with other CCSOs. There is room for more research collaboration among CCSOs active abroad, and between them and those engaged domestically. CCSOs integrate research into their action strategies through methodologies that simultaneously build capacity, raise awareness, engage stakeholders, and influence policy and practice. Other key considerations are identified which donors should keep in mind when evaluating CCSOs' results and influence. Funders should support more adaptive and open methodologies to allow CSOs' key organizational roles to be fulfilled.

Keywords: civil society organizations, knowledge, Global South, development, research, policy

Current relevance

Although use of knowledge is central to civil society organizations' (CSOs) strategies to influence and improve policies and practices for development, the learning from such efforts for CSOs' own growth remains paradoxically

http://dx.doi.org/10.3362/9781780449586.004

limited. Drawing on original research completed in 2012, this study is still exceptional in that it relies on both a nationwide survey and case studies of surveyed CSOs to systematically examine how they use research to influence policies and practices in countries where they work. Distinctively, because it focuses on CSOs that do not have research as a primary mandate, it is representative of situations faced by the majority of CSOs. It examines how Canadian CSOs (CCSOs) – universities excluded – decide to implement strategies for influence in collaboration with their Global South counterparts, to fulfil their objectives, optimize resource use, and achieve greater influence. Finally, it is concerned with processes to influence policy in the Global South to impact local community or institutional practices, and to influence partner CSOs' own programming and approaches.

Given the complexity of the subject, its methodology should be particularly useful to readers, as it categorizes sources of research used, links purposes of research use with the roles played by CSOs, and uses case studies to explore issues raised by an analysis of the data from the nationwide survey. In a context where pressure is on CSOs in donor countries to innovate and deliver on their mandates, and where CSO research funding is increasingly conditional on collaborations with research organizations, two findings suggest ways CSOs and funders can change to address this challenge. First, the noted lack of use by CCSOs of research produced by other CCSOs, although justifiable on some counts, nevertheless curtails their ability to share, learn, and innovate more as a community (select communities of practice are discussed in Chapter 5 of this volume: Smith, 2016). Second, in contrast with the more linear research–dissemination–impact model in academia, the lack of a linear relationship between a CSO's research, influence, and change speaks to the need for CSOs to integrate research throughout their broader strategies for change. Given this, funders not only must do more to support learning collectives that can spur innovation in a sustainable way, but they also need to accept as legitimate the multi-pronged use of research by CSOs and be ready to fund this in ways other than through collaborations with organizations with very different knowledge cultures.

Introduction

Knowledge leads to empowerment, which in turn provides the basis for developing equitable and prosperous societies. Research and corresponding knowledge-sharing activities are essential in both acquiring and disseminating this knowledge. Often associated with academia, research is no longer the realm of universities or research centres alone, nor is it equated with scientific data or left to theorists.

Research has come to include broad categories of methodologies, disciplines, and actors. Not only have the types of research changed with time, but the researchers themselves have also changed. Individuals without research as their main goal and organizations without research as part of their stated mandate can and do conduct a variety of research activities as part of a strategy to further other objectives. Civil society organizations are credited with having a role to play in making research relevant, and in using it to engage in policymaking processes and broaden their impact. With the shift to knowledge-based approaches to development comes the need to examine the role of CSOs, as emerging and underexamined actors, in knowledge creation and distribution. For all actors in the field of international cooperation for development, there is a need to understand the strategies and the contributions of CSOs to the policy process, practice, and overall change in development. Room has been made in international forums and dialogue for CSO voices, but there still seems to be a lack of understanding of the importance they place on research-centred strategies for influence. There is also often confusion about the roles CSOs effectively play and how research relates to these roles.

This chapter presents a study that seeks to examine the strategies put in place by CCSOs, specifically development NGOs. The study addresses how CCSOs make strategic decisions on implementing research-centred strategies for influence in ways that fulfil other organizational objectives, maximize their resources, and make a higher contribution to influence. The study excludes certain types of CCSOs, such as universities and think tanks, which have research as a main goal and generally a much stronger research capacity. Instead, it centres on CCSOs that self-identify as playing organizational roles other than conducting research. These roles include capacity building, advocacy, technical assistance, service delivery, and representation. The aim is to examine attempts at influencing policy in the Global South, as well as influencing local community or institutional practices, and the CCSOs' own programming and ways of working, to provide a less anecdotal and more broad-based awareness of the role played by research in CCSOs' strategies to influence change for development in the Global South. Specific objectives include: identifying the wider range of actors from whom CCSOs access, and with whom they conduct, research to inform their actions; determining the relationship between CCSOs' organizational roles and the purposes that this research serves; and better understanding strategic provisions taken by CCSOs to increase the odds that their use of research will be effective in bringing about positive change.

Following this introduction is an overview of the literature which aims to provide context and present the gap this study serves to help fill. This section briefly summarizes CSOs and their engagement with the policy process. Special attention is given to evidence-based attempts at policy engagement. Recent efforts to incorporate civil society in international dialogue and development cooperation spaces are briefly presented with particular emphasis on the Canadian government's acknowledgement of the central role CCSOs play in Canada's official development assistance (ODA). Next, the methodology section describes the quantitative and qualitative research methods used in this study. The CCSO survey sample is described with details on how CCSOs were selected to take part in this study. The quantitative phase of data collection is explained with a description of the short close-ended survey used. The survey tool provided quantitative data used to answer this study's key questions, but it also served to build and narrow the selection of case studies yielding complementary qualitative data. The selection of the case studies is detailed further with descriptions of the fieldwork activities, which helped capture and analyse these cases. These activities include semi-structured interviews, participant observation, focus groups, and site visits. Following the explanation of this combined-methods approach is the presentation of the study's key findings. The results section addresses findings from the survey and those from the case study analysis separately, but reviews how the two general sets of data complement each other and help achieve a rounded understanding of the strategies and decisions made by CCSOs. The results section includes brief descriptions of each of the four case studies, that is, each of the four CCSOs and their corresponding project or programme, which was being implemented with and by local CSOs in the Global South at the time of the fieldwork. Finally, the chapter ends with some thoughts on the implications of the study findings, recommendations for various stakeholders, and an acknowledgement of where further research is needed.

Review of literature

Civil society organizations' engagement in the policy process

CSOs are in a sense defined by what they are not. That is, they are not organizations of the state, the private sector, or the family domain. Court et al. (2006: 1) define a CSO as 'any organization that works in the arena between the household, the private sector, and the state, to negotiate matters of public concern'. CSOs include NGOs, advocacy groups, trade unions, faith-based institutions, professional associations, academic institutions, research centres, think tanks, networks, and social movements.

As this definition illustrates, civil society and the organizations representing it are as diverse as the roles that CSOs play in international cooperation for development. According to the 2010 report *Civil Society and Aid Effectiveness* by the Organisation for Economic Co-operation and Development (OECD), there are four areas where CSOs engage as development actors: civic engagement; service delivery, self-help and innovation; humanitarian assistance; and as international aid donors, channels, and recipients. Court et al. (2006) also describe five functions of CSOs: representation (citizen voice), advocacy (lobbying), service delivery (implementation of projects and service provision), technical inputs (information and advice), and capacity building (support to other CSOs). Beaulieu (2009) identified three categories of CSOs in Ghana, based on combinations of three main functions: research and advocacy organizations (with research as a primary focus, but supported with advocacy), advocacy and research organizations (with advocacy as a primary focus, but supported with research), and programme delivery, research, and advocacy organizations (involved in all three activities).

Not only have the roles and functions of CSOs grown over time, but the context in which they work has also changed. Democratization, reduction in violent conflicts, government decentralization, increase in the development of information and communication technologies, and opening of markets are all trends that characterize many of the developing countries where CSOs work. As the operating environment for CSOs improves and their roles expand, CSOs find themselves in a better position to work with policymakers (Court et al., 2005). Crediting their contributions, but also recognizing limits on their effectiveness, Court et al. explain:

> Civil society organizations make a difference in international development. They provide development services and humanitarian relief, innovate in service delivery, build local capacity, and advocate with and for the poor. Acting alone, however, their impact is limited in scope, scale, and sustainability. CSOs need to engage in government policy processes more effectively. (Court et al., 2006: iv)

The focus of this chapter is partly to uncover how CCSOs are attempting to heed this advice with the use of research or evidence. Other studies have focused on whether there is room for CSOs in the policymaking process. The OECD report, for instance, includes examples of official recognition of CSOs in policy statements, concluding that a space has been made for these organizations to engage in policy dialogue. According to Court et al. (2006: 1), 'CSOs have become aware that policy engagement can often have a greater impact than contestation' and this engagement can bring about more benefits than service delivery alone. Although there are many limiting factors when it comes to CSOs engaging in the policy process, it is first worth describing the various influencing capacities of CSOs. In other words, how do CSOs attempt to influence policy?

Influencing policy is not necessarily, or even routinely, a direct and easily observable occurrence. Carden (2009) describes three categories of influence: expanding policy capacities, broadening policy horizons, and affecting decision regimes. He explains:

> Affecting a policy or action means: procedures for deliberation and deciding questions of public policy become fairer and more effective when fact-based; scope and competence of governmental policy formulation grows stronger; policy execution is more efficient; citizens secure new knowledge; [there is] a better informed understanding of public policy choices and a wiser judgment about government. (Carden, 2009: 50)

If one understands influencing in this way, then there are several ways that CSOs can be seen to influence policy. In an International Development Research Centre (IDRC) working paper entitled *Evidence Based Advocacy: NGO Research Capacities and Policy Influence in the Field of International Trade*, Paul Mably (2006) identifies four strategies used by NGOs in their attempts to influence trade policies. These are: lobbying (informal process of approaching policymakers), advocacy (formal process of approaching policymakers), promotion or dissemination, and mobilizing public pressure. In their case study of 26 Australian NGOs, Nathan et al. (2002) tried to understand how NGOs take action to influence government policy and practice for health equity. They found that NGOs had taken on the role of advocating for health equity. That is, they made use of tools and activities to draw attention to an issue, gather support for it, foster a consensus around it, and present arguments to get policymakers and the general public to back it. Some of the tools and activities used to achieve these goals were coalition building, media and publicity, letter writing, building community support, and monitoring.

Building and maintaining good relations with governments to influence policymaking and planning was another strategy used by CSOs engaged in advocacy on climate change. Related tools and tactics employed by these groups are analysed in *Southern Voices on Climate Policy Choices: Analysis of and lessons learned from civil society advocacy on climate change* (Reid et al., 2012). How CSOs engage in policy dialogue and the relevance and effectiveness of their policy work is a main theme in the *Joint Evaluation of Support to Civil Society Engagement in Policy Dialogue* initiated by the Donor Group on Civil Society and Aid Effectiveness (Ministry of Foreign Affairs of Denmark, 2012). Nine policy case studies (three each in Bangladesh, Mozambique, and Uganda) were analysed and CSO methods of engagement categorized as direct and formal, direct and informal, and indirect. Direct and formal methods included advocacy and campaigning, invited space for policy reform, evidence-based research, and monitoring (and holding to account). Direct but informal methods included lobbying behind the scenes, networking, and demonstration or mass action. Indirect contribution to policy dialogue described methods such as education and training and capacity building (Ministry of Foreign Affairs of Denmark, 2012). These strategies elaborate on what Thomas (2001) described as the 'four Cs' of influence: collaboration, confrontation, complementary activities, and consciousness-raising. CSOs combine these strategies and do so at different stages in the policy process. In *A Practitioner's Guide to Influencing Public Policy* (2008), Synergos identified various strategies as these relate to the different stages in the policy cycle. Building coalitions, public education, convening stakeholders, and community organizing, for example, are quite logically associated with the agenda-setting stage. Common strategies used to impact policy in the adoption phase include issue advocacy and public/private partnership creation, while litigation is used in the implementation phase. Finally, research and analysis are useful strategies in the evaluation phase. There is, however, overlap, meaning that the same strategy can and is used at different stages. Whatever the influencing strategy used, it is becoming more and more common for CSOs to ensure that this is evidence-based.

Evidence plays a strong role in CSO strategies to influence policy. How does the literature address the question of CSOs collecting and/or using evidence with the aim of influencing policy?

Evidence-based attempts at policy engagement

There is a consensus that the policy cycle is complex and that changes in public policy result from a number of factors and actions by different sets of actors at different times. It is also believed that one of these sets of actors, CSOs, use a variety of different strategies to influence this process. The degree to which CSOs succeed in influencing policy is not the focus here. Instead, examples of evidence-based strategies are examined to illustrate ways that CSOs use evidence to try to influence policy. In the context of international cooperation for development, influencing policy is of course not an end in itself, but rather a means to the end of saving lives, reducing poverty, and improving quality of life in developing countries. It is argued that 'better utilisation of evidence in policy and practice can help policymakers identify problems, understand their causes, develop policy solutions, improve policy implementation, and monitor strategies and performance' (Court et al., 2006: 5).

There is a place for the use of evidence throughout all stages of the policy process. Court et al. (2006) outlined the various ways that CSOs can use evidence in each stage. In the problem definition and agenda-setting phase (in some cases described as two distinct phases), where the need is to convince policymakers that an issue requires attention, CSOs can use evidence to enhance the credibility of their argument; to create links between themselves, researchers and policymakers; and to help support an advocacy campaign. In the formulation phase where the aims are to inform policymakers on available options and formulate a consensus, CSOs armed with relevant and reliable evidence can act as a source of information and channel resources and expertise to policymakers. When a policy is in its implementation phase, the objective is to complement government capacity. Here, CSOs can use evidence to improve the sustainability and reach of the policy and innovate in terms of service delivery. Finally, in the evaluation phase where the goal is to review the implemented policy and understand its impact, CSOs can be the ones providing representative, on-the-ground feedback to policymakers.

In his case study of 22 international NGOs, Mably (2006) noted NGOs found little use for doing research for the sake of research. Instead, they gathered or used evidence to support an action strategy. The most common actions cited for their use of research were: action to influence and change public or corporate policy, popular education or capacity building, building alternatives, and notifying grassroots groups to emerging issues to enable them to take local, regional, or national action. Also mentioned was the use of research as a means to create better (and more informed) dialogue among stakeholders. Their understanding that the policy process is not a straightforward linear one is evident in their cited use of various attempts to involve their constituencies and target groups in the research process. In other words, there is an indication that CSOs can and do find ways to use research as a tool to engage more effectively in the policy process, in hopes of influencing it.

Canadian CSOs' research and policy engagement

Much of what has been written on CSO engagement in the development policy process comes out of the UK, specifically the Research and Policy in Development programme of the Overseas Development Institute (ODI). Based on the literature, case studies, participatory workshops, and an ODI survey, Court et al. (2006: 15) identified key reasons that explain why CSOs have limited influence over policy, noting that the most common barriers were within the CSOs themselves. Among the constraints listed by respondents were insufficient capacity and funding (62 and 57 per cent, respectively). Another 47 per cent cited the closed nature of the policy process as an impediment to their participation, citing the lack of credibility given to CSO evidence by policymakers.

Canada's IDRC has addressed the research-to-policy link, as well as international CSO contributions to policy influence. More specific to Canada, the role that CCSOs could play in influencing policy has been of interest to the Canadian Council for International Cooperation (CCIC), a coalition of Canadian voluntary-sector organizations working to achieve sustainable human development internationally. Between 2003 and 2006, CCIC, with support from the former Canadian International Development Agency (CIDA),[1] carried out a project aimed at strengthening civil society policy engagement with the Canadian federal government. The project was initiated 'to promote knowledge development, learning, and capacity-building on the part of Canadian civil society organizations, their Southern partners, and the Canadian government for effective policy dialogue between government and the international voluntary sector' (CCIC, 2006: 1).

Based on this experience, in 2006 the CCIC published *Building Knowledge and Capacity for Policy Influence: Reflections and Resources*. They found that, from small NGOs to large international networks, CSOs are important development actors and, as such, they bring unique perspectives to the process of public policy development. In addition to describing many of the aforementioned elements in the policy process, and possible methods for involvement in this process, CCIC also pointed to a number of barriers to CCSO involvement. These barriers, identified by an initial 2003 CCIC survey of its members, limit the policy roles that CCSOs can play. Namely, CCSOs do not have a sufficient understanding of the foreign policymaking process in Canada; they often lack an understanding of how best to capture policy-relevant knowledge from their field experience; they face constraints in terms of resources needed to produce policy-relevant research and analysis; they lack the management/ board political will to prioritize policy work; and they are unaware of their legal and regulatory constraints as registered charities.

After this initial survey, the project continued with the development of two new tracks of programming at CCIC: a series of training workshops to build an understanding among the CCIC membership of the foreign policymaking process in Canada, of CSO cooperation in North–South partnerships, and of what policy influence requires – as well as a concrete 'learning by doing' activity on how to create and tell policy-relevant 'stories' or narratives that highlight the roles of CSOs in aid effectiveness. An important focus of project activities was how CCSOs could work with Southern CSOs (SCSOs) as a way to capture knowledge from the field that is relevant to policy development. The CCIC recognized:

> It is not possible for all organizations to have a research department or knowledge-management staff, but much can be achieved through relationships with some of the bigger CSOs, research centres, and interested academics. Northern CSOs should seek out links with sources of intellectual and policy knowledge in the South. They also need to increase efforts to link with, and recognize the knowledge of, citizens' and peoples' organizations. (CCIC, 2006: pp. 5–7)

According to CCIC, these partnerships with Southern actors are a way for CCSOs to access knowledge and glean effective policy messages for their dialogue with different levels of government. In other words, partnering with Southern institutions is a way to build the capacity of organizations in the North. Also, the CCIC suggests that CCSOs might overcome their lack of research capacity by engaging with research in ways other than conducting it themselves. They write, 'Not every organization will have the resources and capacity to collect and analyse field-based knowledge; some may decide that they can be most effective by disseminating and popularizing the research and analysis of Southern organizations' (CCIC, 2006: pp. 3–4). Still, although the CCIC study noted that CCSOs face barriers with regards to influencing policy, one being a lack of research capacity, it did not investigate how some CCSOs use strategies to strengthen this capacity to influence policy. They concluded that CCSOs will need to make strategic choices about what they are going to do, when, and with whom, in terms of the types of activities that they take on to influence, but limited the discussion to influencing Canada's foreign policy.

The review of literature finds a gap in relation to how CCSOs use research (if they in fact choose this activity) – how they produce it, disseminate it, learn from it, and how research fits in their strategy to influence policy and/or practice in the Global South. It was important to add a study to the literature that showcased how CSOs in Canada, despite working in a climate of great funding uncertainty and in often tense relations with the Canadian government, effectively make use of their strengths to maximize their impact with research as a central part of their influencing strategies.

Before turning to how this study was carried out, it is worth pointing out efforts made over the last five years or so to recognize CSOs, their standards and their importance as independent development actors contributing to development effectiveness. The 4th High Level Forum on Aid Effectiveness, held in Busan, Korea, at the end of 2011, marked the first time CSOs participated and were consulted as full and equal participants, alongside partner governments, traditional donors, South–South cooperators, the BRICS

(Brazil, India, China and South Africa), and private donors in the signing of a multilateral agreement that would establish a framework for development cooperation (Open Forum for CSO Development Effectiveness, 2014).

CSOs also joined heads of state and government, ministers, parliamentarians, and leaders from international organizations, business, and foundations at the first High-Level Meeting of the Global Partnership for Effective Development Co-operation in Mexico City in April 2014. Following that meeting, then Canadian Minister of International Development, Christian Paradis, issued a statement in which he said:

> Canada recognizes and supports the vital role that civil society plays in reaching development objectives. Civil society engages citizens in [...] decision-making processes that affect them. Empowered by the fundamental rights of freedom of expression, association and assembly, civil society enables citizens to hold their governments to account, providing legitimacy to the governing institutions, which in turn ensures growth and sustainable development and reduces poverty. (DFATD, 2014)

This public acknowledgement is welcomed by CCIC and its member organizations as it suggests a renewed commitment on the part of Global Affairs Canada to ensure a place for civil society in Canadian ODA funding and programming. Many agree this type of commitment is long overdue. Launched in February 2015, the International Development and Humanitarian Assistance Civil Society Partnership Policy demonstrated a significant turning point in the relationship between the international development and humanitarian assistance community and the then Department of Foreign Affairs, Trade and Development (DFATD). The policy was developed in direct consultation with civil society and established a new framework with clear objectives for how the government engages with civil society. Importantly, it also recognizes CSOs as independent development actors whose work is guided by their own set of values (the Istanbul Principles for CSO Development Effectiveness and the Humanitarian Principles), and acknowledges that governments have a role to play in creating and maintaining an enabling environment for civil society to realize its full potential. The policy also commits to an annual review of its implementation in consultation with CSOs (CCIC, 2016).

Civil society is part of the international cooperation for development dialogue, though questions and critiques remain on whether this recognition is matched by efforts to create and sustain an enabling environment in which CSOs can accomplish their goals. The Canadian policy, issued under the previous government, is being revised by the new government which came into power in late 2015.

Methodology

Readers less interested in the methodology may skip to Results on page 119.

The broad focus of this research project is to understand how CCSOs use research in their efforts to influence policy and/or practice in the Global South.

The narrower focus seeks to (a) assess the extent to which CCSOs conduct research themselves or work in collaboration with others (academics, local CSOs, research organizations, etc.) to produce it, (b) identify the purposes that these uses of research serve, and (c) document what the perceived roles of this evidence are in relation to influencing policy and practice. These questions were addressed by employing both quantitative and qualitative research methods.

The first phase of data collection, yielding quantitative results, centred on a short close-ended survey sent electronically to CCSOs across Canada active in international cooperation for development. For this study, CSOs are defined as organizations that operate outside the private sector, the home, or the government. The list of CCSOs to be surveyed was built by adding to an initial list of Canadian IDRC grantees defined as CCSOs. The sources used to build on this initial list included member lists of the CCIC and other provincial/regional councils for international cooperation, websites of professional associations, and CIDA's International Youth Internship website. The resulting list had over 300 organizations and was later narrowed by analysing each CCSO's website and removing any that did not work primarily in international cooperation for development, did not engage in the Global South, provided only humanitarian relief, or had research as their sole or main objective. This last criterion means that universities, think tanks, and research centres were excluded from the survey sample as it was assumed that their research capacities were larger than other CCSOs. The sample includes international organizations with headquarters or main branches in Canada. The final targeted sample consisted of 129 CCSOs from across Canada ranging in type (e.g. NGO, network, professional association) and focus area (e.g. human rights, health, rural development). Where contact information for the executive director or a senior manager was publicly available, surveys were sent by email directly to them. In cases where names and/or email addresses of directors or managers were not readily available online, surveys were sent to any staff member. In a few cases, surveys were sent to general inboxes. There were 69 surveys returned, a response rate of 53 per cent.

The survey aimed to provide insight on the level of, and reasons for, CCSO research use. Research was defined as the process by which knowledge is produced, inclusive of many types of activities, including, but not limited to, surveys or questionnaires, interviews, focus groups, document review, participant observation, pilot projects and trials, and evaluations, accompanied by analysis. Although there was some room to clarify and elaborate, respondents were generally asked close-ended questions and expected to select one or more responses from among a list of choices. The main survey questions were:

- What role or roles does your organization play?
- Does your organization use research as part of its strategy to influence policy and practice in the Global South?

- If so, who carries out the research that your organization uses?
- For what purpose(s) does your organization use research?
- Do you have ongoing or recent projects that illustrate how your organization uses research, as part of its strategy to influence policy and practice in the Global South?

The first four questions afforded a broad overview of the CCSO landscape, while the last question provided certain qualitative examples of CCSOs with ongoing projects or programmes where research played a role in their attempts to influence policy and/or practice. This helped identify CCSOs that might serve as cases to be studied through a second phase of data collection.

The fieldwork phase of this study was designed to take place in South America, a relatively accessible part of the world where the research budget could be maximized. CCSOs citing ongoing projects or programming in South America were contacted and asked whether they and their local partners would be interested and available to provide background and reflections as part of a more descriptive case study aimed at showcasing particular CCSO strategies for using research to influence policy and/or practice. Four CCSOs confirmed their interest and made the necessary introductions with their partners and/or field staff in four countries: Argentina (Rosario, Córdoba, and Jujuy), Bolivia (Cochabamba, Sucre, and Tomina), Colombia (Bogotá), and Peru (Lima). The selected CCSOs (described in more detail later in this chapter) were Women in Cities International (WICI), Société de coopération pour le développement international (SOCODEVI), Rights & Democracy (R&D), and Save the Children Canada (SCC). From gender-inclusive cities in Argentina to oregano farmers in Bolivia, and from the effects of armed conflict on Colombia's indigenous women to the state of child workers in Peru, each case study highlights unique CCSO influencing strategies, while offering a basis for comparison and insight into CCSOs and their research-centred efforts to contribute to change.

The case study data collection took place over six weeks and comprised four main activities:

- Semi-structured interviews were conducted with CCSO staff (SOCODEVI and SCC) and/or local partner staff in the cities mentioned. These 45–60-minute interviews were in Spanish or English, recorded, and where necessary translated to allow for thorough data analysis. Interviews were also carried out with CCSO staff in Montreal (R&D and WICl) and Toronto (SCC).
- Participant observation was employed and involved attending local CSO meetings with community members, workshops, and awareness-raising activities.
- Focus groups were organized with key project stakeholders, such as the neighbourhood women in Rosario where WICI's programme was being implemented and graduates of a Lima-based Masters programme in child rights.

- Site visits allowed for detailed and accurate descriptions of the project contexts and specifics. Visits were made to neighbourhoods in Rosario where safety audits and improvements to public spaces had taken place, oregano farms and processing plants in Tomina, a group home for ex-child workers in Lima, and to university offices where a virtual think tank is managed in Bogotá.

This combined-methods approach produced quantitative and qualitative data, which helped provide a rounded picture of the links between CCSOs, research, and influence over policy and practice in the Global South. Data in the form of interview notes, field notes, and project-specific publications were analysed and coded by how responses and text related to the project/organization description, the context/issue it addressed, research methodology/purpose, and perceived influence on policy and/or practice.

Results

The findings presented here were drawn from a combined-research methods approach with two main types of data: quantitative data captured through a nationwide survey sent to 129 CSOs and qualitative data collected through interviews and site visits, analysed, and presented as case studies. The findings of this study help answer the following questions:

- Do CCSOs use research in their attempts to influence policy and/or practice in the Global South?
- How active are CCSOs in producing research? In other words, do they conduct research themselves or in collaboration with others, or do they rely on research done by others?
- In what ways do CCSOs use research as part of their strategies to affect change?

Do CCSOs use research in their attempts to influence policy and/or practice in the Global South?

The CCSOs surveyed represent a range of CCSOs working in international cooperation for development. The sample intentionally excluded those with research as their primary or sole mandate. Of the 129 CCSOs surveyed, 69 replied: a response rate of 53 per cent. Three, however, replied stating either that they were not able to provide the feedback required due to time constraints or because they did not fit the description of a CCSO using research as part of their strategy to influence policy and/or practice in the Global South. Another four partially completed the survey but indicated that they did not use research.

The survey found that most CCSOs value and use research to influence policy and practice in the Global South, with 62 of 69 respondents confirming this. This finding challenges a prevalent misconception outside the CSO sector engaged in international cooperation for development and demonstrates the importance of research and evidence-based activities among CCSOs.

How active are CCSOs in producing research?

Outside the CSO sector engaged in international cooperation for development, another misbelief is that CCSOs do not have the capacity or the expertise to conduct their own research. However, of the 62 CCSOs surveyed that do use research, the overwhelming majority (approximately 84 per cent) use their own staff to conduct primary research. This research is then used in their efforts to influence policy and practice directly (e.g. in lobbying decision-makers) or indirectly (e.g. in enhancing their organizational credibility). CCSOs' interns or volunteers are also responsible for carrying out research, with 59 per cent of CCSOs surveyed using research from these sources. Using staff and interns allows CCSOs to retain control over the research process throughout the design, execution, and dissemination.

Findings show there are other important sources of research and types of collaboration used by CCSOs. Figure 4.1 illustrates the frequencies of all CCSOs' sources of research sorted into the same actor categories and divided only by collaboration or none. The light bars correspond to sources in which CCSOs are involved in the research design and process. These include cases where the research is undertaken by the CCSO staff or interns, and also where some type of collaboration is indicated (e.g. with universities). The dark bars, on the other hand, correspond to research being done by someone other than CCSO staff, where presumably CCSOs have less or no control over the research. With only one exception, for each source collaborative research efforts are preferred, pointing to how active CCSOs are in producing the research they use. The survey highlights an interesting finding: while just over 31 per cent of respondents cited

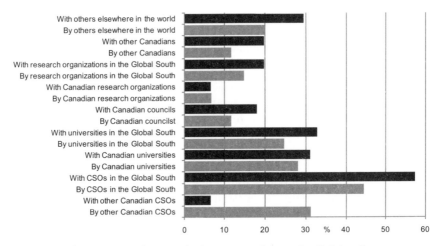

Figure 4.1 Canadian civil society organization sources of research – Collaboration vs. none

using research that is undertaken by other CCSOs, only 6.5 per cent cited using research done in collaboration with other CCSOs, compared to 57 per cent cited using research carried out in collaboration with Global South CSOs (SCSOs). Research done by SCSOs is also a common source, cited by 44 per cent of respondents.

This means that SCSOs are either producing research alongside their Canadian partners or producing research alone (or with other SCSOs), which CCSOs (partners or not) then use. In fact, as the case study analysis will illustrate, engaging SCSOs in the research process serves multiple CCSO purposes, including building capacity, a role that 95 per cent of those surveyed identified as central to their organizational mandates. It is the contexts in which CCSOs work, and the networks that they have built, which encourage CCSOs to collaborate more with SCSOs. Given that very few CCSOs are working without SCSO partners, any collaborative CCSO research initiative would undoubtedly complicate the coordination of managing the research process. Consider that if each of three CCSOs already works with a different SCSO in the same area and on the same issue, a collaborative research effort initiated by the three CCSOs would already involve six organizations, which would then have to agree on the research questions, design, methods, dissemination strategies, and so on. Although carrying out research with CCSOs and carrying out research with SCSOs are not mutually exclusive, case study analysis suggests organizations tend to stick to one model.

The same results from Figure 4.1 are reordered in Figure 4.2 to allow for a better comparison between Canadian and Southern sources of research used by CCSOs. The closest gaps exist within the university category. In fact, research produced by universities in Canada is the only source that is used by CCSOs more (although only slightly) than research by the equivalent source in the Global South. This suggests that Canadian universities are an accessible and credible source of research. There is very little difference between the numbers of CCSOs that use research produced in collaboration with Canadian

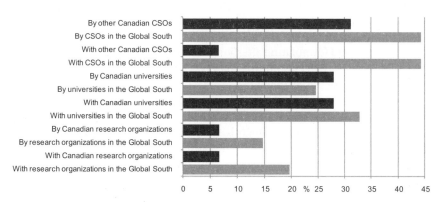

Figure 4.2 Canadian civil society organization sources of research – Canadian vs. Southern

universities (approximately 28 per cent) and those that use research produced in collaboration with universities in the Global South (about 33 per cent). Interviews with CCSO staff confirmed that CCSOs see advantages to using research done by or in collaboration with Canadian universities, but also suggest that CCSOs primarily collaborate within their networks, taking practical approaches and not necessarily weighing the pros and cons of particular sources. Choices are specific to context, established networks, and resources. In some cases, CCSOs might approach Canadian universities for research noting that certain universities in the Global South do not have funding to support research. They may identify an existing partnership as a logical starting point for research collaboration or recognize that working with Canadian interns is more sustainable than working with local professionals.

In what ways do CCSOs use research as part of their strategies to affect change?

As CCSOs work to influence policy and/or practice in the developing countries where they focus their activities, alongside or in support of their local partners, research from various sources is used for a variety of defined purposes in an attempt to achieve these objectives. All the CCSOs surveyed used research for more than one purpose; answers ranged from two to 13, with the average number of purposes cited as eight. This does not mean that a single piece of research is used on average for eight different purposes (although in some instances that may be the case), but rather that CCSOs as a whole, working in a wide range of contexts on a variety of issues over a period of time, understand that research can serve many different purposes and work to engage with the evidence in a variety of ways, to achieve their objectives of influencing policy and/or practice. The most cited purpose corresponds with the most common understanding of what research is used for: to confirm and support understanding of an issue, idea or problem (or as one respondent added, challenge these). This was selected by approximately 93 per cent of respondents.

More surprising is that about 80 per cent of CCSOs use research to help build local capacity. This is addressed later, in the section 'Paying attention to methodological design'. Identifying priority issues, evaluating projects/ organizations, and formulating alternatives through research are also common purposes with 77 per cent, approximately 72 per cent, and 70.5 per cent of CCSOs citing these, respectively.

The particular mandate of a CCSO, including its breadth, seems to bear on the number of different uses that CCSOs make of research. Table 4.1 illustrates the number of organizations categorized by the ranges of their use of research (wide, medium, or narrow) and the breadth of their mandate (specialized, medium, or comprehensive). The arrow indicates the tendency for the purposes of research to increase in range with an increase in the number of roles. In other words, the more roles a CCSO identifies it plays, the more ways it finds to use research in its work to influence policy and practice in the

Table 4.1 The relationship between the number of organizational roles and the number of purposes of research use in Canadian civil society organizations

Roles→ Purposes↓	Specialized (1–2)	Medium (3–4)	Comprehensive (5+)
Wide (9+)	2	15	15
Medium (6–8)	3	11	3
Small (1–5)	3	6	4

Note: n=62

Source: Travers, 2011

Global South. There is a concentration of CCSOs playing several roles and using research for several different purposes. In all, 44 of the organizations surveyed (approximately 71 per cent) described themselves as playing more than three roles and using research for more than six purposes. This implies that, in general, CCSOs work in a variety of ways to achieve their many, yet complementary, objectives and that research plays an important role in their strategies. There is a tendency to use a variety of strategies, and engage with research in a number of ways, since working this way has a better chance of producing the desired results. Also, if results (generally immediate and tangible) are required to guarantee continued funding and secure new funding, then CCSOs must try a number of different ways to achieve these results. Case study interviews with CCSO staff reveal that working in this way, despite running the risk of leaving them overstretched and under-resourced, is, in their view, the best way to engage effectively. Examining these case studies in more depth will provide greater insight into how CCSOs incorporate research into their strategies for influencing policy and/or practice in the Global South, highlight the role of research in achieving CCSO organizational mandates, and showcase proven approaches to affecting evidence-based change across contexts.

Analysing the case studies

Each case study is made up of one South American-based project/programme (ongoing at the time of data collection) implemented by a CCSO and its various Southern partners. At first glance, the four cases might appear to have little in common. The CCSOs selected vary in size, objectives, and focus, while the featured projects and programmes differ in length, stakeholders, and resources. In this way, taken together, they reflect Canadian civil society working in international cooperation for development, a diverse sector united under a very broad goal: sustainable human development. What each case has in common is that it represents an attempt by a CCSO to influence and create change, spelled out in concrete objectives, and to do so in a way that injects and disseminates knowledge. Strategies differ but they are all research-centred attempts at influencing policy and/or practice, doing so through various activities, including the research process itself.

Photo 4.1 Local women identify and record safety concerns in Rosario, Argentina.
Photo: Women and Habitat Network

Case 1: Women in Cities International collaborates with a regional CSO network to identify public policies for greater gender inclusion and equality (Argentina). WICI is a non-profit network organization based in Montreal which works to promote gender equality, prevent violence against women, and strengthen women's participation in local governance and urban development.[2] WICI grew out of the realization that, worldwide, several dedicated individuals and organizations were committed to addressing violence against women, at home and in public spaces. The Gender Inclusive Cities Program (GICP), coordinated by WICI from 2009 to 2012, focused research and action on women's safety and experiences of gender-based violence. It aimed to identify the activities, tools, and public policies that act as enablers of or as barriers to greater gender inclusion and equality, as well as good practices related to gender inclusion, piloted within the GICP (WICI, 2010: 10). One of the four cities where the GICP was implemented was Rosario, Argentina. It was here that WICI chose to team up with the Women and Habitat Network of Latin America (WHN), a local group that had begun addressing the issue of gender inclusion in Rosario several years earlier. GICP activities fell into three stages: data collection, data analysis for intervention planning, and intervention implementation.

Each phase relied on collaborative efforts and local participation. The initial stage brought WICI, the implementing partners, and local women together to develop and use a set of tools to gather data on the condition of women's safety in their cities. One important tool for data collection was the Women's Safety Audit as it works to identify priority safety concerns while engaging local women – a good illustration of how research, specifically its methodological design, can help build capacity (a purpose that 80 per cent of survey respondents associated with research). In Rosario, local government officials participated

Photo 4.2 UNEC General Manager Roberto Muñoz holds up an oregano seedling ready for a farmer's field at the Tomina facility. *Photo:* Stacie Travers

in some of the safety audits. They listened as neighbourhood women walked, observed, and recorded their views on safety-related issues as they noted them. While these safety audits helped women to identify the factors leading to their feelings of insecurity (poor lighting, lack of signage, etc.) and to think about what should be changed, surveys (that they carried out) and focus groups enabled them to understand the types of violence women confront in public spaces, to see how this violence affects different women, and to discuss how to prevent and eradicate these forms of violence (CICSA, 2010).

The second year of the project was spent discussing the findings and planning appropriate interventions, which included the planning of a safe corridor, campaigns to raise awareness of the issue, and events held in public spaces involving the aesthetic transformation of the spaces, as well as having these areas occupied by people, including children, again. WICI coordinated and participated in action and participatory research projects to help build local capacity, identify issues and alternatives, and create awareness among citizens and governments alike.

Case 2: SOCODEVI staff and interns identify a sustainable alternative for small-scale producers in rural Bolivia. Société de coopération pour le développement international, established in Quebec in 1985, is a non-profit international development corporation created when several Quebec cooperatives and mutuals merged with the aim of sharing their experience and knowledge with organizations in developing countries.

SOCODEVI has played a major role in introducing oregano production to Bolivian farmers and in ensuring that this production is sustainable, scalable, and profitable. Years of research are at the heart of making this all possible. They began working with agricultural producers in Chuquisaca in 1998 with an initial grant from CIDA. The first few years were spent carrying out research to identify ways to diversify local income-generating activities. Relying on their network of expertise and much trial and error, the focus soon came to be the growing, processing, and commercialization of herbs and spices, specifically oregano (Villeneuve, 2008: para. 2). SOCODEVI collaborated with the Centre de recherche et de développement de Saint-Hyacinthe of Agriculture and Agri-Food Canada on themes such as the drying of oregano and sensory analysis of the herb. According to CIDA (2011, para. 6), 'by the summer of 2008, ten years into the project, almost 1,000 farmers in 93 communities spanning eight municipalities in southeast Bolivia were growing oregano for cash'. That number has since grown to 2,000 farmers located in 20 municipalities.[3] By not abandoning the growing of their traditional crops, local farmers safeguard their continued subsistence, but also sell their oregano for an extra US$205 per year on average. Agrocentral, an organization of cooperatives in the department of Chuquisaca, coordinates the growing component of the project. It ensures that technical advisers visit the farmers on a regular basis, to help them with any issues that arise and to maximize each producer's harvest (Villeneuve, 2008: para. 6).

Even once a working model had been put in place and Bolivian farmers were successfully growing and starting to profit from this new crop, experimental tests continued with the crossbreeding of different varieties, the production of crops like lavender, dill, and thyme, and the small-scale extraction of essential oils for cosmetic and medicinal products. SOCODEVI was quick to identify and use its strengths to achieve results in this project. Those strengths include a reliable network of Canadian cooperatives with expertise, good relationships with Canadian research centres, and expressed interest from Canadian interns. The first two assets have helped SOCODEVI cast a wide net for solutions, access advanced technologies, and save on material costs. The latter has meant that at least once per year young Canadians use their theoretical knowledge and gain hands-on experience while helping SOCODEVI in areas such as soil analysis, oil extraction, and production of essential-oil products. This strategy has proved efficient and cost-effective. SOCODEVI staff themselves were surprised at the amount of research they were able to conduct with C$2 million.

Case 3: Rights & Democracy coordinates research efforts of local CSOs as they collect information on gender and ethnic discrimination to create jurisprudence and better inform policy (Argentina and Colombia). The International Centre for Human Rights and Democratic Development, more commonly referred to as Rights & Democracy (R&D), was created by the Parliament of Canada in 1988 as a non-partisan arms-length organization that would support and encourage the universal values of human rights and the promotion of democratic institutions and practices around the world. For 24 years, R&D worked with individuals, organizations, and governments in Canada and abroad to fight and promote the rights outlined in the United Nations' International Bill of Human Rights. Shortly after this case study research took place, Parliament closed the centre, announcing it would be continuing its important work through government departments.

In 2005, building on its relationships with certain indigenous organizations in the Americas, R&D began to coordinate and bring together individual country-level research aimed at understanding 'the roots and consequences of the intersection and superposition of indigenous women's multiple identities' (Rights & Democracy, 2008: 6). Consejo de Organizaciones Aborígenes de Jujuy (COAJ) of Argentina and Organización Nacional Indígena de Colombia (ONIC),[4] with coordination, funding and technical support from R&D, IDRC, and La Clinique internationale de défense des droits humains de l'UQAM (CIDDHU), set out to examine multiple forms of discrimination related to the access to education for indigenous girls and the consequences of the armed conflict on indigenous women, respectively, as part of the Ethnic and Gender Discrimination in the Americas project. A carefully crafted methodology was put in place to help meet a set of separate, yet complementary, objectives. The overall objective was to contribute to social and legal changes that would reduce the multiple forms of discrimination faced by indigenous women. This project engaged local teams of indigenous women to document cases of double discrimination against indigenous women. These cases could be used to create jurisprudence both locally and internationally. While systematic changes were ultimately sought, considerable emphasis was placed on building organizational capacity to influence policy and on raising awareness, so that women living in the communities could learn to recognize and question routine rights violations. R&D and its partners aimed to influence policy by helping define the problem, working to get it on the agenda, providing evidence for the development of new policies, and revealing what stood in the way of implementing existing policies and protections for indigenous women.

There is very little information on indigenous women, given that national censuses that do capture data on indigenous people do not disaggregate these data by gender. Also, there have been very few attempts to include qualitative data based on the perspectives and concerns of indigenous women. By developing this project as a research project, R&D and partners began to fill these knowledge gaps, while also helping to build the local capacity of SCSOs. Throughout the project, a participatory and action-oriented approach was used. By involving indigenous women directly in all aspects of the research (from defining the issue, to interviewing and recording stories, analysing and adapting findings and methods, disseminating knowledge, and exchanging lessons), this project aimed to strengthen partnering organizations' research capacity, as well as their capacity to use international legal remedies and tools for future claims. Just as R&D set objectives that went beyond bringing a case of double discrimination in front of the Inter-American court system, its partners also knew that this project was about more than just documenting cases of violations against indigenous women. It was a way to help create awareness among communities, as well as among indigenous women themselves.

By setting objectives that were met by both the process and end result of research, R&D succeeded in strengthening local CSOs in terms of their capacity to engage with and influence their governments and to be heard in other forums as well.

Case 4: Save the Children Canada allies with a regional network of Masters programmes to access knowledge on child workers in Latin America. Save the Children Canada (SCC), a member organization of Save the Children International, focuses on the issues of health and nutrition, education, HIV and AIDS, child protection, emergency relief, and child rights governance. SCC and the 28 other organizations belonging to this international federation cooperate by pooling resources, establishing common positions on issues, and initiating joint projects on child rights, wellbeing, and development. Research and an evidence-based approach are integral components of all Save the Children programming and advocacy. In Latin America, SCC has used its alliance with academia in innovative ways to fill knowledge gaps on the conditions of working children in the region and support training of professionals and future decision-makers. In 2002, with support from Save the Children Sweden, an inter-institutional alliance was formed among three related Masters programmes in Peru, Ecuador, and Colombia – The Latin American Network of Masters in Children's Rights and Social Policies (hereafter referred to by its Spanish acronym, RMI). As the name suggests, each academic programme addresses children's rights. Three years into the network, SCC joined the project and began funding the programme to extend it to Bolivia, to Huancayo in Peru, and to Nicaragua. The growth of RMI further strengthened its ability to collectively generate knowledge on the common problems of children and adolescents, problems that cross national boundaries and affect the region as a whole.

Enrolled students are both mid-level career professionals who apply new theoretical frameworks to their work and contribute relevant practical knowledge and views from the field, and younger professionals who now require graduate degrees to pursue their interest in the field. Both groups of professionals are now occupying important positions in non-profit organizations and government agencies. On its website, SCC claims that children throughout the continent are benefiting from improved local and national policies, as well as higher quality programmes that respond to their needs and those of their families (SCC, 2011). RMI coordinator Juan Enrique Bazán saw the network as having the capacity to get 2,100 students to graduate each year from the affiliated programmes. This accounts for 1.5 per cent of professionals in the field and forms a well-positioned group of innovators.

SCC could not fund each participating university directly, but it contributed indirectly by supporting and initiating several different interactions with the network. These included the following initiatives: (a) funding essay-writing contests encouraging social investigation and critical analysis of child labour, (b) forming working groups of faculty and students to produce country-specific information and analyses of child workers in each RMI country, (c) launching an online platform (virtual think tank) for members of RMI, SCC, and the Latin American and Caribbean Movement of Working Children and Adolescents

(MOLACNATS) to analyse the situations of child workers, as well as discuss gaps in current policies, and (d) creating an online blog where professionals from RMI, SCC, and others can reflect on child rights, society, social policies, and working children while building an online source of information for professionals in the field. Working within its reality of limited resources, SCC found ways to support and capitalize on RMI. As a result of this network and its activities, knowledge on issues related to children and child rights is being produced and applied. Produced, as network members research, discuss, and share, and applied as students and graduates alike find or continue their work in schools, NGOs, governments, and communities. SCC has direct access to this fledgling school of thought and can use what is arguably a very strategic alliance to ensure that its programming and future work contribute to changes in public policies affecting children.

An analysis of these four case studies shows that CCSOs implement research-centred strategies for influence that maximize their resources and increase opportunities for influence by (a) building strategic alliances and partnerships, (b) identifying and using their organizational strengths, and (c) paying attention to methodological design.

Building strategic alliances and partnerships. Understandably, each orga-nization aims to affect change in different ways depending on where it works, what resources it has, and what its experience has been. The cases illustrate how relationships with Southern networks and CSOs are part of CCSOs' strategies for influence. In fact, they are central to the work that they do and the reason behind any perceived influ-ence. WICI collaborated with SCSOs to implement the GICP multilat-erally. R&D advised implementing partner SCSOs as they built cases of ethnic and gender discrimination. SOCODEVI works with Agrocentral, a Bolivian network of cooperatives that monitors and ensures qual-ity oregano production, while SCC supports a Latin American network of universities. These collaborations are not a matter of handholding.

Working with networks and partnering with well-positioned SCSOs allows CCSOs to access a wider body of knowledge and it facilitates the use of this knowledge for influence. A strategic ally or partner, as the case studies show, cannot only access local communities more easily, but also bring with them expertise, experience, and knowledge, which will supplement any new research project. These same allies or partners have contacts and relationships that multiply the opportunities for influence. WICI and SCC both chose to support networks (and are members of networks themselves). WICI, by partnering with WHN in Argentina, accessed a network of women's groups working on the issue of women's safety. This network did much of the data collection and engaged directly with local officials with whom WHN had previously established relationships. The ally that SCC has in RMI provides better access to research and expertise than SCC alone could afford. It also directly involves policymakers and those working to sway policymakers in an open collaborative space. The potential to influence policy through this network is high; not only are professionals interacting and learning how the rights of children can/should fit on the political agenda and what social policies affecting children might look like, but a body of knowledge is being developed for those in and outside the network to apply, including SCC. R&D has partnered with COAJ, whose programme activities of leadership training and local capacity building in Jujuy, Argentina, provided an obvious entry point for data collection and whose director is active in wider political circles. R&D's Colombian partner on the Ethnic and Gender Discrimination project, ONIC, actively engages in policy dialogue and this partnership presents the possibility of inserting their research into this dialogue. By partnering with Agrocentral, a network of co-ops, SOCODEVI reduces direct costs of transportation and administration, allowing it to focus on the research side of the project. This partnership also directly affects the degree to which SOCODEVI and its alternative crop idea was able to assert influence over local farming practice. Acceptance by Agrocentral, an adviser and link to individual co-ops, translates into wider community acceptance. Being strategic about one's partners can go a long way toward strengthening CCSOs' research capacity and widening their sphere of influence.

Identifying and using organizational strengths. Not all CCSOs operate within the same budgets, answer to the same funding requirements, possess the same experience, skills and expertise, or have the same contacts. Strategies that CCSOs use to influence policy and/or practice are, therefore, designed according to their organizational strengths. SOCODEVI has a network of expertise in Canada, as well as the opportunity to host Canadian interns, which they used to produce the research that they needed to implement their project. WICI used their network to disseminate the tools and results of their GICP and to access wider audiences for policy influence. R&D used their experience and credibility to help access and interact with Inter-American agencies, while SCC was able to maintain a regional focus to its work given its multi-country network. These strengths are important in terms of laying out both an influencing strategy and a research strategy. In other words, recognizing what they do well and what defines their organization helps CCSOs to access research and disseminate it in ways that contribute to influencing policy and practice.

Paying attention to methodological design. A carefully designed research methodology works to do more than provide research findings. Action-oriented and applied, CCSOs' research can serve many purposes. As illustrated with the R&D case study, it often involves SCSOs and institutions engaged in participatory processes, which simultaneously builds local capacity. By designing a multi-country comparative project, WICI was able to facilitate exchanges among SCSOs throughout the collaborative research process. This sharing of findings as part of the methodology also helped build each organization's capacity. Designing flexible methodologies that engage local partners not only helps these organizations to acquire skills, tools, and knowledge, but also builds CCSOs' organizational capacity as they learn to adapt their design, facilitate exchanges, and understand new contexts.

In addition, methodologies that avoid as much as possible the subject/ researcher paradigm align particularly well with CCSOs' philosophies and mandates, which add to their credibility. Where academic research is considered sound and credible, and when its findings are logically drawn from a rigorous analysis of adequate evidence, CCSOs' research needs to be transformative. This can only happen if the CCSO involves local people in the process, if it allows research to mix with complementary activities, and if the methodology itself addresses power relations. How CCSOs design their research is part of how they aim to influence the policy process or a particular practice. Key stakeholders and audiences are engaged, tools and methods to build capacity are used, and local ownership is encouraged.

The integrated nature of research in CCSO strategies for influence

Rather than understand the term 'research-centred strategy' as one that counts research as the central and most important aspect of the work, the cases demonstrate that research is in fact one component that is, in many instances, so integrated into other activities that it cannot always be separated from them. Given the multiple purposes that CCSOs' research serves, there is a higher degree of flexibility in research methods and the research process itself becomes quite entangled with raising awareness, building capacity, and implementing new approaches. This allows resources to be maximized and fulfils a wider range of roles and objectives. Not surprisingly, there is no evidence of a completely linear relationship between CCSOs' research, influence, and change. CCSOs' strategies for influence, therefore, do not anticipate this. Instead, CCSOs use a number of means to try and influence policy and/or practice with their research.

This blending of research within a variety of other activities and roles is important for funders to understand. Not only can it be very difficult to frame a CCSO's work in terms of a traditional research proposal, but it is also challenging to attribute impacts of a CCSO's work to specific donor dollars. When asked about the impact of the GICP in Rosario, WHN director Liliana Rainero explained that it is really the combination of efforts, projects, and donor funding that brings about results. Funding a particular piece of research may contribute to change but cannot be entirely responsible for that change. Funders, however, often expect to attribute impacts to specific projects. While recognizing the value and importance of research, CCSOs may not see it the same way as a university would. It may be hard to disentangle research methods from other CCSO activities. Funders understandably have mandates and want to see that their funds are working to support those mandates. The caution here is simply for funders to acknowledge and account for the fact that specific CCSO activities are often multi-purpose and are undeniably linked with one another.

Research collaboration explained

In addition to providing examples of CCSOs' research-centred influencing strategies, interviews with CSO staff in Canada and South America also clarified some of the findings from the survey, specifically with regard to research collaboration and the relationships between organizational mandates and research use.

Survey findings revealed a low number of CCSO–CCSO research collaborations. Support for these and other hypotheses were found in conversations with the CCSOs introduced in the case studies. In relation to the type of technical research involved in the oregano project, SOCODEVI staff explained how collaborating with another CCSO could become complicated. Different CCSOs might share an overall vision, but there needs to be a leader who takes the research down one path. Two heads may lead to disagreement as to what exactly that path is. Roles may not be as easy to define in CCSO–CCSO collaborations. SCC agreed somewhat and noted that based on past experience, there is a tendency for each CCSO to take care of its own priorities and interests, making it difficult for a collaboration to grow. Canadian organizations must also be cautious about which organizations they partner with, as certain Canadian funders are less likely to fund advocacy groups.

It seems SCSO–CCSO collaborations are somewhat different from CCSO–CCSO collaborations. Roles are easier to define as one organization often has the local networks, contacts, and access, while the other provides the funding, technical support, and visibility. Priorities combine and complement more easily and the very collaboration itself aligns with CCSO goals of capacity building and knowledge sharing.

Despite some possible explanations as to why their CCSOs did not collaborate with other CCSOs on research, interviewees did not identify any insurmountable disincentives. In fact, the general response was simply that experience leads them to collaborate with certain organizations over others, but they would not be opposed to working with other CCSOs. Not collaborating with CCSOs does not seem to provide any major disadvantage, while not collaborating with SCSOs would undermine both the chance of bringing about change and the credibility of the CCSO.

Although there appears to be a lack of incentives for CCSO–CCSO research collaborations, there do seem to be incentives for CCSOs to collaborate with Canadian universities, centres, and professionals. The exploration of these CSO–university interactions presented in Chapter 3 (Chernikova, 2016) suggests there are benefits to working with universities, including access to theoretical expertise, research skills, technology, and monitoring and evaluation techniques. Cultural considerations also play a role in this choice. The culture of research is not a universal one. In Bolivia, several informants spoke of the challenge of finding Bolivian professionals, centres, and universities that place as much importance on research as they do themselves. SCC's representative there, for instance, noted the 'lack of tradition of doing research' at the regional level, with organizations instead tending to use an experience-based implementation approach. Silvina Santana, of the Rosario Municipal Government, explained that in Argentina 'there isn't a practice of generating data … everyone does, does things, goes here, goes there, holds workshops, but no one systematizes anything ... including us'. In cases where Southern universities and centres do have the same mindset and can offer the same skills, there is often a very small research budget, meaning the CCSO is expected to fund all the research. Canadian universities or research centres, on the other hand, can usually come up with partial funding, thus lowering the costs for the CCSO.

Aligning research with organizational roles

The idea that a relationship exists between the number of roles that an organization plays (i.e. the breadth of its mandate) and the way in which it uses research (the number of purposes) was introduced with the survey findings. I concluded that the more roles a CCSO plays, the more ways it finds to use research in its work to influence policy and practice in the Global South. This purely quantitatively based relation reflects a higher organizational level, but the case studies show it also manifests itself at the micro-project level. A large CCSO like SCC, which indicated it played eight roles, interacts in a variety of ways with research through innovative initiatives with the RMI, while the other three CCSOs, which indicated that they play three or four roles, focus more narrowly on concrete and defined research projects. The details of each case study also illustrate how these particular research projects help CCSOs fulfil their roles. Table 4.2 lists which roles WICI, SOCODEVI, R&D, and SCC indicated they play (in response to this study's survey) and provides a project-specific example that links research to the fulfilment of those roles. CCSOs surveyed were given five choices (listed on the left), but were able to list others as well. The table focuses on these five as only SCC named more.

When analysing the cases in terms of how research works to fulfil organizational roles, there are two obvious connections between research and these roles: information generated by the research is needed to instruct actions through which CCSOs can fulfil their roles, but the research process itself also works to fulfil such roles. For instance, SCC provides technical assistance (information or advice) to its partners, governments, and others. To provide this advice, it must be well informed on the issue. Initiating research projects in collaboration with RMI on child work gives SCC access to current regional information and allows it to analyse the gaps in information and policies. At the same time, these research projects support local professors and students in strengthening their research capacity, which in turn helps SCC play an organizational role of capacity building. A second example is found in WICI's work. By facilitating exchanges among partners regarding the research methodologies implemented by each partner, it was able to collect information to produce a revised toolkit for future organizations wanting to implement the GICP. The toolkit allows WICI to contribute technical assistance to other organizations and groups, while the research leading to its production and the facilitated exchanges among partners help build local capacity, as each partner owns the research methods.

Table 4.2 Examples of how CCSO research fulfils different organizational roles

	WICI	SOCODEVI	R&D	SCC
Representation				SCC engaged key stakeholders in research analysis and gave them access to a wider set of concerns, which they considered when they spoke as a representative authority on child rights
Service delivery		An initial 2-year research phase pointed SOCODEVI to oregano as a viable alternative for local farmers and supported their decision to begin delivering seedlings and other related inputs to individual farmers	R&D arranged support for local teams in their data collection and background research through its collaboration with CIDDHU students	Knowledge acquired and analysis done by SCC through its initiatives with the RMI fed directly into SCC's programme implementation
Technical assistance	WICI developed a tool kit for all implementing partners and advises local experts on adapting these to local contexts	SOCODEVI hired and worked with local advisers who provided technical assistance to farmers, monitored crop yields and engaged with UNEC research team	R&D developed a research project in collaboration with SCSO-led teams and a Canadian expert in the Inter-American Court system	SCC used the RMI to access relevant and reliable information on which it based its advice and recommendations
Advocacy	Local women engaged in the research process advocated for equal access to their cities, based on what they learned through the Gender Inclusive Cities Programme	The tested model SOCODEVI has developed alongside its partners served to support advocacy efforts for local ownership and research-based alternative crop introduction	R&D's partners used their knowledge and research experience to strengthen their arguments when they advocated against ethnic and gender discrimination	Regional data collected through SCC's link with the RMI helped it focus its advocacy campaigns on pressing issues concerning children
Capacity building	Local SCSOs took on full project implementation after WICI training in research methods and tools	UNEC staff were supported in their research efforts by SOCODEVI interns, and local advisers were hired and trained in technical aspects of oregano farming	R&D chose a research methodology that engaged local SCOs and their consultants in all phases of the research	SCC initiated working groups where local professors and students developed their research capacity

This study targeted CCSOs that did not have research as their sole objective to see how CCSOs with mandates of capacity building, advocacy, and service delivery were also using research. Research can fit within many mandates and is both a tool and a process to fulfil wider organizational roles.

Conclusion

CCSOs working in international cooperation for development, that is to say NGOs, professional organizations, unions, and networks, are using action-oriented research to varying degrees to influence policy and/or practice in the Global South. This study has highlighted the tendency for CCSOs to maintain control over the research process, to collaborate with SCSOs, and to use research in ways that fit with their overall aims, context, and organizational characteristics. CCSOs routinely make strategic decisions with regard to their research-centred influencing strategies, which can combine to effect real change. Based on initial survey responses and case study analysis, this study has explored how CCSOs are using research (producing it, disseminating it, and learning from it) and how that research is part of their strategy to influence policy and/or practice in the Global South. Its key findings are:

- While this study focused on CCSOs that do not declare research as their main objective, research is an integrated component of their work to influence policy and practice. It is combined with related roles such as capacity building, awareness-raising, and technical support.
- Even though the CCSOs studied do not have research as a declared focus of their mandate, they generally retain a degree of control over the research process, either carrying out research themselves or in collaboration with others.
- There is a relationship between the number of roles that a CCSO plays and the range of purposes for which it uses research. The more roles a CCSO plays, the wider the range of ways it finds to use research in its work to influence policy and practice in the Global South.
- Research helps CCSOs fulfil their many roles in two main ways: research is needed to work toward fulfilling roles (e.g. collect data to understand the issue, then use this knowledge to plan an awareness campaign) and the research process itself allows certain roles to be fulfilled (e.g. engage local women as survey takers so they gain certain skills and establish key relationships, thereby building capacity).
- By working this way, CCSOs can: ensure that research complies with their mandates, philosophies, and resources; be flexible and adapt research questions, methods, etc. as needed along the way; and ensure that the research process serves to build the capacity of their partners, but also their own organizational capacity.

- There is relatively little CCSO–CCSO collaboration for research.
  - This is explained by the incentives of other types of collaborations. Collaborating with SCSOs works to build capacity and is seen as more credible. Collaborating with Canadian universities is feasible (in terms of access and available funds) and strategic (seen as credible sources of research).
  - This is also explained by disincentives to collaborating with other CCSOs. Roles are harder to define than with SCSO–CCSO collaborations where the collaboration itself aligns with CCSO goals of capacity building and knowledge sharing. CCSOs with different mandates have different priorities and may be penalized for working with certain types of groups (advocacy groups for instance). In addition, there is competition for a space within certain dialogues on particular issues, both in Canada and internationally.
  - Also, CCSOs tend to draw partners from established networks on the basis of local contexts, resources, and experience. The strategic choice to collaborate based on experience and practical reasoning tends to create more CCSO–SCSO research collaborations than any other.
- Research from various sources is used for a variety of defined purposes to influence policy and/or practice in the developing countries where CCSOs work with local partners. CCSOs recognize the value of multi-purpose research and/or multiple research uses.
- CCSOs can rely on a limited range of sources of research for a wide range of purposes:
  - using limited sources of research, therefore, does not reflect a lack of access to such sources or a CCSO's greater ability to produce the research needed;
  - using limited sources of research for a wide range of purposes is one of a variety of CCSOs' strategies for influence; and
  - CCSOs with a large research capacity benefit more by resorting to fewer, rather than more, sources as compared to CCSOs with small research capacities.
- CCSOs choose strategies for influence that maximize their resources and opportunities for influence by:
  - forming strategic alliances and partnerships: being strategic about partners/alliances can strengthen research capacity and widen the sphere of influence;
  - identifying and using their organizational strengths: recognizing what they do well, and what defines their organizations, helps CCSOs access and disseminate research in ways that contribute to influencing policy and practice; and
  - paying attention to methodological design: how CCSOs design their research can be part of how they aim to influence the policy process or particular processes.

- CCSO research should be seen as sound and credible if it is transformative and involves local people in the process, if it allows research to mix with complementary activities, and if the methodology addresses power relations.

These findings have implications for funders and CCSOs alike. Given the multi-purpose nature of CCSOs' research, it is important for funders, CCSOs, and their partner organizations to have realistic expectations for projects designed to contribute to policy influence or changes in practice (local, institutional, and organizational). Generally, local CSOs seem to have realistic expectations of what they can accomplish in terms of influencing policy and practice; however, despite CSOs on the ground being realistic about what to expect, those further removed (sometimes the Canadian coordinating organization or the funder) have different ideas. It is important that expectations are shared and discussed before, and during, a project and that consideration is given to how this influence will be measured.

These are not always contributions that can be easily measured. A positive change for WICI is that local women in Rosario went on to question why a public green space had yet to be cleaned up by city officials. Years ago, no one looked at this space as something that prevented their free movement and affected their sense of security. Similarly, R&D's partner in Argentina, COAJ, recorded a demand for further awareness workshops and responded by providing local women leaders with the materials to continue them. In certain communities, these women have begun recording changes that have arisen, such as more women now standing up to their husbands or men in the community. These acts may not be directly related to double discrimination, but they are signs of improved self-esteem and a questioning of the status quo: two important conditions for recognizing discrimination and working toward ending it. Of course, remaining realistic about expectations, being open to unexpected outcomes, and trying to capture non-quantifiable indicators of change is not new advice, but the examples analysed here serve to support these recommendations and reiterate their importance.

A key point to keep in mind when measuring or evaluating CCSO research 'results' is that they are not only found at the end of a project. The research process itself can be designed and implemented in a way that brings about positive change, regardless of what data is collected or what is found through analysing that data. It is, therefore, important to look beyond the data and final reports to consider how the very intervention of carrying out research helped to serve other CCSO objectives. Funders may wish to support more adaptive and open methodologies, as the potential exists for CCSOs to further multiple objectives when these methodologies are employed. CCSO research should not be seen as less important or less credible when it is designed to meet broader organizational roles and when as a result the lines are blurred between research activities and raising awareness, building capacity, and/or implementing projects. The grassroots nature of CCSOs influences their research strategies and defines what credible research is by how well it engages local stakeholders, remains adaptable, and maximizes often limited CCSO resources. Therefore, consideration should be given to the fact that sound and credible research may mean something different to CCSOs than it does to universities and other research-mandated organizations. CCSOs aim to achieve reciprocal relationships with their Southern partners and, as such, strongly believe in avoiding researcher/subject divides or North–South transfer of knowledge.

There are obvious reasons for funders to encourage grant seekers to work together. Funders can often identify the synergies in expertise, research area, and capacity among organizations, leading them to suggest how collaborative efforts can achieve more of an impact. They are also able to suggest how funding proposals complement one another and how a joint effort would provide a richer analysis. Despite recognizing the many reasons for Canadian funders to encourage collaboration among Canadian organizations, be they CCSO–CCSO collaboration or CCSO collaboration with Canadian universities, this study suggests that insisting on these types of collaboration can have negative consequences. Organizational mandates and governance structures among CCSOs compared to those of Canadian universities can differ greatly. When working with local CSOs in the Global South, CCSOs often serve coordinating roles, while SCSOs take on implementing roles. This study suggests that defining the roles between CSCOs and their Global South partners is often easier than defining those between CCSOs and other Canadian partners. This study cautions funders to consider the dynamics that may prevent effective collaboration among CCSOs before tying their funding to this type of collaboration.

There are also important recommendations for CCSOs suggested by this study. Namely, CSOs may want to devote greater attention to systematizing their knowledge and making the role(s) that research actually plays within their organizations more explicit to other actors. CCSOs are advised to review their work and reflect on how knowledge production fits (or should fit) into their work. Questions for CCSOs to ask themselves include: How do we know what we know? Is it purely experience-based? If so, is there a way to systematize that experience? How can more accurate data be collected on what we have done and lessons be incorporated into what we are doing or plan on doing? How have we reflected on what we know? Do we learn from others and have we shared our knowledge with others? These questions are important for CCSOs of all sizes and capacities to ask themselves. Research does not need to be a CCSO's niche, nor its main goal. But if CCSOs recognize their work as evidence-based, it is worth taking the time to reflect on the role of research and consider ways to highlight this in their work. Doing so might open doors to more funding opportunities and further strategic collaborations.

A choice to focus on influencing policy and practice in the Global South was made as a singular way to narrow the domain of this study. It is apparent, however, as CCIC (2006: 2–3) writes, that 'many of the factors that contribute in the South are rooted in the policies of the North in areas such as trade, investment, and the environment, as well as diplomatic, security, and aid relationships'. A related but separate focus for future studies would be to look at how CCSOs use research to influence Canadian foreign policy and practices here in Canada that impede development processes in the Global South.

What do these strategies look like? How are the challenges different? What types of strategic collaboration work well in this context? What role does research play in engaging Canadians on issues? USC Canada, for instance, actively works to contribute to policy influence in Canada in the area of food security through policy dialogues, coalition work, and dissemination of information. Further exploration of its work, and other CCSOs like it, could provide useful insights to complement the study presented in this chapter and identify what strategic choices CCSOs working to influence policy and practice in Canada make, and how these compare with their strategies for influence in the Global South.

Another area in need of further exploration is the degree to which this study's findings extend to CSOs in the Global South. An examination of SCSOs and their strategies for influence would help illustrate this and be useful for CCSOs working towards building SCSO capacity and supporting SCSO research. Further research on CCSO coalitions could also help CCSOs in their work. An examination of these groups may help shed light on how effective they are in promoting and building partnerships that lead to CCSO–CCSO research collaborations (see Chapter 5 in this volume: Smith, 2016). An exploration of the channels used by CCSOs to share their results with the larger CCSO community would also bring benefits. In other words, what opportunities are there to share findings of research in areas of concern to other CCSOs? How can CCSOs access the outcomes of projects or initiatives with research components to learn and prevent unnecessary duplication of research?

CCSOs working in international cooperation for development are doing more than delivering services and assistance to the Global South. Through local, often participatory, actions they are working to influence policy and practice. Although very much action-orientated, CCSOs whose research is not central to their role recognize and address the need for their actions to be evidence-based and respond by incorporating research into their work. CCSOs' research is based on the ground, it involves Southern perspectives, it is adaptable and flexible, and it is in no way an end in itself.

Although they often maintain a certain degree of control over the research process, CCSOs examined in this study placed high importance on local SCSO engagement and ownership. CCSO research is not always (though it can often be) as systematized and rigorous as university-based research. In many aspects, it is messy in that research activities cannot always be separated from awareness-raising, capacity-building, or implementation activities. The way in which research is embedded into CCSOs' work is understood in the context of CCSOs working to influence through a variety of means, but also working to meet multiple objectives. Given the blended nature of CCSOs' research, it becomes less visible and suggests to some that their work is based solely on anecdotal experience rather than supported by carefully designed research. How research is accessed and used by CCSOs is ruled by their strategies for influence. These strategies must account for certain constraints: a lack of funds, time, personnel, and sometimes expertise. Therefore, CCSOs must also find ways to maximize their funds, time, and influence; expand their capacity; and access certain knowledge and skills. This is done by forming strategic alliances and partnerships, identifying and using organizational strengths, and paying attention to methodological design. CCSOs use both the research findings and the research process itself to try and contribute to influence over policy and practice. CCSOs' strategies and contributions for knowledge creation and distribution support the claim that these groups are making research relevant, and are using it to engage in policymaking processes and broaden their impact.

Both under its previous (late in its mandate) and its current administration, the Canadian government, traditionally a core funder of CCSOs, has taken steps towards rebuilding trust with a sector that had been subject to a multi-year freeze on new general funding and had been offered very few opportunities to contribute to policy discussion. The steps taken under the previous administration were summarized by Julia Sánchez, President-CEO of CCIC, in an August 2014 call for a strategic partnership between CSOs working in international development and the federal government. In reference to the then draft Civil Society Partnership Policy, she stated:

> This draft policy, recent funding announcements and roundtables, and statements reaffirming the centrality of civil society mark important first steps in an urgently needed process to re-establish a constructive relationship between DFATD and Canadian development and humanitarian organizations. (CCIC, 2014)

Should the new Government of Canada now promote partnership models and funding mechanisms that recognize the different roles played by CCSOs, there will be great potential for CCSOs to more effectively influence policy and practice, and contribute to both reducing poverty and inequality and increasing democratic governance in countries where they have partners. The CCIC has participated intensely in federal government-led public consultations completed in mid-2016 on new directions for its international development assistance.

Notes

1. In 2013, the Department of Foreign Affairs and International Trade absorbed CIDA and was renamed the Department of Foreign Affairs, Trade and Development (DFATD). In 2015, DFATD became Global Affairs Canada.
2. In 2013, two years after the initial report on this research was published, WICI, unable to secure sufficient funding despite submitting six project proposals in that year alone, was forced to let most of its full-time paid staff go and move to a shared office space. Although it continues its work at a

limited capacity, relying mainly on volunteer staff, it fears the trend for donors to fund larger organizations or to reduce funding to the CSO sector altogether will greatly impact its work and that of other social change organizations worldwide.

3. Statistics listed as reported in 2016.
4. Although no interviews or site visits were carried out with staff at their organizations, this project also involved *Abogados y Abogadas por la Justicia y los Derechos Humanos* in Mexico and Quebec Native Women, which represents women from the First Nations of Quebec and Aboriginal women living in urban areas. The latter participated without IDRC funding.

References

Beaulieu, D. (2009) *Développement fondé sur la connaissance : La contribution d'organisations non gouvernementales du Ghana*, PhD dissertation, Université Laval.

Carden, F. (2009) *Knowledge to Policy: Making the most of development research*, New Delhi and Ottawa: Sage Publications and IDRC.

CCIC (Canadian Council for International Co-operation) (2006) *Building Knowledge and Capacity for Policy Influence: Reflections and resources*, Ottawa: CCIC.

CCIC (2014) 'In the fight against global poverty and inequality, the federal government needs to partner with Canadian organizations', Ottawa: CCIC <http://www.ccic.ca/_files/en/media/News%20release%20on%20 CCIC%20Submission%20to%20CSO%20consultation%20-%20 Final.pdf> [accessed 29 July 2016].

CCIC (2016) 'Brief: Moving our common agenda forward', Ottawa: CCIC <http://www.ccic.ca/_files/en/what_we_do/2016_01_25_Brief_New_ Minister_CCIC_priorities.pdf> [accessed 29 July 2016].

Chernikova, E. (2016) 'Negotiating research collaboration between universities and other civil society organizations in Canada', in L.J.A. Mougeot (ed.), *Putting Knowledge to Work: Collaborating, influencing and learning for international development*, pp. 71–106, Rugby, UK and Ottawa: Practical Action Publishing and IDRC <http://dx.doi.org/10.3362/9781780449685.003>.

CIDA (Canadian International Development Agency) (2011) *Lifted from Poverty by Oregano*, Ottawa: CIDA <http://www.international.gc.ca/development- developpement/stories-histoires/bolivia-bolivie/oregano-origan. aspx?lang=eng> [accessed 29 July 2016].

CISCSA (2010) *Las mujeres trabajando por un Distrito Noroeste sin miedos ni violencias: Cartilla de trabajo, Distrito Noroeste, Rosario*, Rosario, Argentina: CISCSA. <http://www.redmujer.org.ar/pdf_publicaciones/art_55.pdf> [accessed 29 July 2016].

Court, J., Hovland, I., and Young, J. (2005) *Bridging Research and Policy in Development: Evidence and the change process*, Rugby, UK: Practical Action Publishing.

Court, J., Mendizabel, E., Osborne, D., and Young, J (2006) *Policy Engagement: How civil society can be more effective*, London: Overseas Development Institute <https://www.odi.org/sites/odi.org.uk/files/odi-assets/ publications-opinion-files/200.pdf> [accessed 29 July 2016].

DFATD (Department of Foreign Affairs, Trade and Development Canada) (2014) 'Statement by Minister Paradis on Canada's Commitment to Protect and Promote an Enabling Environment for Civil Society', Ottawa: DFATD <http://news.gc.ca/web/article-en.do?nid=840289> [accessed 29 July 2016].

Mably, P. (2006) *Evidence Based Advocacy: NGO research capacities and policy influence in the field of international trade*, Ottawa: IDRC <https://idl-bnc.idrc.ca/dspace/bitstream/10625/45959/1/132438.pdf> [accessed 29 July 2016].

Ministry of Foreign Affairs of Denmark (2012) *Joint Evaluation of Support to Civil Society Engagement in Policy Dialogue: Synthesis Report* <https://www.oecd.org/derec/denmark/CSO_indhold_web.pdf> [accessed 15 September 2016].

Nathan, S., Rotem, A., and Ritchie, J. (2002) 'Closing the gap: Building the capacity of non-government organizations as advocates for health equity', *Health Promotion International* 17(1): 69–78.

OECD (Organisation for Economic Co-operation and Development) (2010) *Better Aid: Civil society and aid effectiveness*, Paris: OECD <http://www.oecd.org/publications/civil-society-and-aid-effectiveness-9789264056435-en.htm> [accessed 29 July 2016].

Open Forum for CSO Development Effectiveness (2014) 'An agreement between Donors, Governments and Civil Society', Brussels: Open Forum for CSO Development Effectiveness.

Reid, H., Ampomah, G., Olazábal Prera, M.I., Rabbani, G. and Zvigadza, S. (2012) *Southern Voices on Climate Policy Choices: Analysis of and lessons learned from civil society advocacy on climate change*, London: International Institute for Environment and Development.

Rights & Democracy (2008) *Ethnic and gender discrimination in the Americas: The case of indigenous women*, Project proposal submitted to the International Development Research Centre, Ottawa.

SCC (Save the Children Canada) (2011) 'Where We Work: Bolivia', Toronto: SCC <https://support.savethechildren.ca/sslpage.aspx?pid=1635> [accessed 29 July 2016].

Smith, E. (2016) 'The learning needs and experiences of Canadian civil society organizations in international cooperation for development', in L.J.A. Mougeot (ed.), *Putting Knowledge to Work: Collaborating, influencing and learning for international development*, pp. 143–182, Rugby , UK and Ottawa: Practical Action Publishing and IDRC <http://dx.doi.org/10.3362/9781780449685.005>.

Synergos (2008) 'A practitioner's guide to influencing policy: Learning from the senior fellows annual global meeting', Project 105486, Ottawa: IDRC <http://idris.idrc.ca/app/Search?request=directAccess&projectNumber=105486&language=en> [accessed 29 July 2016].

Thomas, A. (2001) 'NGOs and their influence on environmental policies', in A. Thomas, S. Carr and D. Humphreys (eds), *Environmental Policies and NGO Influence: Land Degradation and Sustainable Resource Management in Sub-Saharan Africa*, pp. 1–22, London and New York: Routledge.

Travers, S. (2011) *Canadian Civil Society Organizations Influencing Policy and Practice – The Role of Research*, Ottawa: IDRC <http://idl-bnc.idrc.ca/dspace/handle/10625/48923> [accessed 29 July 2016].

Villeneuve, Y. (2008) 'Oregano, a unifying project', *Le coopérateur agricole*, 38(9) <http://www.lacoop.coop/cooperateur/articles/2008/11/p58_en.asp> [accessed 29 July 2016].

Women in Cities International (WICI) (2010) *Learning from women to create gender inclusive cities: Baseline findings from the gender inclusive cities programme*, Montreal: WICI <http://femmesetvilles.org/downloadable/learningfromwomen.pdf> [accessed 29 July 2016].

About the author

Stacie Travers is director of International Projects and Education at Tourism HR Canada, an Ottawa-based non-profit. Previously she managed international mobility and award programmes with the Canadian Bureau for International Education and the International Development Research Centre, respectively. She holds an MA in educational studies with a concentration in adult education from Concordia University in Montreal.

CHAPTER 5

The learning needs and experiences of Canadian civil society organizations in international cooperation for development

Eric Smith

Abstract

Civil society organizations (CSOs) have corporate objectives that must be advanced by headquarters-level planning and strategies. This chapter examines how Canadian civil society organizations (CCSOs) are supporting their field activities by improving their knowledge capture, organizational learning, and decision-making. A survey of CCSOs draws a broad picture of their learning needs, while four case studies on organizational learning strategies illustrate how CCSOs are doing more with less, developing purposeful processes for collecting data, and transforming data into information and useful knowledge.

A cross-case analysis identifies elements required for effective learning and planning at the headquarters level that support fieldwork and knowledge capture. Respondent CCSOs actively participate in formal learning activities and have clear learning strategies to guide their work; size is a determinant of the types of internal learning strategies they employ. Key challenges to learning are competing donor and beneficiary demands, documenting knowledge, and a dearth of dedicated resources for learning activities. Effective organizational learning strategies secure senior management and staff support; they balance internal needs with external demands, design purposeful data collection systems, apply knowledge to decision-making, and maximize the use of internal and network capacity. Donors, as key actors that provide critical motivation for CCSO learning, have a responsibility to ensure that changes in policy and procedure help CCSOs improve the work they do. This requires providing time for reflection and learning once project lifecycles have concluded, as well as flexibility in monitoring and evaluation to suit the needs and capacity of recipients and Global South partners.

Keywords: civil society organizations, organizational learning, learning organization, knowledge management, organizational knowledge

Current relevance

Innovation in the new ecosystem for international development not only depends on how civil society organizations (CSOs) find new ways to navigate

http://dx.doi.org/10.3362/9781780449586.005

funder–recipient relationships in agenda setting, how they diversify ways in which they collaborate with other sectors for action research, and how strategic they are in using knowledge to influence changes in local practices and policies. Innovation also, and perhaps more critically, depends on how devoted and agile CSOs are in capturing, sharing, and using knowledge to respond to, or better anticipate, paradigm shifts and to revisit their own niche, structures, and operations, their external engagement with stakeholders, their interventions, and results on the ground. Despite the central role of organizational learning to organizational innovation, other than studies of individual donor agencies and the larger international non-governmental organizations (NGOs), hardly any study can be found on the learning reality of a majority of NGOs in international development. Also, while recent studies have tended to rely on a specific theoretical framework, such as the learning organization (Whatley, 2013; de Wet and Schoots, 2016), this chapter examines strategies used by several NGOs and situates these within a model integrating five theoretical perspectives on OL.

Drawing on original research completed in 2014, including two country-wide surveys and field-researched case studies of NGOs and coalitions in Canada, this study reveals that a variety of learning strategies are used by NGOs of various sizes, and extensively so, to meet different needs even in the face of growing constraints. The case studies identify conditions that are critical for such strategies to be effective. Private-sector practices not only informed the theoretical frameworks for this study; the business-inspired culture of one CSO led it to heighten its virtual ability to learn from and network both internally and with the beneficiaries of its services worldwide. Findings underscore that although they are ever harder to fund and sustain, spaces where groups of CSOs can regularly assemble, share experiences, and learn from each other continue to be vital for a majority of NGOs to reflect and evolve.

Current public policies for international development that prioritize innovation by the civil society sector must recognize learning as a legitimate activity, a necessary outcome, and an essential stepping stone towards innovation, and therefore should expect learning activities to be adequately resourced, reported on, and accounted for. Collecting data for this study was laborious and may explain why similar studies remain scarce; this does reflect the fact that learning processes for a majority of NGOs remain a largely unrecorded enterprise, if not an undervalued deliverable to the public eye. Making their learning strategies more explicit to themselves and to others, in their purpose, means, and uses, is a requisite for CSOs to acknowledge the value of their efforts, advocate funding for these as legitimate, and demonstrate their essential role in evolution, if not innovation.

Introduction

There is a growing interest in organizational learning (OL) and improvements in the not-for-profit sector for sustainable development. This field aims to understand how organizational processes and goals can be improved or strengthened for better development results. CSOs do not simply provide service delivery and project support to their partners in the developing world. They are institutions with corporate objectives and strategies that must be supported by headquarters-level planning and strategies. This study attempts to understand how Canadian CSOs (CCSOs) are working to support field activities by improving their knowledge capture, OL, and decision-making processes. OL is explored through CCSOs' experiences with learning initiatives: how they capture knowledge from fieldwork and apply lessons to their strategies and directions, the challenges and opportunities they face, and the extent to which they share these lessons with others in the wider development community.

A literature review situates the study in the contexts of OL and the Canadian development sector. The review found that available research so far has largely concentrated on donor agencies and large international non-governmental organizations. There are few studies on small CSOs, and even fewer in the Canadian context. The review provided a conceptual framework used to situate four types of learning initiatives: conceptual (related to organizational visions, missions, and strategies); content-based (data that is captured from fieldwork); applied (systems that support data capture and analysis); and process-based (internal operations and structures that facilitate knowledge flow and decision-making). For CCSOs in development, these initiatives are rooted in practice, that is, the fieldwork that they carry out. This might be research, advocacy, interventions, evaluations, volunteer placements, or other forms of support to partners.

Two surveys provide an overview of how CCSOs engage with learning from their fieldwork and activities. One survey targeted CCSOs that produce research from their fieldwork. A second survey targeted coalitions of fee-paying organizations, such as councils and networks, to provide an overview of how these organizations support their memberships in their learning and knowledge activities. These surveys broadly assess the extent of learning strategies, the specific organizational aspects of learning that CCSOs target, the means and activities that they use to incorporate learning into their work, and the challenges they face when doing so.

These surveys indicate that most responding CCSOs participate in many formal learning activities and have clear learning strategies to guide them when learning from their work and practices. Coalitions respond to and support their members' learning strategies by providing opportunities for face-to-face networking, workshops, webinars, and other activities on specific issues. They also provide context analyses by mapping and researching emerging trends that can inform the overall learning strategies of CCSOs. Most, but not all, CCSOs share their lessons with others in the wider development community, either through coalitions or with like-minded agencies. However, the surveys and case studies found that staff prefer to disseminate knowledge through face-to-face activities rather than in published reports and briefs.

Four case studies examine the purposes and challenges of CCSO learning initiatives. These initiatives, undertaken to improve organizational efficiency and impact, have informed monitoring and evaluation (M&E), systems for knowledge capture, organizational processes, and business models and strategies. An analysis of the cases illustrates that CCSOs choose strategies that secure senior management and staff support, that balance internal needs with external demands, that design purposeful data collection systems, that apply knowledge to decision-making, and that maximize the use of internal and network capacity. Barriers to learning include a lack of dedicated funding sources for organizational improvement and knowledge sharing, systematically documenting and using knowledge, and ensuring organizational and/or staff commitment.

It is strongly recommended that CCSOs record their lessons not only about their outcomes in the field but also about processes that effectively support fieldwork, and share these within their networks and through regional councils. In order to continue supporting the work of their member organizations, regional councils should carefully consider the needs of members and their audience – be they newly founded, established, or large organizations – to provide a range of activities that keep their memberships engaged and actively communicating with one another. Donors should keep in mind that they are the exogenous factor that often provides critical motivation for CCSO learning. As such, they have a responsibility to ensure that changes in policy and procedure help CCSOs improve the work they do. This entails providing time for reflection and learning after project lifecycles conclude as well as flexibility in M&E that reflects the needs and capacities of recipients and their partners in the developing world.

Methods

The research combined qualitative and quantitative methods and included three methods of data collection: a literature review, two standardized surveys, and semi-structured interviews. A general framework was developed to guide the approach to research using insight from the literature. The literature review provides a general characterization of OL in the development sector. It begins with a historical overview of OL, followed by the four main theoretical perspectives on OL, main methods used to incorporate learning into organizational activities, and key challenges noted in the literature. The literature review is not intended to be an exhaustive list of how to put theory into practice, but instead provides an introduction to theoretical and practical concerns relevant to OL, such as those explored through the standardized surveys and in three case studies.

Two standardized surveys were distributed to collect basic data and to identify recent learning initiatives, approaches, needs, and attitudes of CCSOs. The first survey (n=27) targeted senior management of CCSOs to assess learning strategies, directions, challenges, and activities. The second survey (n=11) targeted networking organizations, such as provincial councils and other coalitions, to provide basic data on how these organizations support their members' learning activities. The initial surveys were followed by interviews and email exchanges to clarify responses and gather additional information (n=16).

The survey results were analysed and used to identify recent learning initiatives undertaken by CCSOs. The results were used as input for a semi-structured interview guide. Four case studies were selected to represent learning initiatives of organizations that have responded effectively to internal and external pressures. A cross-case analysis was used to draw conclusions and generic lessons from complex and unique contexts.

Limitations

Organizational change and learning cannot be limited to a single intervention, but instead must be understood as a process situated within a particular community of individuals that are working together. The causes and successes of an organizational change initiative with one CSO may not apply to another, given the diversity of roles and stakeholders that share responsibility for development outcomes. The CSOs targeted for the standardized survey were selected on the basis that they have research functions. That is to say that they play a role in documenting, analysing, and sharing their work with the broader development community. The case studies were selected as examples of positive deviancies – organizations that self-identified as having successful learning initiatives that efficiently confronted common CSO challenges identified in the survey. As such, neither the survey sample nor the case studies are representative of the Canadian development landscape. Not all CSOs have a research role, and more work could be done on analysing the experiences of CSOs in diversifying their funding bases through donor outreach.

Literature, theory, concepts

The World Bank's comprehensive definition of civil society states that 'it comprises the wide array of non-governmental and not-for-profit organizations that have a presence in public life, expressing the interests and values of their members or others based on ethical, cultural, political, scientific, religious, or philanthropic considerations' (World Bank, 2013). The term 'civil society organization' refers to a wide variety of organizations and institutions which, according to the OECD's *Civil Society and Aid Effectiveness* (2009), have roles in seven areas: the mobilization of grassroots communities, monitoring and accountability of governments and donors, research and policy, service delivery, networking, aid delivery, and education. For CSOs with an interest in development, these roles incorporate a wide variety of stakeholders which includes Northern and Southern public and private donors, partners, and beneficiaries that often share responsibilities in their work.

The importance of OL and knowledge sharing by CSOs was officially recognized by the Open Forum for Development Effectiveness. The *Siem Reap Consensus on the International Framework for CSO Development Effectiveness* (Open Forum for CSO Effectiveness, 2011) was developed through open consultations with thousands of CSOs over two CSO Global Assemblies. Two major outcomes of the assemblies were the Istanbul Principles for CSO Development Effectiveness and an international framework to guide its implementation. The seventh principle clearly recognizes the importance of OL, knowledge management (KM), and mutual learning. It reads:

> CSOs are effective as development actors when they enhance the ways they learn from their experience and from other CSOs and development actors, integrating evidence from development practice and results, including the knowledge and wisdom of local and indigenous communities, strengthening innovation and their vision for the future they would like to see. (Open Forum for CSO Effectiveness, 2011)

Principle 7 calls on CSOs to be learning organizations and to become 'knowledge brokers' by creating, sharing, and implementing knowledge as a key component of their strategies in areas of collaboration, capacity strengthening, and evaluation.

Those CSOs that conduct research typically do so using their own staff and interns to ensure the credibility and quality of their work, to deepen relationships with partners, to reformulate and target interventions, and to strengthen the capacity of stakeholders (Travers, 2011). However, CSOs typically view research narrowly as it relates to their own purposes: policy action and an instrument for advocacy rather than for the broader development community or their own learning (Gall et al., 2009). Gall et al. (2009) go on to note that CSOs would directly benefit from a culture of research to 'develop a culture of reflexivity [and] learn to question more regularly their own practices and organization'. Research can not only inform advice and policy, but also play a role in refining organizational strategies, directions, and operations. In short, research can contribute to OL.

Theory

Several theoretical directions have been taken when examining learning within the development sector. Krohwinkel-Karlsson's (2007) meta-review of OL theory and practice provides a useful categorization to structure previous work to contrast 'organizational learning', 'the learning organization', 'organizational knowledge', and 'knowledge management'. These are overlapping management practices that guide an organization's approach to knowledge and adaptation. These are complemented by two dichotomies that place them on conceptual–applied and content–process axes. Conceptual approaches have to do with the system an organization finds itself within and how this impacts the organization's vision, mission, strategy, culture, and attitudes towards sharing knowledge with others. Applied initiatives target the systems used to capture knowledge, such as KM and information and communication technology (ICT) solutions to data storage and retrieval. The content–process dichotomy distinguishes between what knowledge is captured and how knowledge flows through an organization to inform internal efficiencies and decision-making. Content-based approaches are concerned with the knowledge and lessons that are captured from activities (for CSOs this might be interventions such as aid delivery, field research, student or professional exchanges, internships, and other collaborations). Process-based approaches have to do with internal operations, such as work plans, team meetings, procedures, and guidelines that facilitate decision-making.

The learning organization (LO) developed out of the corporate sector and the work of Peter Senge. An LO is one 'where people continually expand their capacity to create the results they truly desire, where new and expansive patterns of thinking are nurtured, where collective aspiration is set free, and where people are continually learning how to learn together' (Senge, 1990; quoted in Krohwinkel-Karlsson, 2007: 10). The team is the key learning unit in organizations while 'learning leaders' build shared vision and openness to strategic changes. A later development is Wenger's (2002) study of communities of practice (CoPs) within the corporate environment.

OL is the theoretical analysis of learning processes within organizations. It emphasizes the processes, procedures, and routines that an organization uses to respond to and anticipate external stimuli. This approach is systemic and focuses on the structures that impede or facilitate organizational decision-making and examines connections within organizational systems rather than individual aspects of organizations. As developed by Argyris (1999), OL theory distinguishes between single- and double-loop learning. Single-loop learning's objective is to render organizational activity more efficient, while double-loop learning aims to make an organization open to strategic changes by encouraging organizational staff/members to think critically and creatively about the assumptions and values that underlie their work to improve the organization's strategy and operations.

KM is an approach that emphasizes the collection, codification, and distribution of knowledge. It can be thought of as the process that converts raw information 'into relevant knowledge and us[es] this to achieve [organizational] aims' (Hovland, 2003: 10). It is closely related to the 'first generation' of KM, which focused on ICT interventions to manage and codify the large volume of organizational data that was threatening to overwhelm many organizations in the early 1990s. Early attempts to use ICT threatened to cause information overload on a scale that made knowledge and learning problems even worse. A further concern with KM strategies is that they often do not or are unable to distinguish what data is valuable to an organization, nor does the indiscriminate collection and codification of data allow organizations to apply what they know or innovate. To address these concerns a 'second generation' of KM strategies, including document management systems, intranets, and extranets that include metadata, have helped render these corporate memories more accessible and useable (Britton, 2005).

Organizational knowledge (OK) is an approach to knowledge and learning that acknowledges the differences between tacit and explicit knowledge and provides ways and means of operationalizing implicit knowledge. Explicit knowledge is knowledge that 'can be articulated or documented with relative ease' while 'tacit knowledge is based on personal experience and skills... [it] can only be transferred through socialization processes, such as jointly performed tasks, face to face discussions etc.' (Krohwinkel-Karlsson, 2007: 11). KM strategies that capture and codify data are notoriously bad at capturing the context of the experiential knowledge that is so often crucial in international development and cooperation. The transfer of tacit knowledge requires interpretation and socialization to learn from collective experiences rather than the 'technological fix' provided by KM.

A fifth model, a practice-based approach, which explicitly addresses the role of CSOs in research, was developed by Ferguson et al. (2008) in *Management of Knowledge for Development*. It aims to ground previous theories of learning and knowledge in the understanding that 'the individual's practices, situated at a community level, form the central pivot of knowledge creation' (Ferguson et al., 2008: 10). Connections between practices and contexts allow knowledge flows to occur and stimulate situated learning, the process by which knowledge is co-constructed and embedded within practices. According to Ferguson et al., knowledge and learning activities/practices should reflect the goals of creating and facilitating knowledge flows within and between social networks to achieve mutual learning for more effective development and cooperation.

These five approaches provided a conceptual framework for understanding and placing the learning and knowledge initiatives of CCSOs. It was used to

Figure 5.1 Approaches to organizational learning and practice
Source: adapted by the author from Krohwinkel-Karlsson, 2007

inform a subsequent literature review of common practices, methods, and barriers to learning (see Figure 5.1).

Practices and methods for fostering learning

Organizational culture. Developing an organizational culture that is a supportive learning environment has been recognized as a necessary condition for successful knowledge and learning initiatives. A learning culture 'is one that enables, encourages, values, rewards and uses the learning of its members both individually and collectively' (Britton, 2005: 17). An organization with a learning culture recognizes learning as integral to each individual's work responsibilities, encourages and supports learning activities, gives learning adequate resources, rewards and values learning to incentivize staff, and aims to overcome its internal barriers to learning in a systematic fashion.

Challenges to a learning culture include project lifecycles, lack of time, fear of failure, and the difficulty of systematically capturing knowledge. Many donors require the logical framework approach (LFA) to planning and there is significant evidence this can constrain learning (Sartorius, 1991; Couillard et al., 2009). Project lifecycles with LFAs can generate a constant pressure to produce results, which can result in an 'adrenaline culture' where outputs are the major, or only, measure of success in the field. As a result of these pressures, the incentives for learning for positive change are lost (Britton, 2005). There may also be a fear of repercussions if negative or critical outcomes were to emerge from learning.

Moreover, there is a powerful emotional incentive to (consciously or unconsciously) suppress failure in development, as failures are associated with failing to save or make a positive impact on human lives (Krohwinkel-Karlsson, 2007). Engineers Without Borders in Canada is a notable example of an organization trying to change this systemic challenge to learning through their Failure Reports (Lewis, 2011). Their approach recognizes that while failure is a tragedy, it is worse when we fail to learn from our mistakes to improve future work.

If knowledge 'is acknowledged as a key component of development work, and learning is so important, this would imply that the organization's management needs to be structured in such a manner to optimize the flow, the sharing and the development of knowledge' (Ferguson et al., 2008: 19). An organization's ability to document knowledge may be achieved through KM tools, but to harness this knowledge for future learning and innovation requires a culture and process that can achieve organizational change. This requires a clear organizational strategy that incorporates approaches to learning that are appropriate for that organization. As Ferguson et al. note:

> This involves identifying the unique knowledge assets of the organization, exploring the key organizational processes, and identifying how this knowledge can be streamlined in support of these processes, towards optimal achievement of organizational and, in this case, development goals. (Ferguson et al., 2008: 20)

While the tools and practices that support learning may be easier to apply than management practices that support a learning culture, the management implications of a learning strategy should not be dismissed. Formal tools and practices that can encourage a learning culture include weekly meetings, learning forums, annual or semi-annual retreats, the sharing of staff and travel reports, document retrieval systems, and intranets. There are also more informal practices, such as coffee breaks and learning lunches, which may not be mandatory but provide the opportunity to share knowledge in a less structured manner.

Monitoring and evaluation (M&E). M&E tools are used for four primary purposes: 1) accountability to donors and the government, 2) understanding project outcomes, 3) learning from past work, and 4) accountability to stakeholders and other beneficiaries. Monitoring and evaluation are distinct: monitoring refers to the systematic collection of data as a project progresses to ensure the project is implemented as planned. Evaluation compares the actual impacts of the project with those that were planned; it can be formative (done during a project's lifecycle) or summative (done at the end of a project's lifecycle).

Results-based management (RBM) reporting was the primary means used by CCSOs for planning, monitoring, and evaluation when working with the former Canadian International Development Agency (CIDA), and has continued to be the approach taken since CIDA's merger in 2013 with the former Department of Foreign Affairs and Trade into a new Department of Foreign Affairs, Trade, and Development (DFATD), itself renamed Global Affairs Canada in 2015. RBM approaches, such as the logical framework tool, are intended to offer consistent guidelines to organizations for planning, implementing, and reporting on projects. This type of donor-driven accountability system has been criticized for requiring high levels of investment, training, and time; for not taking into account cultural contexts; and for not taking into account beneficiary needs (Bakewell and Garbutt, 2005). Furthermore, they often make it difficult for CSOs to balance the goal of learning from past work to improve directions and operations with the goal of accounting. It is largely agreed that RBM approaches are also more easily put into practice by donors and large CSOs that have greater experience with RBM and resources for staff training. Smaller CSOs, such as grassroots or community-based organizations with less experience and capacity, may experience frustration when applying an RBM/LFA approach. It has also been argued that RBM/LFA approaches may not account for less tangible results, such as gender equality, that cannot be measured through linear models (see Christie, 2008).

These limitations have prompted a trend towards RBM+ tools. These tools combine RBM with other methodologies to provide financial accountability while taking into consideration the learning and planning needs of the CSOs and their partners in the field. CCIC and the Inter-Council Network have compiled lists of resources (Christie, 2008; Global Hive, 2016) that include social analysis systems (SAS^2, see Chevalier and Buckles, 2008), accountability learning and planning system (ALPS, developed by ActionAid; see Guijt,

2004), outcome mapping (developed by IDRC), and learning before during and after (LBDA). Smaller organizations face significant challenges of capacity, resources, and time in balancing RBM+ models with RBM requirements. In order to address these challenges, Canada World Youth convened a community of practice Bridging Gaps, to facilitate a dialogue between CCSOs, networks, and donors on these alternative approaches.[1]

Knowledge management software. These software programs have evolved greatly since their introduction as tools for KM. The first generation of KM stressed ICTs as tools that increased the ease of documentation within an organization. They were used to collect and codify knowledge and included document-management systems, databases, and organizational yellow pages. This was a far cry from OL, but did improve corporate memory by documenting knowledge. The first generation of ICTs for KM drove 'single-loop learning' to resolve inefficiencies, but could easily lead to information overload due to the volume of data captured without the means to systematically analyse it. This generation of ICTs has been criticized for being unable to capture the contextual embeddedness of knowledge so critical to learning from field results of research and interventions (Ferguson et al., 2010).

The second generation of ICT strategies are document-management systems, intranets, and extranets. These include metadata to enable access and analysis of corporate knowledge using online learning databases and resources. Finally, a third generation has harnessed the capabilities of the internet to create online platforms for communication. These are 'virtual platforms' that facilitate knowledge sharing, learning, and collaboration at a distance. The aim of third-generation ICT interventions for learning and knowledge is to use online, collective learning to share and enhance real-life/offline activities.

Communities of practice. Working groups of individuals, within or across organizations, convene to share knowledge and learning on mutual interests. They develop a unique perspective and a common body of knowledge, practices, and approaches through formal or informal engagement between individuals in a group setting (Wenger, 2002; Britton, 2005). They have received considerable attention in both the corporate and non-profit worlds as essential tools for fostering knowledge sharing by providing situated, context-sensitive sites for mutual learning. A major advantage of CoPs is that practice-based knowledge can be shared and articulated in an accessible and pertinent manner (Ferguson et al., 2010). While many CoPs are face to face, they are increasingly going virtual to connect far-flung geographic partners, which introduces unique challenges in maintaining distributed relationships and common motivation or the long-term investment required in growing and supporting social media (Hildreth, 2004).

Partnerships and collaboration. Partnerships and collaboration between CCSOs, their Southern partners, and universities are a method used by many organizations to learn from their projects. Gall et al.'s 2009 study of the Social Sciences and Humanities Research Council of Canada's Community–University Research Alliance programme showed that deeper CSO engagement with academic research partners can inform not only advocacy but also organizational directions and operations. Chernikova's (2010) analysis of collaboration between universities and CSOs found that working with academics assists CSOs in strategic planning and decision-making. Such collaborations may also grant CSOs access to larger networks, which can result in business development, or access to human resources or expertise they may not otherwise be aware of. In turn, CSOs can share their own expertise and local networks with academics to enhance the 'on-the-ground' experiences of academics and students.

Barriers to learning

Power dynamics and knowledge. A common criticism of knowledge transfer within international development is that it unfairly favours Northern organizations, rather than its intended beneficiaries in the South (Hovland, 2003; Britton, 2005; Ferguson et al., 2008). Hovland recommends combining KM and learning strategies with an explicit focus on Southern knowledge needs and challenges, while Britton recommends that a humble attitude underpins learning and 'also encourages each partner to value and respect the other's experience' to take the focus away from financial transactions that can be the root of power imbalances (Britton, 2005). Ferguson et al. note that action research with a focus on epistemic diversity, inclusiveness, and mutual learning may help to overcome the tensions that result from geographic distance and power imbalances between the North and South.

In Canada relationships between donors – particularly Global Affairs Canada (GAC) – and CSOs favour the collection and analysis of data for the purposes of accountability to the government and taxpayers. Within Canada, GAC-driven evaluations tend to strike a balance between accountability and learning, but it is less clear to what extent evaluations provide accountability to Southern beneficiaries (Christie, 2008). According to the North-South Institute, CCSOs delivered 15.1 per cent (C$559 million) of CIDA-funded aid projects in 2012, down from 17.4 per cent in 2011 (Bhushan, 2013). In 2012, the Canadian government announced an 'aid freeze' and an aid budget reduction of 9.7 per cent over three years (Heidrich et al., 2013). Tomlinson (2016) found that CIDA/DFATD cuts disproportionately affected small and medium-sized CCSOs: 70 per cent of the organizations that lost their funding were small organizations, and 22 per cent were medium-sized. Since 2012-13, growth in GAC funding to CCSOs has resumed, but only so if humanitarian funding is included; it is focused on Africa and now benefits fewer CCSOs, with core funding continuing to decline (CCIC, 2016).

Trust and competitive behaviour. A competitive market for funding can create perverse incentives to keep knowledge within an organization. Forsyth and MacLachlan (2009) note that information on NGO attitudes towards interorganizational learning is lacking, and seek to address this gap. They reaffirm the importance of context of relationships and interorganizational learning as a crucial site of learning (see also Britton, 2005; and Ferguson et al., 2008). Despite these difficulties, Forsyth and MacLachlan identified a number of opportunities for CSOs to partner for research on learning and knowledge, for greater influence over public perceptions of CSOs, and for joint fundraising. These are mechanisms that a number of CCSOs have been able to use, such as CoPs (Bridging Gaps, coordinated by Canada World Youth), councils (the Inter-Council Network's seven thematic Knowledge Hubs), and joint appeal instances (the Humanitarian Coalition).

Competing beneficiary and donor demands. These are a common challenge to all CSOs. Each is a distinct group that requires a different strategy for interaction and change. The strategic knowledge of how to influence each may be split within organizations by necessity. Thus, contrary to Senge's (1990) assertion that an organization ought to be treated as a harmonious entity, CSOs may require distinct learning strategies that allow them to learn from, and adapt to, donor and beneficiary needs (Hovland, 2003; see also Krohwinkel-Karlsson, 2007). As key intermediaries between donors and beneficiaries, CSOs have responded by developing new approaches to learning and knowledge, such as the aforementioned RBM+ models that strive to balance learning from research and experiences with financial accounting and results monitoring.

Geographical distance. Physical separation between partners or between headquarters (HQ) and field operations can also hinder learning and knowledge strategies. These can lead to information gaps and tensions when trying to balance information flow between far-flung actors. Field staff are often overwhelmed with the contextual situation 'on the ground' and with making immediate decisions concerning programming, while head offices are focused on funding, donors, and strategic decision-making related to organizational concerns. This leads to a gap between the expectations of each group, with HQ requesting information from field staff who may not have the time to respond quickly or in the manner requested (Suzuki, 2004). Suzuki makes no strict recommendations for overcoming this challenge, which may be inherent to the nature of international business and development. Instead, he stresses that organizations must create processes to alleviate the tension as best as they can, given their organizational structures and needs.

Survey findings

A standardized survey was sent to 126 CCSOs, of which 27 responded. The survey was not intended to be exhaustive, but instead to provide some insight into how CCSOs tend to benefit from learning activities, what internal and external activities they use for learning and knowledge sharing, and what challenges they have experienced in learning and knowledge-sharing activities. Of the 27 respondents, nine were small (one to five staff), eight were medium (six to 15 staff), and 10 were large (16 or more staff). The survey found, as

hypothesized, that the size of the organization is a major determinant in its selection of particular approaches to learning and the challenges experienced.
The survey found that:

1. Larger organizations tend to have broader learning strategies that incorporate internal operations (i.e. internal efficiency, procedures, guidelines, and work plans), KM (ICT solutions such as virtual platforms, intranets, and extranets), and human resources (such as recruitment, contracting, supervision, reporting, and staff learning/training) (see Figure 5.2).
2. The size of an organization determines what methods it uses to incorporate learning into evaluations and fieldwork. While nearly all organizations surveyed, regardless of size, used partnerships to incorporate learning into their evaluations and fieldwork, the small organizations surveyed used LFAs less frequently than large organizations. Large organizations surveyed were also more likely to use KM e-tools, but less likely to use outcome mapping techniques (see Figure 5.3).
3. Internal activities that organizations use to collect and share knowledge also varied according to size, with formal processes and learning forums and annual/semi-annual retreats more likely to be used by larger organizations (see Figure 5.4). Follow-up interviews indicated that small organizations do not feel the need to formalize their knowledge collecting and sharing activities, as their small staff and office size facilitate this process naturally and continuously.
4. To share knowledge and lessons, both small and large organizations were more likely than medium-sized organizations to take part in interorganizational activities such as CoPs, working groups, and conferences. Surprisingly, small organizations were most likely to share their knowledge and lessons through publishing reports, papers and briefs (see Figure 5.5).

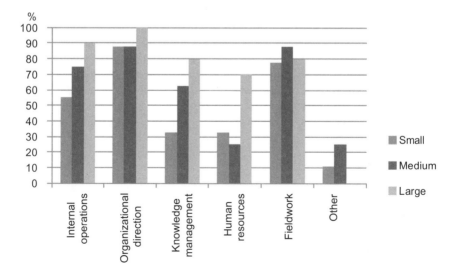

Figure 5.2 Learning strategy directions

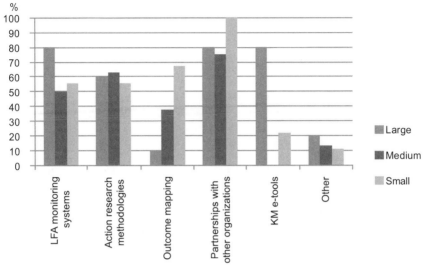

Figure 5.3 Methods used to incorporate learning into field activities by staff size

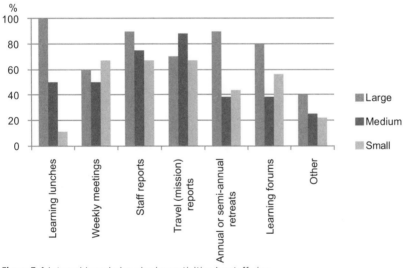

Figure 5.4 Internal knowledge-sharing activities by staff size

5. The most common challenges organizations experience in learning and knowledge-sharing activities are competing beneficiary and donor demands, documenting knowledge, and a dearth of resources and capacity. The incidence of these challenges is also highly dependent on staff size, with eight out of nine small organizations reporting that their primary challenge is competing beneficiary and donor demands. Medium-sized and large organizations reported documenting knowledge is their primary challenge at 75 per cent and 80 per cent, respectively. Some 40 per cent

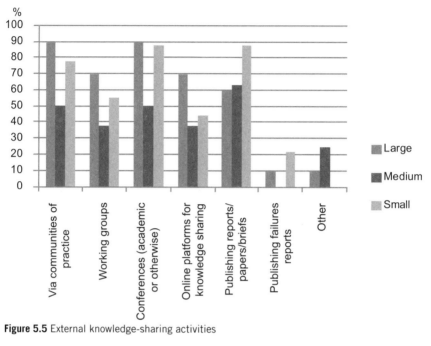

Figure 5.5 External knowledge-sharing activities

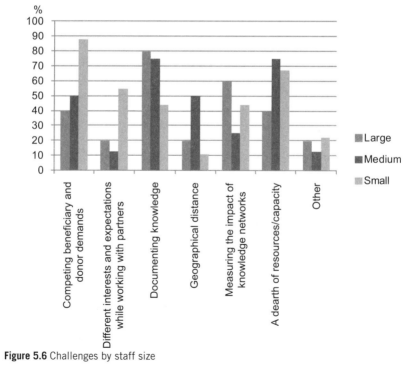

Figure 5.6 Challenges by staff size

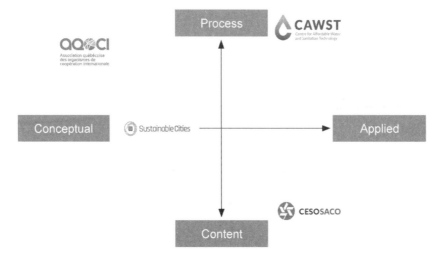

Figure 5.7 The four case studies of learning initiatives within the conceptual framework

of responding large organizations reported that a dearth of resources and capacity is a challenge while 67 per cent of small and 75 per cent of medium-sized organizations reported this as a challenge (see Figure 5.6).

Based on these findings and subsequent follow-up interviews, four case studies were selected to examine the purposes of recent CCSO learning initiatives. Cases were selected to respect differences in size, types of learning initiatives, and key challenges identified through the survey.

The case studies

Four learning initiatives were selected as the basis for four case studies on the processes that support OL. While learning by doing occurs in the field, the cases examine HQ-level processes that support the synthesis, analysis, and application of knowledge. Two of the cases are large organizations, one is a small organization, and the final case is an interorganizational learning initiative housed within a provincial council. The four cases were analysed to determine the organizational need, learning strategy, barriers to implementation, and key factors of success. Figure 5.7 places the cases within the conceptual framework. This placement does not reflect the sum total of each organization's learning strategy or approaches, but places the particular initiative within an ideal-type (specific quadrant) for analysis.

The Centre for Affordable Water and Sanitation Technology (CAWST) is placed in the process-applied quadrant as it has formalized and systematized KM processes to complement face-to-face learning and capture of experiential field knowledge from staff and partners. To do so it created a new knowledge management system (KMS) to increase efficiency in decision-making processes and knowledge sharing. The Canadian Executive Service Organization (CESO) is in the content-applied quadrant. CESO's new monitoring, learning, and evaluation (MEL) framework aimed to consolidate and streamline the data it was collecting to reduce information overload and more effectively report on development outcomes. Sustainable Cities International (SCI) is on the conceptual line, as it developed a new business strategy to move away from public funding. Finally, Genre en pratique, a CoP coordinated by l'Association québécoise des organismes de coopération internationale (AQOCI), is in the conceptual-process framework as this initiative focused on the process of interorganizational learning and systemic concerns about the institutionalization of gender equality. The following section provides a narrative overview of the four cases and is followed by a cross-case analysis that draws generic lessons and recommendations.

Case 1: The Centre for Affordable Water and Sanitation Technology

Founded in 2001, CAWST is a Calgary-based NGO that provides technical training, consulting, and expertise on water and sanitation technologies in developing countries. The organization began by promoting a biosand filter and with the mission of providing education and training on the device to increase local capacity to build, use, and maintain the filters. Since 2008, the organization's water, sanitation, and hygiene programmes have expanded significantly with the launch of its Water Expertise and Training (WET) programme. The staff size increased to reflect this wider mandate and this presented a challenge to the organization's learning strategy.

CAWST's OL strategy is informed by three key priorities: cutting-edge knowledge on water and sanitation, understanding failure, and a flat organizational structure. These priorities are supported by a commitment to face-to-face and iterative learning through two two-week learning forums each year for staff. Partnerships with universities, client and partner feedback, and a full-time staff researcher help the organization to remain innovative in the field of water and sanitation. To understand and improve from 'failure', the organization's management encourages staff to reflect on projects that do not work or finish as anticipated, and to have these lessons inform organizational processes and structures. Within each project, short- and long-term feedback loops are explicitly designed in the planning phase to validate plans and to readjust projects as necessary. A flat organizational structure encourages staff to take advantage of new opportunities and assess the needs of partners and clients. Weekly one-on-one meetings between each staff member and their director allow them to discuss current priorities, new opportunities, and time available. This frequent feedback harmonizes needs at the individual, team, and organizational levels.

This approach was appropriate until it was challenged when CAWST's staff size, number of clients, and partners grew after the launch of the WET programme in 2008. While CAWST's approach to OL was effective, it required frequent communication and at times lengthy iteration to translate tacit experience into explicit and transferable knowledge. Recognizing this, CAWST moved towards a 'trust the process' approach to ensure that both internal and external communication and information exchange remain efficient.

An important consideration for CAWST was that this system acts not just as a technical database for articles, but is integrated with CAWST's internal analyses of their products and services. According to Zoran Gligorov (ICT Coordinator, CAWST), this is where 'tacit to explicit knowledge is shown and advice is given. It's not just the factual information from this research paper or the factual knowledge from the publications, but advice that is tailored to the question that is asked. So tacit to explicit.' The organization found that its staff were answering the same questions frequently and that some staff were not aware of internal organizational knowledge that would contribute to their duties. The goal became to create a KMS that all staff could contribute to and access. This required formalizing decision-making processes, feedback loops, communication, and knowledge capture.

To achieve this goal, CAWST invested in a new knowledge management strategy to support formal and informal learning pathways. This would enable staff training, knowledge capture from clients and partners, and knowledge dissemination, such as updates on technology and implementation, to others. CAWST created a KM platform it calls the Household Water Treatment and Safe Storage Knowledge Base. This online platform was developed to change and integrate knowledge capture processes into a single database system that harmonized with current practices, would suit future needs and growth, and provided bidirectional communication between CAWST staff and clients. To meet these requirements, CAWST chose to leverage in-house resources and personnel to ensure that there was no time lost in communicating needs to external consultants. A staff member with coding experience undertook a project to fast-track the system and develop it at minimal cost.

The Household Water Treatment and Safe Storage Knowledge Base is now an interactive virtual platform for users of biosand filters that enables their successful implementation by sharing technical expertise and experiential knowledge (see CAWST, n.d.). Different sections allow users to share designs and technical updates, experiences on implementation, questions and answers, research papers, project evaluations and case studies, and an online forum for informal discussion. This allows CAWST to rapidly train its own staff, capture the concerns and lessons of clients and partners for analysis, and provide the users of the filter with a way to interact with one another. The Knowledge Base is also available to download for offline use in the field.

While a full evaluation of the Knowledge Base has not yet been undertaken, clients have been able to share their feedback through an annual survey that determined that many of CAWST's clients actively use or contribute to the Knowledge Base. By leveraging internal knowledge of ICTs, CAWST developed the system brick by brick to ensure that it was targeted to current needs, but capable of being adapted and scaled to future priorities. As designed, the Knowledge Base enables CAWST to leverage the tacit knowledge of clients and staff by translating it into explicit knowledge that can be used by others. While the challenges of documenting knowledge, including time constraints, cannot be fully eliminated, they were reduced by developing user-friendly and efficient tools.

Case 2: Canadian Executive Service Organization

Founded in 1967, CESO is a volunteer-based development organization that aims to strengthen economic and social wellbeing in Canada and abroad through cooperative work with partners and clients. It provides services in strategic planning, business development, accounting and finance, organizational development, community development, governance, and production and operations.

In 2010, CESO conducted an internal review and restructured to improve operations and develop a culture of nurturing, sharing, and learning. This was prompted by dissatisfaction among staff and partners with its current MEL system, as well as an increasingly competitive external environment for funding. Before this, CESO's M&E strategy was largely limited to capturing outputs, such as the number of volunteers sent abroad and their personal experiences. The review found that longer term benefits and outcomes for their partners that resulted from their programming were assumed, but not systematically measured. Like many CCSOs, its M&E system was designed to provide accountability to donors and did not systematically capture the collective impact of knowledge transfer and skills development. The review also found that strong organizational silos had developed between the organization's different Canadian offices as well as between its national and international programme areas.

A new strategic and operational plan was developed to address these challenges through four key areas: cultivating a culture of learning and accountability; programme planning, delivery, evaluation, and reflection; building an engaged workforce; and improving both communications and administration. This built on a new approach first introduced in 2008 which aimed to create closer collaboration between CESO and its partners to support longer term relationships and better meet partners' needs. A critical element of this strategy was a renewed emphasis on MEL to bridge gaps between different areas of work.

To develop a revised MEL strategy, CESO's Evaluations Department brought together key staff from the international programme to determine which areas of M&E should be prioritized. A participatory approach was taken using SAS^2 dialogue tools to identify priorities and concerns in a manner that was sensitive to variations in language, levels of seniority, and M&E needs. This initial series of meetings identified key challenges, such as delays in providing feedback to stakeholders and inconsistent sharing of key lessons and best practices. Canadian staff from other locations were soon involved in the consultations to share their experiences and needs. As the review proceeded and the M&E system was developed, 60 volunteers and partners were brought into the dialogue to refine and develop M&E tools.

Throughout this process, SAS^2 dialogue techniques provided a participatory framework to capture tacit and previously unarticulated knowledge that could then be made explicit and analysed systematically. Programme staff, volunteers, and partners were actively involved in the process to provide accountability and ownership of the framework. The revised MEL framework created new reporting forms that combined staff and client feedback to reduce paperwork and provide a vehicle for participatory evaluations, when required. Conversation guides were developed to replace written reports where appropriate, which allowed staff to gather feedback over the phone or in person to combine communications and reporting activities. Dissemination of final evaluations was made a key priority to ensure that volunteers and partners receive pertinent information in a timely manner.

CESO's systematic and brick-by-brick approach to mainstreaming evaluations helped the organization confront two key challenges: competing beneficiary and donor demands, and documenting and using knowledge. The first challenge is related to the specific project information required for reporting back to major donors. This can isolate evaluations from programme operations and planning because M&E becomes reactive to donor demands and thereby neglects to document knowledge (successes, lessons, and best practices) for future planning. CESO's revised framework captures not just outputs, but also outcomes that inform planning and are used to provide additional evidence of innovation and efficiency to donors. The second challenge is due to the large volume of information and data which is produced through projects and provided by volunteers and partners. These data include informal feedback, stories of progress and success, and formal feedback. CESO ensured that processes strategically collected and transformed the data into useable knowledge for partners and strategic planning.

CESO's initiative shows that targeted and strategic M&E can mediate between these competing needs by responding to the financial, communications, and planning needs of partners while creating an improved data collection process at the same time.

Case 3: Sustainable Cities International

SCI is a small civil society organization based in Vancouver, British Columbia. It was founded in 1993 to connect Canadian experts in sound city planning to their private, public, civil society, and academic peers around the world. Its staff support urban growth management, urban infrastructure, poverty reduction, resource efficiency, and renewable energy. In 2003, SCI launched the Sustainable Cities Network to build capacity for long-range urban sustainability planning and implementation. This peer-to-peer platform was driven by the learning needs of its members, and has become the major facet of SCI's operations. It now includes 40 cities in Africa, Asia, Latin America and the Caribbean, and North America. This network serves as a repository which can be drawn on to implement projects and identify expertise.

As a small organization, SCI depends on its partners and associates to provide targeted and timely interventions and knowledge transfer. While a small staff size has the advantage of flexibility, small CSOs engaged in international development can be particularly affected by shifts in public policy and priorities. In light of this and a more competitive external environment for sources of funding, SCI engaged in a strategic reorientation to diversify its revenue base. This was deemed necessary due to changes in the CIDA/DFATD Partnerships for Development Branch, which disproportionately affected small and medium-sized CSOs (Tomlinson, 2016).

A strategic planning exercise, followed by working groups of staff and board members, helped SCI to refine its business model. The revised model prioritized moving away from programmes dependent on public funding by expanding fee-for-service components, building relationships with academics, foundations, and the corporate sector, and reducing overhead. This multi-faceted strategy was supported by a number of initiatives that would better position SCI to deal with funding fluctuations and access new opportunities for research and advocacy.

To diversify the organization's revenue base, the organization added fee-for-service components to its traditional offerings. These included municipal leadership training, infrastructure costs, and urban growth management consulting. To build relationships with academics and others, SCI assigned a higher priority to research by beginning an affiliated researcher programme and taking part in university colloquia, while continuing outreach to large foundations and the corporate sector. To reduce operational expenses, SCI moved from a traditional office environment to a shared non-profit workspace (HiVE Vancouver) with access to essential infrastructure such as business equipment, internet, and a receptionist. SCI enjoys an academic affiliation with the Sustainable Community Development Centre of Simon Fraser University in Vancouver.

While SCI continues to face challenges in accessing core funding for operational expenses, its small staff size meant it was flexible enough to quickly react to new realities by moving to a shared workspace and reorienting its business strategy. This has enabled SCI to continue doing its core work while also launching the SCI Energy Lab in 2013, initially funded in part by Siemens Canada, the Alberta Real Estate Foundation, and National Resources Canada. SCI's network of 10 cities addresses the barriers that prevent the large-scale uptake of renewable energy technology, and it is expected to help create a business case for cross-sectoral approaches to sustainable energy development.

Case 4: Genre en Pratique, a community of practice

Genre en Pratique is a CoP established in 2010 as an informal working group after the Montreal 'Conference on women's rights and gender equality in Canadian cooperation' (AQOCI, 2013). There, participants reflected on the challenges of integrating gender equality into their own programmes and organizations. While the conference was successful, it became apparent that there was a sense of isolation and a need for continued exchange. This led to a recognition that working together on the institutionalization of gender equality might be more effective in confronting this complex issue, which touches on an organization's culture, partners, projects, and staff attitudes.

AQOCI was approached by several conference participants to convene and coordinate an informal working group. While AQOCI was unable to dedicate additional financial resources to the topic, it provided some staff time and identified a graduate student intern in support of the working group. Over the following year, the group met informally to share experiences and thoughts on institutionalizing gender equality. Learning spaces are critical to innovation (Hayman et al., 2016) and this working group created a space in which practitioners could think about shared challenges and overcome them. Its members saw a further opportunity to deepen their work on gender by examining, sharing, and creating tools and strategies to advance gender equality.

However, there were two challenges to formalizing their partnership. At the institutional level, a sense of competition impeded interorganizational knowledge sharing. In a competitive funding environment, the institutions involved were wary of engaging in deeper knowledge sharing. Also, staff were cautious of sharing too much information that had not been approved by senior management for external audiences. The second challenge, closely related to the first, is that of a general dearth of dedicated resources for reflection and learning in the development sector. Funding for NGOs tends to focus on outputs and work in the field. With strict project lifecycles and a constant pressure to generate results, it can be difficult for organizations to prioritize and value reflection. As such, there is limited funding or paid staff time for learning activities.

To address these challenges, the working group developed a formal strategy to ensure clear organizational commitment to the CoP and to maximize use of limited resources and time. They proposed an environment in which staff representatives from each organization would work collectively to reflect on, consolidate, and develop knowledge on gender. The members' organizations were asked to ensure their commitment to devoting staff time to a formal CoP. To gather additional resources, the members wrote a proposal for funding that formalized their roles and responsibilities and committed them to formal outputs and reports to be disseminated within their own organizations and with others in the development community. Both these approaches ensured managerial commitment and leveraged limited resources and capacity to come together to work on shared challenges.

The funding proposal was successful and AQOCI assumed coordinating responsibilities. The success of the application increased the confidence of members, attracted institutional support, enabled training by university and other experts, and provided incentives to create and share written outputs. While the group would likely have continued operating on an informal basis, funding was critical to having a deeper impact.

The formalized learning strategy adopted by the group combined building knowledge and skills, providing peer support, and carrying out innovative and experimental practice. Individual institutional representatives benefit from these, but the group has created processes to transfer knowledge and lessons back to members' organizations and partners. The documents and reports created are also made available to the public through AQOCI's website. Short- and long-term feedback loops were built into the process through informal feedback, participatory mechanisms, and regular evaluations and self-assessments. These are used to adjust activities and strategies to ensure members' needs are being addressed and that learning occurs at the individual, institutional, and partner levels.

To address changing needs, the CoP revised its strategy to create small working groups to concentrate on shared institutional challenges, such as gender policies and committees. This was a new point of departure to create concrete initiatives within organizations, with the support of the CoP.

Language barriers provided some challenges to disseminating outputs (training kits, documents, etc.) as some documents were unilingual and not available in French, English, or Spanish. These were translated and shared as needed by CoP members. Connecting with academics working in gender was difficult due to different research rhythms, priorities, and networks. The CoP has attempted to bridge the gap between researchers and practitioners; however, it still has to figure out how to effectively identify, connect, and partner with researchers.

The CoP made important contributions to individual, team, and institutional learning. The dedicated and committed membership upon which the CoP draws expertise and experience, outside expertise the group has been able to access, effective participatory coordination, and the creation of documentation have enabled the CoP to assess the needs of members, to respond to specific needs, and to transmit knowledge beyond the individual CoP members. At the institutional level, the group has developed indicators which member organizations can use to measure their progress on the institutionalization of gender equality: at least nine members have re-evaluated and invigorated their organizational approaches to gender equality, four have created gender committees to involve their co-workers in the subject, two have integrated lessons from the CoP into their most recent funding proposals, three others have integrated gender equality into their M&E frameworks, and five have developed a toolkit for MEL from gender-sensitive programmes. The members have supported their partners in integrating gender-sensitive questions into their projects and increased exchange and conversation on gender issues. A training kit for international organizations was created along with five technical manuals on gender equality.

Cross - case analysis – why, what, how, and for

OL and improvement is a broad topic. However, the approaches to learning initiatives examined in this chapter – a KM strategy, a new MEL framework, organizational refocusing, and a CoP – share common strategic elements. While some NGOs were dealing with growth, others with downsizing, all wanted to increase the capacity of their staff and the efficiency of their field interventions. There are key ingredients to the learning strategies CCSOs have been implementing or improving. No initiative – whether it best fits the ideal-type of conceptual, content-based, applied, or process-oriented – was conducted in isolation from other aspects of the organization. A conceptual understanding of why an organization exists (its mission) inform what data is collected, which in turn influences which applied KMSs are used to collect data. Organizational processes and structures inform how captured data is turned into knowledge that can be used for improving field activities and may also inform visions, missions, strategy, and decisions. This virtuous circle does not always occur, and is certainly not the only manner in which knowledge flows within organizations. Exogenous and endogenous factors affect at which levels of the organization decisions are made and how they inform strategic thinking and knowledge capture.

All four cases were compared to distil commonalities between these strategies and organizations to identify elements required for effective learning strategies, planning, and processes at the HQ level that support fieldwork and directions. The following analysis of the cases illustrates that CCSOs choose strategies that secure senior management and staff support, that balance internal needs with external demands, that design purposeful data-collection systems, that apply knowledge to decision-making, and that maximize the use of internal and network capacity. A final item, interorganizational learning, is also analysed in the context of these four case studies.

Identifying internal needs. Each organization took a different path to improve its learning strategy, based on its mission and partners. The four cases show how learning strategies are not one-size-fits-all, but require a targeted identification of areas where there is a need to improve organizational directions and/ or fieldwork in the future. How these areas can be improved requires an assessment of constraints (financial, human, political, funder requirements, volume of data, knowledge silos) and opportunities (funder flexibility, internal capacity, support from partners, size). All the organizations studied used a variety of methods to identify internal needs through feedback loops, which include informal pathways, face-to-face interaction, and annual climate surveys of staff. Larger organizations tend to require more formal pathways to ensure that staff input on work plans, processes, and strategies do inform management practices.

CAWST recognized that as its organization grew, face-to-face physical learning approaches were being stretched to their limit by finances and geography. It chose to complement its face-to-face iterative learning with a virtual platform that could help capture tacit and experiential knowledge to make it explicit. CESO initiated an organization-wide review which led to a new strategic and operational plan that focused efforts on six pillars, one of which was programme planning, delivery, evaluation, and reflection. This focus on M&E was designed to help CESO document, manage, and use large volumes of documentation.

The identification of internal needs and the opportunity to address these can also come from external sources. The Genre en Pratique CoP evolved from an AQOCI-led conference at which delegates realized they could support gender equality within their organizations and with their partners by collaborating with one another. Facing an increasingly competitive and challenging funding environment, SCI moved to broaden its revenue base by refocusing its business model. While there is certainly a difference between internal and external motivations for learning, planning for both is a sign of an agile and adaptive organization that is able to take advantage of emerging trends and opportunities.

Identifying partner needs. The case studies show that successful learning initiatives go beyond identifying internal needs to involve partners and stakeholders. This can be a challenge because stakeholders may have priorities that do not include reporting, may be reticent/unable to provide sensitive or confidential information, and may have multiple donors. However, successfully identifying and taking into account partners' and beneficiaries' needs and capacities can lead to mutual strengthening. Engaging with them in a conversation about what they are reporting, how they report it, and what guidelines they have in place can help identify reporting synergies.

To address these challenges, CESO and CAWST engaged their partners with participatory and iterative approaches to harmonize reporting and develop key indicators for organizational planning, learning, and accountability. CAWST, for example, examines what information it needs internally to improve performance and provide evidence. It then integrates the reporting requirements of funders and donors within its existing framework so that additional reporting is kept to a minimum. If the requirements of particular donors are burdensome or are not useful to CAWST or its partners, it may simply turn funding down.

CESO has moved towards one standard of RBM+ reporting across its organization that accounts for financial reporting requirements while satisfying learning requirements. Close and participatory engagement with partners and beneficiaries helped identify their respective needs and examine areas and outcomes not included in its previous evaluation approach. The new system has enabled CESO to use its resources effectively and, in collaboration with partners, identify information which is relevant to demonstrating the achievement of programme goals.

As Genre en Pratique began its second year, the members recognized that they were not achieving the institutional impacts that they had anticipated. They have since revised their strategy to create smaller working groups to concentrate on shared institutional needs and ensure that concrete initiatives take place within the organizations supported by the CoP.

Cultivating cultures of learning. Output-driven workloads and project lifecycles can impede this. Further, there can be a powerful emotional incentive to consciously or unconsciously suppress talk of 'failure' or learning from errors, as these can be associated with failing to make a positive impact on the lives of beneficiaries. Organizational norms can impede or encourage this, and the cases show that organizations are trying to reframe how they think about failure and put it into a more positive light to inform projects, processes, and plans. The CCSOs examined sought to create and nurture cultures of adaptation and learning by using incentives and rewarding initiative. This required dedicated and passionate staff who think critically about the work they do, as well as senior management and board commitment to OL initiatives, participatory planning that makes use of staff skills, and processes that optimize the flow and development of knowledge.

Securing senior management and staff support. To move learning and knowledge initiatives toward the centre of operations and processes, the organizations studied secured senior management and staff support. While two cases were initiatives by senior management (SCI and CESO) and the other two (CAWST and Genre en Pratique) were initiatives by staff, they all strove to include multiple levels of the organization to accomplish their goals. This is not to say that major lessons cannot occur at the individual level, but rather creating and involving teams accesses institutional expertise, breaks down silos, and creates the critical mass needed for organizational change. When space and time is created for knowledge sharing, and when change to knowledge processes and daily tasks are beneficial, staff come to see OL as part of their duties. Harmonization and alignment of priorities at the staff, management, and board levels allow learning initiatives to extend beyond the individual to the organizational.

The case studies imply that learning directions initiated by upper management must seek conceptual changes from staff to secure ownership and positive attitudes towards changing work processes and procedures. CESO's M&E teams worked hard to proceed with a participatory process to ensure that staff recognized the benefits of a revised evaluation strategy. This work is ongoing, and management engages employees through M&E training and opportunities to refine MEL processes. SCI's small size aided organizational change; staff already worked closely and recognized the need to rapidly alter their strategy and business model. Behavioural changes such as the reallocation of resources can be quickly initiated by management, but conceptual changes require ongoing commitment and course correction to ensure that staff needs are being met.

The opposite challenge is apparent in those cases initiated by staff. CAWST and Genre en Pratique had to secure senior management commitment to foster behavioural changes. CAWST staff proposed the allocation of human and financial resources towards a revised ICT system. Members of Genre en Pratique secured written commitments to interorganizational knowledge sharing, including institutional uptake and human capital to attend meetings and create documentation. In both cases, staff secured senior management support by documenting organizational needs, the purpose of the action, and the benefits to the organizations. Each secured conceptual changes of staff by proceeding in a participatory manner and assessing if staff were willing and able to contribute.

Understanding and challenging donor requirements. The literature review, survey, and subsequent interviews found that using reporting requirements for OL can be challenging for CCSOs. LFA and RBM accountability systems do not necessarily help organizations learn from their work, nor provide useful and timely feedback to partners. Reporting on political activity and finances for not-for-profit purposes is an additional requirement that CCSOs must often fulfil.

The cases of CAWST and CESO show that M&E systems can be designed to meet donor requirements while supporting OL. In both cases, staff developed key indicators that suited the LFA and RBM requirements of donors, supported the organizations' internal knowledge needs, and could be used to provide feedback to partners in the field. They did so by moving beyond a particular funder's needs towards setting their own standards for knowledge and creating programmatic categories that apply across all their contracts.

This was confirmed by interviews with organizations that were not part of a case study. These organizations indicated that strategies for designing useful and minimally burdensome reporting standards are: (a) to have key organizational indicators, (b) to communicate the utility of these frameworks to partners and build their reporting capacity, and (c) to be flexible in measuring indicators. Additional factors that aided organizations in reporting were to have dedicated evaluation staff, experience with LFA and RBM systems, and consistent donor agency liaisons.

Maximizing the use of internal and network capacity. Some organizations have the in-house capacity to proceed with their plans in isolation. CAWST had the expertise and resources to develop a full KMS itself, but had to re-organize staff roles to allow an employee the time to lead the development of the KM platform. This situation tends to be the exception rather than the rule. Most learning initiatives benefit from outside expertise. CCSOs can use their internal and network capacity to minimize constraints and their use of resources. Not all CCSOs have the budgets for external expertise, nor do they necessarily need or require it when engaging in learning initiatives. Thus, these four learning initiatives used wider networks to minimize the use of costly, and potentially inefficient, external consultants.

While CESO dedicated members of its evaluation staff to its initiative, it was also part of a CoP which greatly accelerated its project and provided opportunities for interorganizational learning. SCI had the support of its member organizations and board of directors. Genre en Pratique was the clearest example of leveraging network capacity and the benefits of interorganizational learning. Interviews confirmed that larger aggregates of CCSOs, such as provincial councils, provide crucial venues for face-to-face knowledge sharing. These directly connect organizations on thematic or sectoral issues (such as CCIC's working groups), but also indirectly stimulate conversations and build informal relationships.

Designing and using purposeful data-collection systems. The survey found that CSOs working in international development have difficulty in documenting, managing, and applying knowledge. This is even more pronounced for tacit or experiential knowledge which can require socialization and iterative, face-to-face conversations. The organizations under study moved towards KMSs that capture and share these lessons and recognized that capturing raw data is not enough. Data must be used and incorporated within formal and informal learning pathways to inform organizational directions, planning, and fieldwork.

Strategies for this include both informal conversations, written reports, virtual KMSs, and face-to-face knowledge-sharing activities. Depending on their needs, as well as those of their beneficiaries/partners, CCSOs may prioritize formalized knowledge capture and analysis or may choose to share experiential knowledge through more conversational aids, such as structured webinars. The choice between written reports or more conversational means is based on perceived return on investment, but also general appetite for networking and face-to-face learning opportunities.

The cases show that indiscriminate data capture does not inform OL, as it causes information overload. To be effective, manageable, and applicable to OL, data capture must be purposive and targeted towards the needs of an organization, as well as its donors and partners. The four organizations chose data capture strategies that ask pertinent questions, engage partners and beneficiaries in analysis, and share documented knowledge with relevant internal and external stakeholders, including the public.

Applying information to decision-making processes. To help data inform decision-making, the organizations studied examined their internal formal and informal knowledge pathways. This helped them understand their own operations and decision-making processes to improve upon them. This allowed the organizations to design project- and organization-level strategies to transform information into useful knowledge. The Genre en Pratique CoP dedicated time to clarifying roles and responsibilities, and formed a coordinating committee that would balance member needs and interests. Similarly, SCI created small working groups of staff and board members to draft a new business model. These smaller groups worked closely together to ensure that institutional knowledge would inform the organization's renewed strategic direction.

CAWST integrated aspects of its KM into an ICT system. This formalized data capture and provided a central repository for knowledge and innovations. CESO's MEL system allowed staff to flag cases and stories for communications, planning, and inquiry so they are able to inform future directions. Both organizations put an emphasis on communicating results and feedback to stakeholders in a timely manner to strengthen relationships and improve fieldwork.

As these organizations moved forward, they built short- and long-term feedback loops into their projects and programmes to receive regular updates on how activities were reinforcing their ultimate objectives. These processes reinforced and validated plans, but also resulted in the opportunity to introduce course corrections and recognize why deficiencies occurred. The organizations did not look at these deficiencies as failures, but as opportunities to learn and revise processes to ensure they would not repeat them. Incremental initiatives allowed them the time to better understand how these would contribute to or constrain their learning, while giving better control over financial, human, and time constraints.

Interorganizational knowledge sharing. The case studies and further interviews helped determine the extent of sharing with other Canadian organizations working in the development sector. All organizations engaged in interorganizational knowledge sharing, primarily with their partners in the developing world. Within Canada, knowledge sharing typically happens through virtual networks, newsletters, and websites. There is some demand-driven knowledge sharing when organizations contact one another on sectoral themes. While these methods of sharing knowledge are important, surveys and informants noted that presentations, conversations, and conferences are the most important means of creating dialogue and sharing results. The individuals interviewed appreciated the rich debate and deeper learning that face-to-face meetings provide; these are an opportunity for reflecting, thinking, and coming to a common ground in a manner that cannot be achieved through reading a written report or a newsletter.

All the organizations studied or contacted as part of follow-up interviews to the survey indicated that there are few dedicated sources of funding for face-to-face dialogue, which results in few opportunities to connect. Further, council activities often occur in major cities, leaving rural organizations or those based in small cities with few options to come together. Knowledge sharing thus remains within the narrower networks that NGOs cultivate, typically along historical ties or sectoral links. However, the British Columbia Council for International Cooperation (BCCIC) model of four sub-provincial networks, convened around universities, has enabled membership to engage with one another, academics, and the public. This model could be duplicated elsewhere. The Atlantic Council for International Cooperation rotates its annual general meeting and symposium between the Atlantic provinces to provide equivalent opportunities.

Key findings and recommendations

Several key findings and recommendations can be drawn from the literature review, two surveys, and case analyses in this chapter. The study explored how CCSOs learn from their activities, the means by which lessons are documented and shared, and how these lessons inform projects, programmes, and organizational strategies.

What are CCSOs' recent experiences with learning initiatives?

In recent years, CCSO learning initiatives have been prompted by reactions to the unpredictability of public funding for development. While this makes prioritizing learning difficult, it also pushes organizations to re-examine what they are doing and rigorously document the impacts of their work. As King et al. (2016) point out, this is becoming critical to CSOs' reinvention. It seems that CCSOs had previously been complacent with learning initiatives as their government funding was more predictable. This removed incentives for learning, working together, and sharing knowledge. Now that government funding is less consistent, organizations must show the value of their projects and programmes, and work together to share resources on important issues.

However, these pressing exogenous factors have resulted in few endogenous learning initiatives. A lack of funding has pushed learning to the margins of CCSO activities. As a result, organizations concentrate their learning along existing processes and systems (such as evaluation or KM) or sectors. Furthermore, beyond the two IDRC-supported CoPs noted in the case studies, there seem to be few activities for innovative and concentrated interorganizational learning.

Particular areas that CCSOs are learning about are the implementation of the Istanbul Principles (supported by CCIC and the regional councils), the development of key performance indicators to minimize the burden of M&E, the diversification of funding, and working with the private sector. On some of these issues there is interorganizational learning, but this is often predicated on personal knowledge of others or active membership in regional councils. For other issues, such as working with the private sector, CCSOs are still very much working in isolation.

What and how do organizations learn from these exercises?

CCSOs are interested in understanding how other organizations work, the challenges they face, and how some may have overcome them. Interviews indicated that staff glean the richest information from face-to-face conversations. Though these lessons are often undocumented, they inform projects and programmes because staff are able to apply them directly to their work. When such lessons are documented, they can more easily feed back into projects, programmes, and strategies because they provide a written record for colleagues who were unable to attend. This requires purposeful documentation that relates to key areas of interest to the organization.

To learn from their projects, CCSOs use a variety of means including RBM frameworks, travel reports, participatory action research, outcome mapping, and reports or documents from partners. These are often used in conjunction, not in isolation, to gain a holistic understanding of the projects they are supporting. Smaller CSOs may be required to use LFA systems, but may lack the capacity to actively learn from them. To balance this, they use outcome mapping and participatory research to better understand the impacts they are having, and what methods or activities have helped them reach their objectives. Larger organizations, which may have dedicated evaluations staff, often find LFA to be sufficient for their own learning requirements, though this is often used in conjunction with travel reports and documentation from partners.

Regional, national, and international councils or networks can play a significant role in convening and supporting interorganizational learning activities. These include working groups on regional or sectoral issues and the Istanbul Principles, as well as other research- and policy-related topics. Council activities can encourage member organizations to share their successes and lessons from both field research and interventions, so that organizations do not duplicate previous work and are able to apply new ways of addressing their goals of development and social change.

From these activities, organizations learn about the Canadian development landscape, including the challenges faced by other organizations, innovative activities or projects, and emerging trends.

How do CCSOs apply these lessons to their directions and operations?

CCSOs apply lessons to their directions and operations in a number of ways. First, by documenting them they provide a means through which knowledge can inform programmes and organizational strategies. Suitable organization-wide processes ensure that lessons are drawn from across the organization. Data thus transformed into knowledge enables organizations to understand their development outcomes and to target future activities.

To inform directions and operations, it is helpful for CCSOs to build feedback loops into their projects and programmes for regular updates on how activities are supporting corporate and programme-level objectives. These processes reinforce and validate plans, but also provide the opportunity to introduce course corrections and identify deficiencies. To push learning from the margins towards the centre, organizations secure senior management and staff support to ensure that lessons are documented and that processes are followed. Involving multiple levels of the organization through iterative or participatory processes can help organizations access institutional expertise to ensure effective operations and inform strategic directions.

What challenges and opportunities do CCSOs face?

CCSOs face significant challenges in learning and improvement. However, there are also opportunities for internal and interorganizational learning. Challenges include a lack of resources, a pressure to lower administrative costs, an adrenaline culture that prioritizes reporting rather than reflection, and LFA systems that do not prioritize learning. Surveys and interviews indicated that CCSOs aim to diversify away from CIDA/DFATD (now GAC) funding to finance their core activities and salaries and benefits.

A lack of resources was mentioned by nearly every organization as a serious constraint. This was not just for learning, but for their work in general. CCIC and Aidwatch Canada's analysis of *Budget 2013* notes that 'general funding for civil society organizations (CSOs) and specific funding for the volunteer-sending CSOs has been put on hold for the past two years, and new projects approved for specific purposes have been significantly delayed' (CCIC and Aidwatch, 2013). The Inter-Council Network found that small and medium-sized organizations were marginalized following the government's implementation of an exclusive call-for-proposal funding mechanism (Tomlinson, 2016).

The Inter-Council Network, provincial council, and CCIC networks were actively engaged in the 2016 International Assistance Review. CCSOs and their wider networks can work together to demonstrate their value, innovation, and effectiveness. Surveys and interviews indicated increasing pressure for CCSOs to lower their administrative budgets. However, this may reduce opportunities and resources for organizational and interorganizational learning. Moreover, uncertainty about what constitutes administration can challenge organizations. Supporting the administrative budgets of partners may constitute important capacity building, but cannot necessarily be documented as such. Learning and a budget to do so are part and parcel of an effective organization, but it is often unfunded or comes out of the administration budget.

CSOs often have an adrenaline culture, which is created partially by logical framework approaches and RBM systems for project planning and reporting. These can create a constant pressure to generate results where outputs might be seen as the major, or only, measure of success in the field. Within project lifecycles, incentives for reflection and learning can be lost or there may not be time to implement changes. There can also be a fear of repercussions if negative or critical outcomes were to emerge from learning initiatives. These have implications for funding and for credibility, and can prevent organizations from sharing openly.

This said, CCSOs are highly interested in and motivated to make LFA and RBM systems work for their own learning and that of their partners. This requires liaising with donors and working closely with staff and partners to develop targeted learning systems. Small organizations may not have dedicated staff with expertise in organization-wide M&E systems. Medium and large organizations may have a variety of funders and partners with different reporting requirements. However, M&E can be a catalyst for project-based and OL because it relates to fieldwork and systematic knowledge capture. There is an opportunity for CCSOs to work together on revised MEL systems that can highlight their work and successes. This might continue the work that CCIC as well as the Bridging Gaps CoP have begun, or it might look at revised systems. Looking ahead, it will be important to work with and share the results of any such initiatives with government, private donors, and the public.

Other opportunities for CCSOs include continuing to create opportunities to learn about critical issues together to bridge internal gaps in expertise.

These might include sharing experiences of working with the private sector, developing codes of conduct for doing so, sharing experiences and challenges of collaboration with academia, developing KM platforms, and strategies for diversifying funding. Regional councils provide an important opportunity and catalyst for such initiatives by bringing CCSOs together on a range of topics.

To what extent do they share these lessons with wider communities?

The research showed that CCSOs tend to share with their counterparts in Canada by uploading documents to their websites, publishing newsletters or organizational updates, and meeting face to face at conferences/forums. Personal or professional relationships are a core means of sharing lessons and knowledge. Knowledge sharing thus remains within the narrower networks that NGOs themselves have cultivated, typically along historical ties or sectoral links.

The CCSOs studied prioritize communicating with their partners in the developing world, but do engage frequently with their Canadian counterparts. However, there is likely room for greater sharing and knowledge of one another's work. Most organizations indicated that there is little funding available for face-to-face dialogue, which results in few opportunities to connect. Dedicated government funding for interorganizational learning activities is desired, but there are few mechanisms for this.

How do regional councils support these activities?

Regional councils are a key stimulus of OL. For example, each has a particular area of expertise, which they have expanded on through the Inter-Council Network's Global Hive Toolkit (Global Hive, 2016).[2] They actively support their memberships in these areas, and through the Inter-council Network support of CCSOs across all of Canada. They are a crucial venue for CSOs for networking, collaboration, and interorganizational learning on issues, such as codes of conduct, the Istanbul Principles, and public engagement. The councils also document issues of importance to CSOs and emerging trends while providing training and support to organizations.

Some of the CCSOs studied are members of provincial councils, but do not actively participate in council events. Several cited the fact that regional councils typically support smaller and recently established organizations. Others perceived CCIC as a coalition composed of large national CSOs that did not offer opportunities tailored to small and medium-sized CSOs. Council activities may not closely relate to their particular sectors or challenges; more topical issues could be interesting subjects for discussion. Nevertheless, these organizations used the resources, tools, and networks provided by regional councils and CCIC.

Recommendations

The findings of this study are pertinent to CCSOs, regional councils, and donor organizations. Several key recommendations, which are not necessarily distinct, can be made for each group. CCSOs are seen by some as 'boutique organizations': they do important and effective work, but they lack the capacity to scale up their work and share innovations. While this is not a fair characterization of small and medium-sized organizations as a whole (Tomlinson, 2016), it is clear that organizational and interorganizational learning is a challenge for small, medium-sized, and large organizations. There is a clear role for donor organizations to increase opportunities for interorganizational learning in support of development effectiveness and innovation. CCSOs have a role to play in publicizing their ongoing knowledge creation and innovative solutions with each other, councils, and the public.

Recommendations for CCSOs. CCSOs should attempt to bring learning to the centre of their work, rather than leaving it at the margins. This can be difficult due to underfunding and an inability to consistently access official development funding, but it should be a priority of organizations that wish to be innovative, effective knowledge creators and brokers. With this said, CCSOs should be realistic about what they aim to achieve with learning initiatives, and target the most crucial aspects of their organizations where inefficiencies and knowledge breakdowns occur. When contemplating organizational improvement, CCSOs must think about what needs to be strengthened – reporting, internal processes, strategy, or fieldwork, for example. They might ask themselves which elements are missing, where are lags occurring, and where transactional costs are highest. Engaging staff when identifying these areas is crucial, and may require rebalancing work priorities. M&E seems to be a critical nexus of knowledge creation and sharing, and CCSOs could improve their M&E work by ensuring that reporting is limited to the most pertinent outcomes and results. Smaller organizations might engage in capacity building with their in-country partners so that they are able to fulfil most reporting requirements.

Taking time for reflection is critical. Annual retreats or days away from typical work provide the opportunity to reflect on work processes, projects, and emerging issues. These also provide a moment when experiential knowledge can be transferred through socialization, and then systematically recorded for planning purposes. Knowledge can be produced all along, not just at the end of the project lifecycle in project completion reports or evaluations. This can allow organizations to highlight how their approaches succeed, how they have been improved, and may aid in communicating field activities to others.

CCSOs should strive to actively share their knowledge, either through regional councils or their wider networks. They should ask themselves if their knowledge is pertinent, and if it has been shared with others. This allows the opportunity to make connections for future collaboration and knowledge sharing, which can strengthen their work and that of others. Both the Genre en Pratique and Bridging Gaps CoPs began as informal and unfunded working groups of organizations interested in gender and M&E. These provide interesting models for working together informally on timely issues and then seeking out funding once the initial exemplar has proven useful.

Recommendations for regional councils. Regional councils support a diverse membership, and should continue to carefully consider the needs of members and who they aim to support, be they newly founded, established, or large. They should ask themselves if they provide a range of activities that can keep their memberships engaged and actively sharing with one another. For organizations in large provinces, they might follow the example of BCCIC, which has convened four sub-provincial councils at colleges and universities to better support its geographically distant members. They might also consider which staff they target – is it programme officers or upper management – as some CCSO staff are not aware of council activities and how these might contribute to their work.

Councils might also want to consider systematically documenting the impact of their networks on professionals, institutions, and overall development outcomes. This was a challenge noted by 56 per cent of councils, and they might come together to better understand how these networks contribute to organizational and collective objectives.

The Inter-Council Network's Global Hive initiative is to be commended, and councils could continue supporting targeted interventions on topical issues. The Genre en Pratique CoP demonstrates how councils can provide expertise and coordination for these activities. CIDA once supported thematic networks that provided opportunities to share and create knowledge, but interviews indicated that the former DFATD was less actively supporting broader opportunities to learn, and instead supporting issue-based networks such as the Maternal, Newborn, and Child Health Network. The regional councils may be able to provide broader opportunities for thematic learning, depending on their capacity to do so.

Recommendations for donors. The study found that exogenous factors often provide critical motivation for CCSO learning. Some donor accountability mechanisms have pushed CCSOs to revise their M&E strategy so that they can report to donors, while also enabling themselves and their partners to learn from the work they do. This is often not the case. Donors occupy a position of great power, and with this should come a responsibility to ensure that reporting improves and contributes to CCSOs' work. They should strive to ensure consistency in staff liaisons with CCSOs to ensure that their reporting needs and requirements do not shift, as this increases CCSOs' administrative burden significantly.

Donors ought to ensure that there is time for reflection and learning after project lifecycles conclude. This might entail providing funding for CCSOs to meet with partners and other stakeholders to reflect on impacts and on what did and did not work. Donors can also ensure that these lessons are recorded and shared so they can inform future projects and strategies. They might also consider providing greater funding for CCSOs to come together for discrete learning activities, events, and conferences. This can also provide an impetus for CCSOs to document and share knowledge with one another. CCSOs yearn to learn from one another, but are stretched for time and resources. Donors can help satisfy this need, while supporting development effectiveness and innovation.

Finally, donor organizations might consider adjusting their reporting requirements to the needs and capacities of the organizations they support. Interviews indicated that small organizations are held to the same reporting and monitoring standards as large organizations. This prevents expansion, growth, and innovation as they are continually stretched by reporting requirements. Donors might consider, in conversation with these organizations, alternate means of holding smaller organizations to high standards.

GAC is to be commended for its 2016 International Assistance Review. Consultative processes like these enable CCSOs to contribute to Canada's development agenda. Such virtual and face-to-face interactions provide rich opportunities to engage with the government, but also with regional councils and development organizations and to share knowledge with one another. GAC, in particular, should provide specific funding tools that encourage innovation and OL, and support knowledge networks for CCSOs.

Notes

1. A concise table of RBM+ methodologies is available in Christie, 2008. For a study of the potentials and limitations of RBM+ methodologies see Christie, 2010.
2. This project brought together the regional councils on the following topics, with each taking the lead on one of the following themes: How Change Happens, Global Education, Integrating Gender Equality into Public Engagement, Monitoring and Evaluation, Partnerships and Collaboration for Public Engagement, Public Engagement Policy, and Youth-Based Public Engagement.

References

Association québécoise des Organismes de Coopération internationale (AQOCI) (2013) *Communauté de pratique (CDP)* <http://www.aqoci.qc.ca/?Communaute-de-pratique-CDP> [accessed 31 October 2016].

Argyris, C. (1999) *On Organizational Learning,* 2nd edn, Malden, MA and Oxford: Blackwell Business.

Bakewell, O., and Garbutt, A. (2005) *The Use and Abuse of the Logical Framework Approach,* Stockholm: SIDA.

Bhushan, A. (2013) 'Global Development Trends 2013: An Analysis of Data Available on the Canadian International Development Platform', Ottawa: North-South Institute.

Britton, B. (2005) *Organisational Learning in NGOs: Creating the motive, means and opportunity,* Oxford: INTRAC.

CAWST (Centre for Affordable Water and Sanitation Technology) (no date) *Household Water Treatment and Safe Storage (HWTS)* <https://www.hwts. info/> [accessed 30 October 2016].

CCIC (Canadian Council for International Cooperation) and Aidwatch Canada (2013) 'Budget 2013: Implications for Canadian ODA', Ottawa: CCIC.

Chernikova, E. (2010) 'Shoulder to shoulder or face to face? Canada's university–civil society collaborations on research and knowledge for international development', Ottawa: IDRC <https://idl-bnc.idrc.ca/dspace/handle/10625/46120> [accessed 29 July 2016].

Chevalier, J. and Buckles, D. (2008) *SAS² Social Analysis Systems: A Guide to Collaborative Inquiry and Social Engagement*, Ottawa: IDRC.

Christie, J. (2008) *Evaluation of Development Action – Why? of What? for Whom? The Challenges of Evaluation, as seen by some Canadian CSOs*, Ottawa: Canadian Council for International Co-operation <http://www.ccic.ca/_files/en/what_we_do/002_dev_effectiveness_2009_01_report_ccic_evaluation_review.pdf> [accessed 29 July 2016].

Christie, J. (2010) *Expanding the Evaluation Repertoire: Summary Observations on Four Case Studies in Evaluation Design*, Ottawa: Canadian Council for International Co-operation.

Couillard, J., Caron, S., and Riznic, J. (2009) 'The logical framework approach–millenium', *Project Management Journal* 40(4): 31–44 <http://dx.doi.org/10.1002/pmj.20117.

De Vet, J.P. and Schoots, J. (2016) 'The learning organisation: conditions of possibility in a feminist NGO', *Development in Practice* 26(1): 64–76. <http://dx.doi.org/10.1080/09614524.2016.1118017>.

Ferguson, J., Mchombu, K. and Cummings, S. (2008) *Management of knowledge for development: meta-review and scoping study*, IKM Working Paper 1, Bonn: European Association of Development Research and Training Institutes <http://wiki.ikmemergent.net/files/080421-ikm-working-paper-no1-meta-review-and-scoping-study-final.pdf> [accessed 29 July 2016].

Ferguson, J., Huysman, M., and Soekijad, M. (2010) 'Knowledge management in practice: pitfalls and potentials for development', *World Development* 38(12): 1797–810 <http://dx.doi.org/10.1016/j.worlddev.2010.05.004>.

Forsyth, C. and MacLachlan, M. (2009) 'Head office attitudes towards inter-organisational learning in Irish non-governmental organisations', *Knowledge Management for Development Journal* 5(1): 4–20 <http://dx.doi.org/10.1080/18716340902875860>.

Gall, E., Millot, G., and Neubauer, C. (2009) 'Participation of Civil Society Organizations in Research, Science, Technology and Civil Society', in *Research: Final report of Science Technology and Civil Society (STACS) Project*, Paris: Fondation Sciences Citoyennes.

Global Hive (2016) <www.globalhive.ca> [accessed 30 October 2016].

Guijt, I. (2004) *ALPS in Action: A Review of the Shifts in ActionAid towards a new Accountability, Learning and Planning System*, London: ActionAid <http://www.eldis.org/vfile/upload/1/document/0708/DOC21745.pdf> [accessed 29 July 2016].

Hayman, R., King, S., Narayanaswamy, L., and Kontinen, T. (2016) 'Conclusion: negotiating knowledge, evidence, learning and power', in R. Hayman (ed.),

Negotiating Knowledge: Evidence and Experience in Development NGOs, Rugby, UK: Practical Action Publishing.

Heidrich, P., Kindornay, S., and Blundell, M. (2013) *Economic Relations between Canada and Latin America and the Caribbean,* Ottawa and Caracas: The North-South Institute and the SELA Permanent Secretariat.

Hildreth, P. (2004) *Going Virtual: Distributed Communities in Practice*, Hershey, PA: Idea Group.

Hovland, I. and ODI (Overseas Development Institute) (2003) *Knowledge Management and Organisational Learning – An International Development Perspective: An annotated bibliography*, London: ODI.

King, S., Kontinen, T., Narayaswamy, L., and Hayman, R. (2016) 'Introduction: Why do NGOs need to negotiate knowledge?' in R. Hayman (ed.), *Negotiating Knowledge: Evidence and Experience in Development NGOs*, Rugby, UK: Practical Action Publishing.

Krohwinkel-Karlsson, A. (2007) *Knowledge and Learning in Aid Organizations. A literature review with suggestions for further studies*, SADEV Working Papers 1, Karlstad: SADEV.

Lewis, S.E. (2011) 'Forward', *Failure Report 2011,* Toronto: Engineers Without Borders Canada.

Open Forum for CSO Effectiveness (2011) 'The Siem Reap Consensus on The International Framework for CSO Effectiveness' <http://cso-effectiveness.org/-InternationalFramework-.html> [accessed 29 July 2016].

OECD (Organisation for Economic Co-operation and Development) (2009) *Civil Society and Aid Effectiveness: Findings, Recommendations and Good Practice*, Paris: OECD <http://dx.doi.org/10.1787/9789264056435-en>.

Senge, P. (1990) *The Fifth Discipline: The Art and Practice of the Learning Organization*, 1st edn New York: Doubleday/Currency.

Sartorius, R.F. (1991) 'The logical framework approach to project design and management', *Evaluation Practice* 12(2): 139–47 <http://dx.doi.org/10.1016/0886-1633(91)90005-I>.

Suzuki, N. (2004) *Inside NGOs: Managing conflicts between headquarters and the field offices in non-governmental organizations*, Rugby, UK: Practical Action Publishing.

Tomlinson, B. (2016) *Small and Medium-Sized Canadian Civil Society Organizations as Development Actors: A review of evidence*, report prepared for the Inter-Council Network, Ottawa: AidWatch Canada <http://aidwatchcanada.ca/wp-content/uploads/2016/07/ICNSMOStudy_Final_kg_Graphics_3.pdf> [accessed 15 September 2016].

Travers, S. (2011) *Canadian Civil Society Organizations Influencing Policy and Practice: The Role of Research*, Ottawa: IDRC <https://idl-bnc.idrc.ca/dspace/handle/10625/48923> [accessed 29 July 2016].

Whatley, B. (2013) 'Improved learning for greater effectiveness in development NGOs', *Development in Practice* 23(8): 963–76 <http://dx.doi.org/10.1080/09614524.2013.840563>.

Wenger, E. (2002) *Cultivating Communities of Practice: A Guide to Managing Knowledge*, Boston, MA: Harvard Business School Press.

World Bank (2013) *Civil Society Engagement: Review of Fiscal Years 2010–2013*, Washington, DC: The World Bank.

About the author

Eric Smith is Writer, Grants and Proposals, at Saint Francis Xavier University's Coady International Institute in Antigonish, Nova Scotia, Canada. Before joining Coady, Eric worked with Genuine Progress Index Atlantic, supporting youth learning initiatives in India. From 2013 to 2015, Eric worked with IDRC's Canadian Partnerships programme, and later its Fellowships and Awards programme. Eric holds a Master's in Political Science from Carleton University and a BHum in Humanities and Philosophy from Carleton University.

CHAPTER 6

Conclusion: Main findings, messages, and pending knowledge gaps

Luc J.A. Mougeot

Abstract

This collection makes a strong contribution to the conversation on the rising importance of knowledge management for civil society organizations in the new ecosystem for international development. Given an emphasis revived by Global North bilateral funders on North–South research partnerships, Putting Knowledge to Work *reignites the debate on donor–recipient power imbalances in such partnerships. Alternative funding partnerships are on the rise and deserve greater research attention. In Canada and other high-income countries, the sociopolitical context calls for more collaboration between practitioners and academia; this book offers a rare account of the impressive range of knowledge-centred collaborations at work between these two communities in a Global North country.*

Beyond individual, small-scale, punctual collaborations, it is difficult to see how synergies between these two communities can become more strategic, sustainable, and impactful in a more competitive ecosystem without their investing in structural innovations. Knowledge use may be central to influencing practices and policies in development contexts, but knowledge on how this actually works remains strikingly thin. This book explores strategies devised by non-governmental organizations (NGOs) to create, access, share, and apply knowledge to influence positive changes in practices and policies of stakeholders in the Global South. Finally, the book documents efforts by small and medium-sized development NGOs to improve their knowledge capture, organizational learning, and decision-making processes; challenges to more effective learning are highlighted. In Canada at least, the NGO community would benefit from stable and better-resourced structures to coordinate learning exercises and disseminate results widely.

Keywords: civil society organization, international development, knowledge, collaboration, influence, learning

The collected works in this book bring forward a number of new elements discovered to be happening in Canadian civil society organizations (CSOs),

http://dx.doi.org/10.3362/9781780449586.006

while confirming others found in different contexts. All these elements are important considerations for CSOs in developing more comprehensive approaches to managing knowledge and sustaining their relevance in the new ecosystem for international development. In addition, the collection brings forward its own contributions in the form of findings, messages, and some pending knowledge gaps.

Main findings

Central to defining what knowledge should be created or used, by whom and for which purpose, is the role of power, politics, and priorities wielded by those involved in donor–recipient partnerships. With recent evidence pointing to a persistent under-representation of recipient-country actors, and given the revived emphasis placed by Global North bilateral funders on North–South research partnerships, the chapter in this book by Bradley (2016) will re-ignite the debate on power imbalances in donor–recipient research partnerships in three ways. First, her study offered a unique review of experimentation on innovations from the first decade of this century by a couple of the more progressive and reflective OECD agencies that were trying to redress the donor–recipient power imbalance in such partnerships – the Dutch 'demand-driven' and the British 'excellence-focused' approaches. Second, Bradley scrutinized often-under-rated implications and obstacles in the way of more equitable Southern engagement in setting agendas pursued under such partnerships. Third, she explored first-hand Global South researchers' own motivations for entering into North–South partnerships, the obstacles that they face in agenda setting when doing so, and strategies used to ensure their concerns are met or to opt out. Such alternatives reflect a diversification of funding sources available to Global South researchers and organizations, as well as growing pressure for local control over agendas, noted in the introductory chapter (Mougeot, 2016) of this book. Through querying both donor agencies and their officials on one hand, and recipient organizations and their researchers on the other, Bradley submitted a rounded appreciation of the political economy at play in North–South development research partnerships.

In Canada and other OECD countries, the sociopolitical context calls for collaboration between civil society and academia to be more relevant and effective for positive change in international development. Chapter 3 (Chernikova, 2016) offered one of very few countrywide survey-based studies on knowledge-centred collaborations between development non-governmental organizations (NGOs) and research institutions in the Global North. This not only revealed that universities and civil society do work together in multiple ways, but also suggested that they have been trying to do so in a gradual and orderly fashion, and for good reasons; they should be supported in continuing to do so in a way that is respectful of their differences. Various ways in which universities and NGOs collaborate were identified and such relationships were qualified as potentially evolving from simple interactions to more formal partnerships. Cross-sectional data on the types of joint activities in which universities or NGOs are involved suggest that these vary in diversity from organization to organization. Still, overall casual and low-risk interactions are more frequent, while fewer NGOs have added to these other forms of collaboration that call for more sustained and comprehensive commitments.

Given the lack of more recent similar studies, Chernikova's findings remain the most accurate available, as they offer initial guidance for growing a rapprochement between academia and CSOs as advocated by donor governments in international cooperation for development. Data suggest that, when working together, universities and NGOs tend to proceed in a prudent way, developing mutual trust and only taking their relationship to the next level when this is perceived to be for mutual benefit. Moved by 'pracademic' or 'integrator' individuals, these collaborations sometimes blossom into fully fledged partnerships. However, we still know too little of how these partnerships develop and what incentives, if any, exist or should exist in either community to promote such multi-pronged partnerships. So, while the experiences reviewed offer guidance for growing the aforementioned rapprochement, advocated by donor governments, more research and incentives are needed to understand and expand current collaborations between these two communities into more powerful ones for development.

Knowledge use is central to influencing the practices and policies of a range of stakeholders in local development contexts. Yet, published learning on which knowledge is used and how it is used by Global North CSOs for this purpose remains strikingly thin. This collection also explores strategies devised by development NGOs to create, access, share, and apply knowledge to influence positive changes in the practices and policies of stakeholders in the Global South; particularly, how Global North-based NGOs join forces with their Global South counterparts to do so. It explains how Canadian NGOs decide to implement strategies in collaboration with Global South counterparts to fulfil their objectives, optimize resource use, and achieve greater impact. Chapter 4 (Travers, 2016) is exceptional in its reliance on both a nationwide survey and case studies of selected respondent CSOs to examine their use of research for influence, focusing quite originally on CSOs representative of a majority of those which lack strong research capacity.

Travers' case studies clearly illustrate how specific development NGOs go about using partnerships, research methodologies, and capacity building to impact local community or institutional practices, including partner CSOs' own programming and approach (including Women in Cities International on improving women's safety in public places; Rights & Democracy on reducing multiple forms of discrimination faced by indigenous women; private-sector inspired SOCODEVI on fomenting fine herbs value chains through the cooperative model; and Save the Children Canada's link with academia for building professional capacity in agencies engaged in protecting working children).

Given the pressure on CSOs to innovate better ways of delivering and conditioning research funding to cross-sector collaborations, changes may be in order for CSOs and funders to support innovation: there needs to be more exchange between domestic and internationally engaged organizations and a more explicit recognition and communication by CSOs to others, funders included, of the role of research throughout their strategy for change. For donors, there is a need for more support to learning collectives for innovation and to CSOs' research activities outside cross-sector collaborations as well. Travers' study tested a methodology which allows categorizing the sources of research used, linking the purposes of research use with the roles played by CSOs, and using case studies to verify hypotheses raised by survey data.

The collection finally documents efforts by small and medium-sized development NGOs to support field activities by improving their knowledge capture, organizational learning, and decision-making processes (Smith, 2016). It identified elements required for effective learning, planning, and processes at the headquarters level that support fieldwork and knowledge capture. It also found that respondent NGOs actively participate in formal learning activities, have clear learning strategies to guide their work, and that organization size is a determinant of the types of internal learning strategies used. Challenges were also underscored that stand in the way of more effective learning: competing donor and beneficiary demands, documenting knowledge, and a dearth of dedicated resources for learning activities.

Case studies exemplified how specific NGOs applied different approaches to learning in order to tackle challenges hindering their performance as organizations. CAWST created a new knowledge management system to increase efficiency in decision-making processes and knowledge-sharing among staff and with beneficiaries. CESO's new monitoring, learning, and evaluation framework aimed to consolidate and streamline collected data to reduce information overload and more effectively report on development outcomes. AQOCI's Genre en Pratique community of practice developed a gradual and coordinated approach for interorganizational learning and for monitoring progress indicators toward mainstreaming of gender equality within members' structures and processes. Finally, cross-case analysis indicated that in order to be effective and durable, organizational learning strategies must secure senior management and staff support. They need to balance internal needs with external demands. They have to design purposeful data-collection systems, apply knowledge to decision-making and, for all this, maximize the use of internal and network capacity.

Some key messages

Truly, as depicted in Figure 1.1 in the introductory chapter, the various contributions cover a wide span of knowledge-relevant relationships among development actors. Although depicted in a linear way to stress the organization of the book, the studies collected here clearly show that in actual fact these relationships overlap and intersect with one another; funding, collaboration, influence, and learning are highly interrelated in the lives of CSOs, just as they are for other types of organizations. While the following overarching messages are mainly rooted in evidence from particular contributions, they also feed on information drawn from other chapters in this collection.

First, innovative approaches to North–South partnerships, such as the demand-driven and worldwide competition models experimented with in the early 2000s by the Netherlands and the UK, can improve Global South researchers' ability to influence collaborative agendas. However, their sustainability over time is very much at the mercy of changes in the political climate and attitudes of influential donor-country civil society stakeholders (academia and NGOs), as well as the mandate and structure of institutions responsible for implementing such collaborative funding programmes. Such partnerships can generate negative externalities locally in the Global South, of which both donors and recipients should remain aware. There can be plenty of reasons why Global South organizations may decide to walk away from such partnerships, just as there are many why they would decide to join in.

Alternative partnerships, such as with private foundations, corporate enterprises, or with other Global South organizations, or between low-income and emerging-economy organizations, are on the rise and deserve greater research attention in the future.

Second, despite the many challenges faced by universities and other types of CSOs in their collaborations with each other, there is a widely shared recognition in both the academic and practitioner communities that the rapidly evolving ecosystem of international development calls for more, not less, collaboration between them. This is not only to render the design and process of research more purposeful and responsive, and the findings more relevant and actionable, but also for CSO strategies to professionalize their personnel, better assess their external environment and own ability to add value, skilfully tap into their own and their partners' ground-level experience, and develop more robust and varied approaches to major challenges through the methodical systematization and synthesis of their individual practices.

Beyond individual, small-scale, punctual collaborations it is difficult to see how synergies between these two communities can become more strategic, sustainable, and impactful in a more competitive ecosystem without these communities investing in further innovation at a structural level, including new hybrid institutions.

Third, Global North CSOs are indeed using action-oriented knowledge to various extents to influence policy and practice in the Global South. Their own research, or that borrowed from others, is part of their strategy, for both the information and the capacity building that research affords. As noted in other countries, it is still felt that there isn't enough research collaboration between CSOs in Canada, and between those working domestically and those working internationally. This could undermine CSOs' ability to draw on domestic experience to grow their competence and credibility in international collaborations, as well as to expand alliances and coalitions for comprehensive impact on policies affecting development. It can also hinder the ability of a country's civil society to access its collective stock of experience and innovate with new approaches. These will be increasingly needed, given changes in the global development ecosystem discussed here.

Lastly, less preoccupied until recently with investing in more formal learning (while government funding was more predictable), development NGOs in Canada and other OECD countries are now paying more attention, albeit perhaps reactively so, to self-reflection for their own organizational growth. Still, few communities of practice (CoPs) animated by CSOs could be identified in Canada that are effectively producing innovative and concentrated inter-organizational learning in international cooperation for development. Those CoPs which do function have been addressing, with limited means (and much to their credit), issues of common and pressing interest, such as how to implement international codes of conduct, how to manage viable performance indicators, how to diversify funding, and how to engage with the corporate private sector. The need for more systematic and sustained attention to learning, as a dedicated and normal activity, is very likely to grow under new partnership strategies introduced by donor countries, Canada included. The need is clear, but resourcing still less so. The new partnerships call for investment in experimentation and innovation for greater efficiency, synergies, and impact at scale.

In Canada at least, the NGO community would greatly benefit from stable and better-resourced structures with national reach that could coordinate learning exercises and disseminate results widely. Provincial or regional councils of development NGOs, an inter-council network, a dedicated think tank, or a research institute, affiliated with a university or not, are options for structures that could play a leading role in this area.

Pending knowledge gaps

Clearly, this book explored only part of the picture schematized in Figure 1.1 of the introductory chapter. Many pending questions remain to be addressed, where filling knowledge gaps can further assist CSOs to remain valued players in the new ecosystem for international development.

For instance, beyond national government ministries and agencies officially mandated in the Global North to deliver international development assistance, a growing number of ministries and agencies elsewhere in central governments are increasingly active internationally. Their sectoral policies do have consequences on development outcomes in the Global South, be this in the area of immigration and labour, justice and security, international trade and industry, or health and social welfare.

There is little collected knowledge on the ways in which Global North CSOs might have been involved in advising, implementing, monitoring, or influencing international activities of their own and other countries' government entities which have a bearing on development outcomes in low- and middle-income countries (LMICs).

Likewise, beyond central government, more meso-level (provincial, departmental, state, etc.) and local governments are engaging in development-relevant international activities: how is their engagement with CSOs different from that of central governments particularly given the growth of first- and second-generation immigrant populations from LMICs in many places, the creation of diasporic organizations, and the interest of community foundations in cross-border policy issues?

Also, regarding university–CSO relationships, there is a growing range of disciplinary fields whose curriculum now includes international development issues and which send student volunteers to work with development-oriented CSOs. We need to know how academic departments, faculty, and students in finance, journalism, law, engineering, and technology, for instance, are engaging with development CSOs. Additionally, it would be interesting to examine how much mutual learning takes place between these relatively new groups and disciplinary groups traditionally more engaged in international cooperation.

Mention was made in Travers' chapter of a lack of knowledge sharing among NGOs (working domestically and/or internationally). Greater coordination between these two communities on influencing national policy, separately or in collaboration with Global South counterparts, could potentially wield considerable impact on public opinion. More exchange is needed between Global North CSOs working domestically and those working overseas on how they go about influencing government policy that affects development outcomes both at home and abroad, so as to inform each other's approaches. The practices of Global South partner CSOs in dealing with related domestic issues also deserve more research and coordination with Global North partners. Reviews of inspiring practice on particular subjects, such as labour migration, agricultural and trade policy, and human rights could be very useful to those working in other subject areas.

With regard to CSO–corporate-industry relationships, it is interesting that the dynamics examined by Chernikova between universities and other CSOs prompts the following question: to what extent could a gradual approach used by CSOs and universities to expand the range and depth of their collaboration with one another inform similar approaches for CSOs when they begin to engage with newer actors such as corporations? Where this is already happening, what role if any is played or could be played by CSO–private-sector 'integrators' – who may straddle both industry and activism? Can some of the social impact investors play this role? Vocational and technical training colleges have been developing extensive linkages with industry over the years, drawing both faculty and staff from that sector. They are also increasingly active on the international scene: how active might 'integrators' based in such colleges be in facilitating CSO–industry collaboration?

Finally, while Global South CSOs also create and use knowledge to inform their relationships with donors, partners, stakeholders, and beneficiary communities, this book concentrates on Global North actors, and only indirectly on Global South actors. The gap between knowledge generated by these CSOs and, of this knowledge, the share that is available in published records, could possibly be larger than what is found in the Global North, and it is a gap that should be narrowed for the benefit of the whole system, including Global North CSOs.

References

Bradley, M. (2016) 'Whose agenda? Power, policies, and priorities in North–South research partnerships', in L.J.A. Mougeot (ed.), *Putting Knowledge to Work: Collaborating, influencing and learning for international development,* pp. 37–70, Rugby, UK and Ottawa: Practical Action Publishing and IDRC <http://dx.doi.org/10.3362/9781780449685.002>.

Chernikova, E. (2016) 'Negotiating research collaboration between universities and other civil society organizations in Canada', in L.J.A. Mougeot (ed.), *Putting Knowledge to Work: Collaborating, influencing and learning for international development,* pp. 71–106, Rugby, UK and Ottawa: Practical Action Publishing and IDRC <http://dx.doi.org/10.3362/9781780449685.003>.

Mougeot, L.J.A. (2016) 'Introduction: Knowledge for civil society in the rapidly changing ecosystem for international development', in L.J.A. Mougeot (ed.), *Putting Knowledge to Work: Collaborating, influencing and learning for international development,* pp. 1–36, Rugby, UK and Ottawa: Practical Action Publishing and IDRC <http://dx.doi.org/10.3362/9781780449685.001>.

Smith, E. (2016) 'The learning needs and experiences of Canadian civil society organizations in international cooperation for development', in L.J.A. Mougeot (ed.), *Putting Knowledge to Work: Collaborating, influencing and learning for international development,* pp. 143–182, Rugby, UK and Ottawa: Practical Action Publishing and IDRC <http://dx.doi.org/10.3362/9781780449685.005>.

Travers, S. (2016) 'Canadian civil society organizations using research to influence policy and practice in the Global South', in L.J.A. Mougeot (ed.), *Putting Knowledge to Work: Collaborating, influencing and learning for international development,* pp. 107–142, Rugby, UK and Ottawa: Practical Action Publishing and IDRC <http://dx.doi.org/10.3362/9781780449685.004>.

Index